INTRODUCTION TO GERMAN
LITERATURE, 1871–1990

Introduction to German Literature, 1871–1990

Malcolm Humble

and

Raymond Furness

St. Martin's Press   New York

First published in the United States of America in 1993

Printed in Hong Kong

ISBN 0–312–10084–1 (cl.)
ISBN 0–312–10068–X (pbk.)

Library of Congress Cataloging-in-Publication Data
Humble, Malcolm, 1943–
An introduction to German literature, 1871–1990
p. cm.
Includes bibliographical references and index.
ISBN 0–312–10084–1. — ISBN 0–312–10068–X (pbk.)
1. German literature—20th century—History and criticism.
2. German literature—19th century—History and criticism.
I. Title.
PT401.H86   1993
830.9'008—dc20   93–17724
                                                CIP

Contents

Preface

To write a history of the literature of the German-speaking peoples of the last one hundred and twenty years, from the foundation of the Second Reich under Bismarck to the breaching of the Berlin Wall and the subsequent reunification of Germany in 1990, is by no means an easy task. For the journey is a momentous one, and the literary responses to the vicissitudes of modern German history are manifold and complex. The literature of the *Gründerzeit* will reflect or reject the values of Wilhelmine Germany; the experiments of the Naturalists, and the cultivation of aestheticism which followed them, both owe much to the awareness of international trends; the explosion of Expressionism, that 'gash of fire across the world' of which Paul Celan spoke, is a major German contribution. The literary and cultural achievements of the Weimar period are acknowledged to be of outstanding merit; the jejune and eccentric offerings of the Third Reich betray, in contrast to the writings of *Exilliteratur*, a Germanness both sterile and banal. The collapse of 1945 is an obvious caesura, and the literary historian has then to contend with ever more divergent literatures – those of the erstwhile German Democratic Republic, the Republic of Adenauer and his successors, of Austria and, to a lesser extent, of Switzerland. The theme of *Vergangenheitsbewältigung* will loom large, as will the reaction to materialism, student disaffection and to terrorism. The literary response to the far-reaching events of 1989 and 1990 will conclude the volume, the response of those writers to the challenge facing Germany as the country moves towards an uncertain future. Many of the texts under discussion will reflect, then, the world around them – but there will also be a place for those writers who seek inwardness and utopias (or dystopias) in their aesthetic re-enactments.

It was Franz Kafka who demanded that a book be an axe to break open the frozen sea within us. And axes the German literature of the last century or so will provide aplenty, some to wield, others to grind. The uncertainties, restless energies and tortuous attempts at self-definition of the German-speaking peoples of the twentieth century will provide many fascinating formulations. And as the century nears its end it may well be seen that the German contribution to world literature has perhaps made the most striking impact.

The authors of this book have attempted to give a survey of the major figures and of those works which, in their opinion, are the most significant. They have for the most part eschewed quotations in German and also cumbersome footnotes in order that the reader may be presented with an unimpeded and lucid narrative. Although we have been guided by our personal knowledge and judgement, our work would not have been possible without resort to the many publications on the history of twentieth-century German literature which have recently appeared, many of them supplying new emphases, and which are listed in the bibliography. The present volume is in part a reflection of the sifting process undertaken and the critical conspectus developed in these volumes, to which acknowledgement is due. Because the view which emerges from these works conforms to present-day reading patterns, it can be claimed that most of the texts referred to, with the exception of the literature of the Third Reich, are generally available in book-shops and libraries in German-speaking countries and that a good many have been translated into English.

We may reasonably be accused of having given the literature of German-speaking Switzerland short shrift. Faced with the decision whether or not to include a consideration of it, we settled for the compromise of placing the two major figures of post-1945 Swiss literature, Frisch and Dürrenmatt, within the context of developments elsewhere.

Raymond Furness wishes to acknowledge a term's leave of absence from the University of St Andrews and the generosity of the Carnegie Trust which enabled him to complete those chapters for which he was responsible. Both authors are deeply indebted to Hazel Dunstan for her patience and efficiency in preparing the typescript.

M.H.
R.F.

1

The Period of Transition

It is a commonplace of literary history to designate the generation born in the 1880s as that which so altered modes of writing and thinking as to be called modernist or revolutionary; it was this generation which, in late adolescence, rejected the values of the previous one and continued to map out new frontiers in works which, although originally deemed alien, are now accepted in any list of modern European classics. It would seem appropriate, therefore, to begin this book on twentieth-century German literature with the *Jahrhundertwende*, to look at that febrile artistic and intellectual concoction with which the nineteenth century ended and the twentieth century began, a time whose plethora of conflicting styles Robert Musil (born 1880) so well described in his gigantic novel *Der Mann ohne Eigenschaften*. But another writer of that generation, Gottfried Benn (born 1886), when discussing the intellectual preoccupations of his contemporaries, insisted that practically everything that they had discussed and suffered, everything, that is, that became part of the stock-in-trade of the European mind, had received authentic formulation already by a man who had anticipated the whole of psychoanalysis, and the whole of existentialism: he was, according to Benn, the 'earthquake of the epoch' and the 'greatest genius of the German language since Luther'. This is Friedrich Nietzsche, who died, clinically insane, in 1900, on the threshold of the new century, and who is indeed indispensable for any understanding of the intellectual and artistic climate of the last decades of the nineteenth century and most of this. It is consequently with the 1870s that we shall begin, to consider the literature of the first thirty years of the new German *Kaiserreich* and to detect those innovatory tendencies which anticipate much of what is to come. Our survey must necessarily be succinct and selective, but the period of transition described is one which, it is to be hoped, will contain much that is surprisingly modern amongst the stilted and the genteel.

Monumentalism and grandiloquent gestures characterise much

of the art of the 1870s: the second *Reich*, proud of its conquests in the field of battle, and secure, despite the financial crash in 1873, in its industrial might, demanded self-glorification, a literature of sycophantic praise for the Hohenzollerns, such as was provided by Ernst von Wildenbruch, author of numerous patriotic plays. Prussia's defeat of France called forth much nationalistic fervour and writing which commemorated German power and *Nibelungentreue*: the ending of Felix Dahn's *Ein Kampf um Rom*, a novel which rapidly became a best-seller on its appearance in 1876 (and which the self-righteous hero of Gerhart Hauptmann's *Vor Sonnenaufgang* extolled as being an exemplary book, a work which pointed the way ahead), describes in colourful prose the return of the Vikings with their dead heroes to the North. The gleam of helmet and spear, the streaming flags and purple waves, create an obvious set-piece reminiscent of the paintings of Anton von Werner or Hans Makart or, in literature, of Conrad Ferdinand Meyer's historical tableaux, the Swiss writer whose powerful novel *Jürg Jenatsch* appeared in the same year. The portentous motto from Emanuel Geibel at the beginning of Dahn's novel, advocating fortitude in the face of implacable destiny, seems very much of its time, deriving from a mentality compounded of defiance, dedication and heroic attitudinising. This year, 1876, witnessed the most important cultural event in Germany – or even Europe: the opening of the Festspielhaus in Bayreuth and the performance of Wagner's *Der Ring des Nibelungen* before emperors, kings, artists and patrons: a sophisticated nineteenth-century audience saw unfolded before it a world of mythical archetypes, a profound fairy-tale plot suffused by music of overwhelming intensity. A work redolent of the *Gründerzeit*, perhaps, but also atavistic and ultramodern, as Thomas Mann well knew; Nietzsche had likewise, in his brilliant analysis of the overture to *Die Meistersinger* (in *Jenseits von Gut und Böse*, 1885), talked of Germany's uncertainty, despite the apparent successes of the day, of its place in the scheme of things.

He had, as early as 1873, warned of the defeat of the German spirit, of its extirpation even, at the expense of the new German *Reich*: victory over the French at Sedan should not, he claimed, be thought by his fellow countrymen to signify superiority in cultural matters. His preoccupation, obsession even, with cultural values led Nietzsche again and again to look at developments within the *Kaiserreich* and to criticise them most harshly. Of crucial importance was his first major work, *Die Geburt der Tragödie* of 1872, which, inspired by Wagner's music-dramas, posits the distinction between the Apolline and the Dionysian, the former representing serenity and repose, the latter darkness, chaos and violence. Greek art, the argument runs, is exemplary in that it represents a synthesis of these two forces, a synthesis achieved only after a struggle: the art of modern times should recognise the chthonic powers, the world of the subconscious (as Sigmund Freud would later argue) and draw from this fecund source. The striking image of the tree which must put down deep roots into the earth in order that the branches may soar into the light, found within *Also sprach Zarathustra* (1883–92), contains the idea *in nucleo*: this vast prose-poem showed Nietzsche to be an unparalleled *Dichterphilosoph* and would inspire a whole generation with its provocative imagery and rhapsodic fervour. The hectic emphasis on heroism and the call for the destruction of the moribund would appeal above all to the young; the euphoric excesses and daring apostacy, rarely found elsewhere in Nietzsche's elegant prose, could, however, be seen as advocating a dangerous irrationalism. The immense range of Nietzsche's writing was such that the Naturalist writers of the 1880s could applaud his attack on bourgeois complacency; the aesthetes of the 1890s would learn much from his aphorisms on art; and the Expressionist generation would extol his emphasis on the daring transvaluation of all values and the vision of the New Man.

Nietzsche's voice, in extreme isolation, grew increasingly more shrill: the full scope and impact of his thought would only become apparent in the century which he did not see and which, he prophesied, would be convulsed by wars the like of which the world had never experienced. His influence, as Gottfried Benn explained in his essay *Nietzsche–nach fünfzig Jahren*, was all-pervasive, and his world stature assured. Less extreme, more provincial and more typical are the descriptions of Bismarck's Germany, and later the Germany of Wilhelm the Second, to be found in the novelists of the day. Felix Dahn's bestseller, which spoke of Goth and Viking but which was very much of the 1870s, has been mentioned; very popular were also the novels of Friedrich Spielhagen, whose portrayal of the opulence, concupiscence and material values of that decade makes exemplary reading. *Sturmflut* (1877), in three volumes, describes a world of financial speculation and lavish style, a world shot through with ruthless managerial ambition. The flood of the title is symbolic of that inundation of finance, greed and market values which threaten to drown altruism and selflessness. Gone are the resigned, introverted heroes of many of the novels and *Novellen* of the 1850s and 1860s: Spielhagen portrays the world of the predator. The rapid rise of industrialisation, and the related problems of poverty and slum-dwelling will later be prevalent in the works of Naturalism; a writer like Wilhelm Raabe, however, anticipates this concern in his short novel *Pfisters Mühle*, written in 1883–4, where the destruction of the old mill, the demolition of the chestnut trees and the contaminated stream, polluted by chemical waste, point to a new, brash Germany which threatens to oust the old. Raabe, born when Goethe was still alive, lived until 1910. His earlier novels, which brought him a wide readership, are sub-Dickensian; later his narrative style, with shifting authorial stances, approaches a self-reflective complexity which is far ahead of its time. (Hermann Hesse visited him in 1909 and noted Raabe's 'extra dimension', that quality which, so difficult to categorise, nevertheless showed through and demonstrated the master.) The absurd, the grotesque element in literature will become prevalent in the twentieth century, but the later nineteenth century produced, in F. Th. Vischer's *Auch Einer* (1879), a remarkable example, loosely constructed, aphoristic and manic in the portrayal of the hero's struggle against truculent inanimates.

It has been persuasively argued that nineteenth-century German prose fiction, unlike the fiction of France, England and Russia, deals more successfully with man in isolation than man in society and thus anticipates the twentieth-century concern with existential loneliness and dread. Raabe's small compass, the emphasis on the parochial and the narrow, contains character-sketches of individuals which would not be out of place in Samuel Beckett's work; 'outsiders' are the order of the day, and isolation the common human condition. The same may be claimed for Stifter, a writer who died by his own hand in 1868; Theodor Storm likewise comes to mind, a writer normally associated with a narrative style of melancholy lyricism. Storm died in 1888 on the eve of the Naturalist breakthrough, but the powerful Novelle *John Riew* (1884–5), dealing with hereditary alcoholism, predates Hauptmann's first masterpiece *Vor Sonnenaufgang; Ein Bekenntnis* (1887) with its discussion of euthanasia, demonstrates again Storm's awareness of modern concerns, this theme being widely discussed at the time. With *Der Schimmelreiter* (1888), his last work, Storm depicts Nordic man in his struggle against the elements and the disbelief of his fellow-men, a theme which, with hindsight, has a disquieting ring. Thomas Mann speaks of an extremism in Storm, something almost pathological, and disagrees with Fontane's comments on 'Provinzialsimpelei' in his essay on Storm of 1930. To claim that Storm was in any way a precursor of modernism would be false, but nor is he to be categorised solely with purveyors of genteel fiction such as Paul Heyse, the first German recipient of the Nobel prize for literature who died reviled by the Naturalists in 1910. This 'almost indecently prolific epigone' (the phrase is again Thomas Mann's) had written one hundred and fifty Novellen, eight novels, sixty plays, innumerable poems and published five volumes of translations; Storm, in 1879, in a letter to Gottfried Keller, had commented on the work as being ultimately barren ('dürftig') and even Theodor Fontane would lose his patience with Heyse's posturing. To the new generation he was unreadable, and Conrad Alberti, in 1889, came out with the brutal statement that to read Heyse meant being without taste, and to admire him meant to be a wretch.

The prose fiction of the last two decades of the nineteenth century is necessarily dominated by the genius of Theodor Fontane, arguably Germany's greatest novelist and a writer who can take his place among Europe's masters of realistic narrative. His tolerant, ironic style, his magisterial ease in the portrayal of late-nineteenth-century Prussian society particularly, and his delightful *causeries* have no equal in German fiction; his mastering of the novel is seen at the time when the firm ground of the nineteenth century is elsewhere rapidly disappearing, and even in Germany the new, aggressive experiments of the Naturalists were beginning to oust the traditional narrative and theatrical forms. Yet the seventy-year-old was keenly aware of the new developments and greeted the young Gerhart Hauptmann, then not yet thirty, as Ibsen's successor in a famous review of the latter's *Vor Sonnenaufgang* in 1889 (he would also, in 1895, come to the defence of Oskar Panizza's scurrilous and blasphemous play *Das Liebeskonzil*). Fontane belongs in any discussion of nineteenth-century narrative fiction, a novelist who effortlessly eclipses such writers as the Austrians Marie von Ebner-Eschenbach and Ferdinand von Saar, his contemporaries. Suffice it here to note that he was keenly aware of the new, that he greeted it, that his criticisms of Prussian arrogance and vanity would appeal very much to the young generation who, in the 1880s, proclaimed themselves to be 'Jüngstdeutsche' and who sought 'die Moderne' above all. (The deliberate echo of 'Jungdeutschland' was meant to demonstrate the similarity of aims: a new sense of material reality, of political commitment, and an undeniable social-democratic tendency.) The time was ripe, it was felt, for a new, abrasive literature, one dealing with modern problems, without the pompous facade of the *Gründerzeit*: women's emancipation, social justice, the portrayal of the proletariat – these were the new themes to which the playwrights and the novelists known as Naturalists sought to address themselves.

As so often in Germany, the theoretical justification for an uncompromising modernity in the arts preceded the actual works themselves. The 1880s were characterised by a wealth of periodicals, pamphlets, admonitions and manifestoes, each attempting to define the basic position. (The publication of Büchner's *Woyzeck* in 1879 should be noted, whose fragmentary sequence of scenes, coarse language and moving portrayal of the inarticulate soldier struck many as being quintessentially 'modern', that is, raw, unpolished and brutal in its impact.) Of great importance was the journal *Die Gesellschaft*, edited by Michael Georg Conrad, a 'Realistische Wochenschrift für Literatur, Kunst und öffentliches Leben'; the *Freie Bühne für modernes Leben*, founded by Otto Brahm, was also of seminal importance (from 1894 it became the *Neue deutsche Rundschau*). The *Kritische Waffengänge* of Heinrich und Julius Hart (1882–4), Wilhelm Bölsche's *Die naturwissenschaftlichen Grundlagen der Poesie* (1887) and Karl Bleibtreu's *Revolution der Litteratur* (1885–6) were also significant documents in their attempts to describe the new attitudes: the latter is enlightening in its division of German literature into the older generation (Heyse, Freytag, Keller and Spielhagen), the fashionable and popular contemporaries (Felix Dahn amongst them) and the 'Stürmer und Drängler'. Indeed, both writers and readers require courage to 'put up with *true* reality' – this was Bleibtreu's credo: courage, presumably, to face and describe the sordid, the banal and the brutish, with no attempt to transfigure or conceal. It is Zola above all who is extolled, particularly the writer of *Germinal*, that overpowering portrayal of a mining community which appeared in 1885. The German novelist Max Kretzer, who was hailed as the German Zola, achieved great popularity at this time but little lasting success (Karl Bleibtreu compared the last chapters of his novel *Die Verkommenen* to Shakespeare; the poet Detlev von Liliencron immodestly claimed that it could have been written by Jesus Christ himself, the humanity being so profound). Famous above all as being a writer of Berlin novels, Kretzer is now remembered for *Meister Timpe* (1888), a portrayal of the antagonism between man and machine and the destruction of traditional values. Kretzer may be seen in many ways as following in the footsteps of Freytag and Spielhagen, but his social-democratic stance and keen awareness of the problems facing the proletariat place him close to the Naturalist camp. The description of the first train of the new Berlin *Stadtbahn* which steams past as Timpe dies is a rather strained symbol for the modern age which, ruthlessly, has no place for sentimental nostalgia. Kretzer could well lay claim to the ability to portray urban suffering in a realistic manner; Hermann Sudermann's *Frau Sorge* (1887) and Wilhelm von Polenz's *Der Büttnerbauer* (1895) portray rural tragedies.

The year 1885 also saw the publication of Wilhelm Arendt's anthology *Moderne Dichter-Charaktere* and Arno Holz's *Buch der Zeit. Lieder eines Modernen*, two works which contained in their titles the obligatory epithet proclaiming a break with the past. Poetry as well had to face topical issues: there was to be no escape into stale Romantic versifying or faded Victorian fiction. And as Zola had showed the way in the novel, so Ibsen had dared to tackle the problems of heredity and women's emancipation in his uncompromising drama, writing of ordinary people in everyday prose, eschewing artificialities of plot and refining the art of conversation. In Austria Ludwig Anzengruber had showed remarkable originality in his *Das vierte Gebot* (1877), a tragedy dealing with the tensions between old and new in a direct and bold manner, and running into trouble with both church and censorship. But the violent hostility which it invoked was as nothing before the uproar which greeted Gerhart Hauptmann's *Vor Sonnenaufgang* on 20 October 1889, and which has entered literary history: the crude Silesian dialect, the brutishness of alcoholism, the screams of pain of the woman in labour (and forceps brandished in the audience), and hero who, unable to help and to love, causes suicide. Here was indeed, as Fontane noted, a German successor to Ibsen. This was a 'soziales Drama', but there is nothing crudely political about the work which is concerned with human suffering above all; it is a drama of compassion. The first edition was dedicated to 'Bjarne P. Holmsen', the pseudonym used by Arno Holz and Johannes Schlaf (such being the impact of Scandinavian literature at this time) in

Papa Hamlet, a group of prose-sketches written in *Sekundenstil*, a technique of minute realism midway between narrative and drama. Hauptmann had published his stories *Bahnwärter Thiel* and *Fasching* one year before *Vor Sonnenaufgang*, but it was as a dramatist that he became famous throughout Europe – that 'stilvoller Realist' (Fontane) who, keeping within the conventions of the well-made play, revealed with remarkable skill the feel of a situation, the intonation of a voice and the latent instincts of a human being; a dramatist of compassion and keen psychological insight.

Arno Holz and Johannes Schlaf, advocates of *konsequenter Naturalismus*, that most extreme of attempts to reproduce reality exactly, published *Papa Hamlet* in 1889. These sketches contain little 'action' in any traditional sense: each second of time is faithfully registered and each spoken word recorded, with any linking narrative approximating to a stage-direction. The milieu is generally proletariat, or petty-bourgeois bankruptcy. A certain mechanical sterility may ensue, but later twentieth-century linguistic experiments are also adumbrated here (certain aspects of Beckett, for example, or Peter Handke). Holz and Schlaf published their drama *Die Familie Selicke* in the following year, 1890: the exact reproduction of human speech, fragmented and formless, led Fontane to claim that the play was a more progressive work even than *Vor Sonnenaufgang* which, although capturing the speech of illiterate peasants and crude nouveaux-riches, did not indulge in *Sekundenstil*. *Meister Oelze* (1892), written by Schlaf alone, is a grim portrayal of murder and fraud. It was Arno Holz who attempted to supply the definitive contribution to German Naturalist theory with the following tenet, an extreme 'scientific' approach to literature, a desire to go beyond Zola in the quest for an absolute, consistent Naturalism: 'It is the tendency of art to become nature again. It achieves this according to the prerequisites of reproduction which it has at its disposal, and their manipulation.' This formula he reduced to an absolute minimum: 'Kunst = Natur − x ', where ' x ' is to be identified with Zola's 'tempérament' in the latter's famous statement concerning the 'coin de la nature'. An undeniable aridity is detected in such theorising, and Holz's uncertainty concerning the relationship between objective form and subjective response, as well as the emphasis upon mimetic verism which reduces reality to a fragmentation not far removed from *pointillisme*, lead Naturalism to a sterile impasse. The appearance of the first version of Holz's gigantic *Phantasus* in 1898, with its concept of the symmetrical, ornamental *Mittelachse* poetry, betrays a flirtation with *Jugendstil* decoration, and the notion of the fusion of self with cosmic processes shows that the world of Mombert and Morgenstern is not far.

If Naturalism is associated above all with early Hauptmann rather than with the jejune theories of Arno Holz it is because of the vital energy of his talent and his potential for organic development. In a series of plays written between 1889 and 1911 Hauptmann conquered the German stage with works not necessarily concerned with the industrial proletariat, nor with the city, but frequently with middle-class problems and the plight of common people. *Das Friedensfest. Eine Familienkatastrophe* (1890) and *Einsame Menschen* (1891) show the presence of Ibsen, the former dealing with lack of communication within a family, and the latter a sensitive portrayal of a protagonist caught between traditional beliefs on the one hand and more progressive views on the other, the catastrophe being triggered by the arrival of an attractive, emancipated woman. Hauptmann is concerned with personal and psychological problems and betrays a reluctance – a reluctance shared by many of the Friedrichshagen circle who flaunted their modernism – to contemplate the social predicaments of the day as the Naturalist writer is often expected to do. But Hauptmann's fame was assured with the success of *Die Weber*, produced on 26 February 1893 in the Freie Bühne; this play is indeed Germany's classical drama of hunger, exploitation, strike and abortive revolution, the 'hero' being the Silesian people themselves who speak with a natural force and directness which come over even more forcefully in the dialect version *De Waber*. Despite imperial disapproval, and the fact that a genuine working-class drama is enacted, the play is, in Hauptmann's own words, 'certainly social, but not socialist' ('wohl sozial, aber nicht sozialistisch'): no political drama (as Büchner knew) can remove the ultimate suffering of the world. What is indeed remarkable in Hauptmann's plays at this time is his ability to portray the vulnerable nature of human existence, to give dramatic shape to the trapped and the pursued. This is seen most strikingly in *Rose Bernd* (1902) and *Die Ratten* (1911), Hauptmann's last successful plays in the Naturalist mode.

The German theatre had been revitalised by these plays, also by the great success of Sudermann's *Heimat* (1893) and Max Halbe's *Jugend* of the same year. But what is extraordinary about German Naturalism is how short-lived the movement was. The movement may well have been a necessary breakthrough to a more forceful, less effete way of writing, but the restrictions placed upon the imagination by the strait-jacket of scientific verisimilitude were felt to be irksome, and the emphasis on the sordid stultifying and jejune. The dream-play *Hanneles Himmelfahrt* was performed in 1893, a rude shock to those admirers of Hauptmann who expected another play from the Naturalist canon. This play is certainly set in sordid surroundings, but the blank verse employed, and the mystical, child-like vision of a paradise at the end demonstrated that Naturalism had been superseded. The spirit-world was, admittedly, present only in Hanneles's febrile delirium, but in *Die versunkene Glocke*, that German fairy-tale drama of 1896, Hauptmann portrays the elemental spirits, dwarfs and elves to be as real as Heinrich the bell-founder, his wife and their neighbours. The strange *Glashüttenmärchen* of ten years later, *Und Pippa tanzt!*, contains a fusion not only of Naturalism with Neo-romanticism, but also tendencies which the critic Alfred Kerr would describe as Expressionistic *avant la lettre*.

The rich confusion in artistic styles prevailing at the end of the nineteenth century to which Musil refers, as was noted at the beginning of this introduction, is fascinating in its divergence. Two strands are discernible: the 'Naturalist' and the symbolic-aesthetic (Musil calls them the 'robust' and the 'morbid'). At the same time that Holz, Schlaf and Hauptmann were writing one detects the opposite tendency, variously known as impressionist, or Neo-romantic, or *symboliste*: decadence and *Jugendstil* are further offshoots. Important in an analysis of the rejection of, or disdain for, Naturalism, are the comments of Hermann Bahr. An habitué of the Café Griensteidl in Vienna, and companion of such writers as Arthur Schnitzler, Hugo von Hofmannsthal, Peter Altenberg and others, Bahr, sensing that Naturalism had been surpassed by a new movement, wrote in his essay *Die Überwindung des Naturalismus* as early as 1891 that Naturalism was a thing of the past, and that a 'nervöse Romantik', 'eine Mystik der Nerven' was the order of the day. Bahr stressed predominantly the direction in writing away from a faithful reproduction of reality to the cultivation of inner visions and sensibilities. Three years later, in his *Studien zur Kritik der Moderne*, Bahr used the term *décadence* to describe the new, anti-naturalistic writing, the new preoccupations and aversions: of paramount importance was the debt to French symbolism, the Neo-romantic cult of the soul, the Wagnerian element (derived

paradoxically from France) and the portrayal of exquisite sensi-
bilites. After the lean years of Naturalism, where the imagination
had been largely harnessed to social issues and the reproduction of
frequently inarticulate speech, the time had come for the exploration of mysterious realms and of subtle nuances of feeling. The
Viennese critic Franz Servaes preferred the term *Impressionismus*
to describe the subtle reproduction or registration of the visual
and the aural, thus linking the tendency with photographic
Naturalism; the importance of Ernst Mach's *Analyse der
Empfindungen* (1886) may be noted here, and Robert Musil's
attempts in his early stories to capture sense-impressions in as
accurate a manner as possible. The linguist-philosopher Fritz
Mauthner likewise attempted to describe the literary scene around
him, as did Theodor Lessing. Hermann Bahr, however, came closest to summing up the temper of the age, and it was in Vienna, a
city where Naturalism had never gained a significant foothold,
that Bahr experienced a talent of the highest order who perfectly
exemplified the new mentality.

This was Hugo von Hofmannsthal, whose precocity amazed
such writers as Arthur Schnitzler and Stefan Zweig: the flawless
perfection of the poetry and the lyrical dramas, the obvious indebtedness to Maeterlinck, Wilde and Huysmans exemplified an aestheticism infinitely remote from the crassness of Naturalism. The
early 1890s saw Hofmannsthal's concern above all with the fascination of amoral beauty (*Gestern*, 1891 and *Der Tod des Tizian*, 1892):
in 1893 the play *Der Tor und der Tod* demonstrates the dangers of
aestheticism, the sterile nature of a life spent in the contemplation
of beauty. In the following year the powerful story *Das Märchen der
672. Nacht* appeared, a more sombre portrayal of a similar theme,
where the aestheticising of death is shown as fraudulent and
deceptive. Hofmannsthal increasingly felt the need to distance
himself from a poet such as Stefan George, who had approached
him in the winter of 1891 with suggestions for the formation of a
new, élite, literary sodality: the poem 'Der Prophet' expresses the
fascination but also the reservations. For Hofmannsthal will see
with ever greater clarity the need to reach out to a wider reading,
and also listening, public, and his later collaboration with Richard
Strauss and the foundation of the Salzburg Festivals showed that
this had been put into practice: no arrogant isolation, but a living
theatrical and musical tradition. Other names associated with
Viennese *fin de siècle* include Richard Beer-Hofmann (whose *Der*

Tod Georgs, 1900, is much indebted to Hofmannsthal but also uses the technique of inner monologue which Schnitzler will perfect in his *Leutnant Gustl* of the same year), Leopold von Andrian, Felix Salten (creator of the deer Bambi and also the hilariously pornographic *Josefine Mutzenbacher*) and Felix Dörmann, author of *Neurotica* (1891) and *Sensationen* (1896). Of equal rank to Hofmannsthal is, of course, Schnitzler, the success of whose plays led him, an eminent doctor, to devote his life to writing. Mach's *Analyse der Empfindungen* might have been an appropriate name for Schnitzler's artistic method which was qualified by a typical brand of Viennese self-deprecating irony and gentle scepticism. The seven dramatic episodes of *Anatol* (1891) have much of the impressionistic sketch about them and Schnitzler, acknowledged by Freud to be a *Doppelgänger*, expertly analyses Anatol's erotic egotism, his insufficiency in emotional responses. In *Reigen*, begun in 1896, sex is portrayed as being the force before which all levels of society are equal. A wider concern is present in Schnitzler's later writing, particularly the autobiographical novel *Der Weg ins Freie* (1908) and the play *Professor Bernhardi*, which deals with the tension between a Jewish doctor and a Catholic priest. But Schnitzler never resorts to cumbersome polemic: intelligence and irony prevent an all-too-earnest commitment. His reputation rests quite rightly on his subtle portrayal of erotic entanglements and sexual frustration of *fin-de-siècle* Vienna, on his status as *Jungwien*'s analyst and ironic practitioner.

The cult of aestheticism was, however, not a Viennese prerogative: Stefan George's name has been mentioned, and it is with Munich above all that he is associated. In 1889, twenty-one years old, George arrived in Paris from Turin, having left the city at the same time Nietzsche left it as the clinically insane. In Paris, particularly from Mallarmé, George absorbed an atmosphere redolent of French symbolism and returned to Germany with a sense of mission, namely, to rid German poetry of provincialism and stale, nineteenth-century mannerisms and to elevate art – and life – to the highest ideal. In 1892 the plan to found an exclusive journal, modelled on the *symboliste Ecrits pour l'art* and entirely devoted to the cult of beauty, came to fruition: the first number of the *Blätter für die Kunst* appeared, a periodical which survived sporadically until 1919. George's own work had hitherto been printed privately and given to close friends (*Hymnen*, 1890; *Pilgerfahrten*, 1891; and the decadent *Algabal* poems, 1892): the *Blätter* would now be an outlet for his poetry and that of his initiates. The ornamental *Jugendstil* type-face by Melchior Lechter, the individualistic punctuation and orthography, emphasised the exclusive nature of the enterprise. (*Jugendstil*, incidentally, is a label which was first used in art history but which later came to describe the decorative formalism used by the artists associated with the Munich journal *Jugend* which first appeared in 1896; the designs frequently used arabesques and swirling lines, and showed a predilection for tendrils, foliage, swans, dancing maidens and swirling hair, streaming incense and flying clouds.) In the *Blätter für die Kunst* 'l'art pour l'art' tendencies prevail, but George also saw himself as educator and magus, desirous of purifying a debased culture: later collections exemplify this. A circle of devotees, most famous of whom were Gundolf, Wolfskehl, Bertram and Derleth, composed the *George-Kreis*, a circle associated with a striving for perfection and, after the earlier decadence had been transcended, with Grecian discipline and vision. In 1903 George met in Munich a fifteen-year-old boy who seemed to be the incarnation of perfect aesthetic form: his death soon afterwards led to a deification which alienated certain members of the circle. The collection *Der siebente Ring* (1907) extols masculine youth and its role in the cleansing of civilisation. George's later insistence on discipline and classical sobriety led him to reject the turgid hyperbole of Alfred Schuler and Ludwig Klages, those *Kosmiker* who, initially close to him, turned to an irrationalism which George could only deplore. His internationalism also led him to deplore the incipient chauvinism of the *Kaiserreich*, as well as the carnage of the First World War and the ugliness of National Socialism; he chose to die and be buried in Switzerland.

Munich is also the city of Thomas Mann, who moved from Lübeck to the Bavarian capital in 1893. Mann was fascinated by that city and its literati, decadents and overwrought pseudo-philosophers such as Ludwig Derleth: many of his early stories touch upon the impotent aesthete *vis-à-vis* the vulgar *bourgeois*. Mann associated with many aesthetes and *enfants terribles* such as Kurt Martens and Arthur Holitscher, the latter's *Der vergiftete Brunnen* being recommended by him for publication, and the former's *Roman aus der Décadence*, with its theme of 'Verfall' being of importance to him at this time. For *Buddenbrooks* has, as its subtitle, 'Verfall einer Familie', and it was the publication of this novel in 1901 that made its author an immediate celebrity. ('Decay' was the literary watchword of the time, ever since the publication of Max

Nordau's vulgar diatribe *Entartung* in 1892, an attempt to claim that all contemporary art was pathologically sick.) The novel ironically portrays collapse, but also an increase in intellectual and artistic awareness: both Schopenhauer and Nietzsche provide the philosophical sub-structure, but the novel is solidly based on nineteenth-century narrative models (Fontane). The relationship between art and disease may be called an obsession in Thomas Mann's *oeuvre* at this time, reaching its climax in the acknowledged masterpiece *Der Tod in Venedig*, published in 1912. There is much of Thomas Mann himself in this *Novelle*, also George (the Munich milieu of the beginning) and Richard Wagner, who died in the Italian city. Mann's greatest work belongs in the period of Weimar and the time of exile: his artistic beginnings, however, are of equal importance, with the 'trinity of eternally united spirits' (Schopenhauer, Nietzsche and Wagner) in constant attention. The self-styled 'chronicler and commentator of decadence, lover of death and the pathological' (see his *Betrachtungen eines Unpolitischen*) learned much from the literary scene in Munich, as had his brother Heinrich: *Wälsungenblut* (1906) may well be the finest example of German *décadence*.

The attempt to look at the various forms which the literary reaction to Naturalism took in the German-speaking world must finish by looking briefly at Prague and Berlin. Prague is associated with fantastic literature (Meyrink's *Der Golem*, 1915), but it is also the city of Rilke's beginnings, and also Franz Kafka, a writer to be discussed in Chapter 2. Rilke's Neo-romantic effusions, frequently embarrassing in their mawkishness, cannot compare with the pellucid *finesse* of Hofmannsthal and are strangely at variance with the later work. Rilke's attempts at obligatory Naturalist drama are now forgotten; the early collections of poems (*Leben und Lieder*, 1894, *Larenopfer*, 1895, *Traumgekrönt*, 1896 and *Advent*, 1897) convey, in effortless facility and sentient waves of feeling, the cliché-ridden world of Neo-romantic escapism. Rilke's *Arme-Leute-Poesie*, plus a morbid introspection, together with a Franciscanism concerning 'die Dinge' are unpalatable to the modern reader. The *Stundenbuch*-cycle of 1905, with its vapid spirituality and arrogation of Christian (Byzantine) symbols into an aesthetic view of existence, is very much of its age. The effulgence of the 1890s and of the *Jahrhundertwende* will give way to a clearer, harder line in Rilke's poetry which will warrant his comparison with poets such as Valéry and Eliot: the beginnings in provincial Prague are, however, not auspicious, and it will be the years in Paris, the experience of loneliness, *Angst* and modern alienation that will produce poetry and prose of sublety, precision and extraordinary refinement. But Rilke's great popularity rested on the early work, particularly the prose-poem *Die Weise vom Leben und Tod des Cornets Christoph Rilke*, published in 1903, Neo-romantic velleities proving more accessible than the imagism of the *Neue Gedichte* collection (1907–8) and the existential agonies of the *Aufzeichnungen des Malte Laurids Brigge* (1910) and the *Duineser Elegien* (1923), to be discussed in the following chapter. The months in Worpswede, the artist colony in North Germany, should not, however, be forgotten, that lonely moorland where Rilke learned to see and describe a landscape in a manner reminiscent of certain aspects of Georg Heym's poetry; his enthusiastic review of Gustav Frenssen's *Jörn Uhl* (1901) showed an appreciation of North German *Heimatdichtung* at its best.

This section will now close with a reference to Stanislaus Przybyszewski and his memoirs (recently reissued), an indispensable account of the Berlin literary world at the end of the nineteenth century. Przybyszewski, despite his strained satanism and exaggerated bohemianism was an acute observer of the literary scene, both in Friedrichshagen, the artists-colony outside the city, and also in 'Zum schwarzen Ferkel', that tavern which was the Berlin equivalent of the Café Griensteidl, frequented by Strindberg and other Scandinavian artists. Przybyszewski took pleasure in denigrating German Naturalism and cultivated a decadent aestheticism: his *Totenmesse* (1893), *Satanskinder* (1897) and *Androgyne* (1900) brought him the reputation he avidly sought. His insistence on the primacy of 'the naked soul', however, anticipates certain Expressionist preoccupations, and the descent into subrational darkness of much of his writing looks forward to certain aspects of Hermann Hesse. Przybyszewski's friendship with Paul Scheerbart is also of interest here: the Polish visionary and the writer from Danzig with his dreams of glass temples and space travel are not at home in the world of *Asphaltlyrik*.. Przybyszewski's most vital friendship was with Richard Dehmel, whose *Aber die Liebe* (1893), ecstatic and outspoken, belongs on the periphery of Expressionism, as is the commitment to a fervent socialism. Dehmel, together with Alfred Mombert, will exemplify a proto-Expressionism and point the way to a more urgent, dynamic approach to human existence that would later take extreme and often strident forms. And Berlin will be in the vanguard of the

Expressionist exploration of life, the city of the two seminal journals *Der Sturm* (1910) and *Die Aktion* (1911).

This period of transition which we have attempted to describe, characterised by Naturalism, aestheticism and the beginnings of Expressionism, is a rich and confusing one in German literature, implying a profound uncertainty in man's emotional response to the world around him. Nietzsche's *aperçus* were seen later to be prescient and uncannily accurate; his comments on Wagnerism, on the *Kaiserreich*, or decadence and the preoccupations of the 1880s, together with his rapturous and vital call for the new, the fervent and the amoral would reverberate throughout the beginnings of the new century. His writings on language and its limitations will achieve a profound resonance, as will his vision of a godless universe, his views on nihilism, and his insistence on the need for affirmation and creativity. The following quotation from *Menschliches Allzumenschliches* marks an appropriate end to this chapter and introduction to what is to come:

> Our age makes the impression of being an interim-condition: the old ways of looking at the world, and the old cultures, are still partly in existence, the new are not yet secure and part of the order of the day, and consequently without firmness and consistency. It looks as if everything were chaotic – the old has gone, the new is worthless and increasingly invalid . . . We are vacillating, but we must not lose heart, we must not abandon that which we have recently achieved. And apart from this – we *cannot* go back to the old ways, we *have* burnt our boats behind us, and all we can do is be brave, come what may. Let us stride forward – let us move into the unknown!

2

From the Jahrhundertwende to Weimar

One year into the new century Hofmannsthal wrote an essay in letter form entitled *Brief des Lord Chandos*; it was published in 1902 as *Ein Brief*. Using an alienating historical mask Hofmannsthal expressed the consternation experienced by the young lord and the *impasse* he had reached, the inability to think and speak coherently, the awareness of the inadequacy of language and the reluctance to attempt to use generalisations and value-judgements; those words which had hitherto come to him so easily, those words which were glibly used to pronounce and pontificate, he explained, crumbled in his mouth like rotting fungus. Words had lost all coherence for him, and the pattern of reality was totally fragmented: all became a vortex which swirled in vertiginious confusion. This *Sprachkrise*, endemic in Vienna at the turn of the century (we think of the closing proposition of Wittgenstein's *Tractatus*), betokened a deep-seated malaise in man's attitude to language: in Hofmannsthal's case that effortless ease with which he had written poetry of exquisite refinement had been superseded by crisis, and although he did not abjure writing he nevertheless sensed that lyrical self-indulgence was not enough, and that the twentieth century would bring with it more challenging and more disturbing modes of experience. At the same time that Hofmannsthal published *Ein Brief* (it appeared in book form in 1905) another work was in progress which, appearing in 1906, again takes as one of its central themes the problem of communication – Robert Musil's *Die Verwirrungen des Zöglings Törleß*. This remarkable short novel has little in common with the rash of descriptions of pedagogical cruelty to be found in many of the popular novels of this time (including Hesse's *Unterm Rad*), nor is it essentially a study in homosexuality.

The central concern is expressed in the motto from Maeterlinck which prefaces the book: to describe means to debase, for human experience is utterly ineffable, a mystery made banal by man's crude attempts at portrayal. Young Törleß, cadet at an exclusive military boarding school, encounters sadism, violence, and a world both repugnant and fascinating, that which Musil will later describe as the dual nature of things: language seems woefully inept at expressing this complexity, the awareness, dimly felt, of a world beyond reason and of situations manifold in their impact. Yet clarity, in a certain sense, is achieved, and Musil's precision, subtlety and skilful psychological penetration mark him out as a highly accomplished and sophisticated author. As a scientist Musil sought exactitude and clarity: as an artist he strove to convey the baffling world of sense impressions. *Törleß* is certainly a highly skilful piece of narrative prose, prescient in the portrayal of atavistic forces lurking behind the façade of respectability and extremely subtle in the description of adolescent confusion and of the education of a writer, one who knows the parameters of language and the need for ironic detachment.

The new century, then, begins with a note of scepticism concerning language and its ability to convey meaning unambiguously; Nietzsche had also expressed his doubts in the 1880s. Hofmannsthal's previously unthinking acceptance gives way to reservation, particularly concerning the use of abstractions and aesthetic self-indulgence in facile word-spinning; Musil will think of language and its limitations for much of his life, and in his gigantic novel *Der Mann ohne Eigenschaften* (see the next chapter) will posit a possible 'language' which would be at the same time more imaginative and more precise. Garrulous attitudinising will be one of the targets in this novel, the debasement of language and the consequent cheapening of concepts. Another Viennese should be mentioned here, Musil's contemporary Karl Kraus, a writer surely unique in his constant vigilance and punitive satire against clichés of all kinds. Kraus detested the poseurs of the Café Griensteidl and singled out Hermann Bahr for vitriolic attack: the famous *Die demolirte Litteratur* of 1896 delights in debunking the aesthetes with their *préciosité* and deliberate cult of decadent lassitude. What the young Kraus despised most in Bahr was his lack of integrity, and the conviction would grow within him that a man's art – or his aesthetic pretensions – were intimately bound up with his moral character. It is in a man's use of language that Karl Kraus found a valuable clue to his ethical core, and the language of most of his Viennese contemporaries he found either cliché-ridden, hollow, pretentious or inflated beyond measure. Not yet twenty-five years old, Kraus founded his own satirical journal, *Die Fackel*, the first number of which appeared in April 1899: from 1911 onwards it would be written entirely by Kraus himself until his death in 1936. Many of the younger, avantgarde writers of the day appeared in the early numbers (such writers as Heinrich Mann, Frank Wedekind and Franz Werfel), but the literary establishment and the aesthetes of Vienna were castigated without mercy: even Hofmannsthal was not spared. Writing, like Kafka, late at night, and besieged by spectres of human folly, vanity and viciousness, Kraus took it upon himself to be the Cassandra of his age and the champion of the new, of that which was vital and above all honest. (The poem 'Nach zwanzig Jahren' succinctly summarises his *credo*.) His defence of Adolf Loos, Georg Trakl and Oskar Kokoschka and the writers associated with Ludwig von Ficker's journal *Der Brenner*, the support given to Peter Altenberg and Stanislaus Przybyszewski, are also matched by his love of late Goethe and his deep devotion to Nestroy: the greatest emphasis is upon renunciation of specious glitter (Heine) and the praise of authenticity and integrity. The triumph of the mendacious, the mediocre and the banal Kraus feared above all, a triumph achieved predominantly through the medium of the press, for he saw with unusual clarity that the manipulation of words by thoughtless, third-rate minds blurred the reader's critical receptivity, and the unscrupulous have their way prepared for their more sinister purposes. Kraus's greatest achievement, the enormous drama *Die letzten Tage der Menschheit* (1918–19), is a forerunner of documentary drama in that it reproduces the speech of cafés, of clubs, of the Ringstraße and of politicians and generals: Kraus lets men condemn themselves by their own phrases, phrases born of greed, stupidity and gullibility. Only occasionally does a constructive voice sound in the general Babel which accompanies the Apocalypse (and Messianic terms *are* appropriate to Kraus's vision); in a welter of rodomontade and tergiversation all sanity is eclipsed and the 'banality of evil' (the term is Hannah Arendt's) unflinchingly exposed.

Kraus sought above all the clear, authentic voice: like Wittgenstein he greatly admired the work of Georg Trakl, that poet who, dying by his own hand in the psychiatric wing of the military hospital in Cracow in November 1914, exemplifies well the transition from Neo-romantic, even decadent, attitudinising to a harsher, proto-Expressionistic exploration of reality. The world of crepuscular decay and haunting euphony in Trakl has much of the early Hofmannsthal in it; the use of parataxis, unusual topoi and above all of compressed, laconic imagery creates a decidedly original tone. Trakl's poetry may be called 'modern' in its complex use of metaphor, where metaphors become unfamiliar images which radiate an evocative power. His colour adjectives are characteristic and bewildering, there being no key to their understanding; they are not always private and abstract, for some concession is made to conventional usage. The world Trakl portrays is half-familiar to the reader, and its reflection in painting would be Franz Marc rather than, say, Kandinsky, of whom he has been called the literary equivalent. Another great admirer was Rilke, that major European poet whose vapid beginnings were mentioned in Chapter 1. The movement away from effusion and self-indulgence towards a greater objectivity was paralleled elsewhere in Europe by the Imagist demand for a rejection of flabby Georgian verse: Rilke's admiration for the ruthless objectivity of Cézanne and for the fearless truth of Baudelaire's 'Une charogne' reminds the reader of Ezra Pound's plea for the imitation of Gautier and Eliot's appreciation of Laforgue. In Paris Rilke learned much from Rodin, above all from the latter's insistence on craftmanship, persistence and dedication, and a corresponding tautness and muscular suppleness emerges in his poetry. The *Requiem* of 1908 states the new position unequivocally: emotion must be controlled, if not entirely expunged; the poet must shape and transfigure experience into an objective statement. The *Neue Gedichte* of the same year are supreme examples of this new outlook, acknowledged masterpieces of clarity, refinement and precision, with only rare lapses into a manneristic self-consciousness. There is no sterile *l'art pour l'art*, however: a subtle symbolism is present in many of the poems, including the famous *Dinggedichte*, these recreations of objects (or animals, patiently observed) in a language that is objective, yet evocative and allusive. 'For verses are not feelings, as many people believe (we have enough of these, from an early age) – they are experiences': this is what Rilke has learned, and what the *Neue Gedichte* exemplify. The words are spoken by Rilke's *alter ego* Malte Laurids Brigge, whose *Aufzeichnungen* he started as early as 1904 in Rome, and on which he worked intermittently for nearly five years. The book (or, rather, 'notes') appeared in 1910 and is undoubtedly the expression of a crisis in the poet's life, a coming to terms with the problems of aestheticism and harsh reality. Rilke is one of the first in German literature to register the full terror of loneliness, dread and isolation, of 'Grenzsituationen' and the predicament of 'faceless' modern man. Those descriptions of the minor Danish aristocracy show that Rilke has not entirely succeeded in exorcising those *précieux* and somewhat effete aspects of his earlier work, but the descriptions of Parisian streets, of decaying buildings, sickness and deformity have a directness lacking in the earlier writings: here is no sentimental *Arme-Leute-Poesie* but uncompromising portrayals of squalor. The work is also stylistically ahead of its time: the traditional narrative has been replaced by a new, more tentative approach, the tenuous nature of which being better suited to convey the uncertainties of Malte's experiences. The narrative technique in *Malte Laurids Brigge* springs from the conviction that all 'finished' forms of literature impose a false order: there can be no omniscient narrator in a work that is a fragmentary expression of one man's individual vision. Malte's consciousness is presented directly; no other perspectives are given. The result may be solipsistic, but is also a highly effective way of portraying isolation.

The work of Rilke in the decade preceding the First World War demonstrates on the one hand a unique ability to create perfect art-forms – the sonnets of the *Neue Gedichte* – and yet also a reluctance to use the traditional form of the novel, and the preference for a fragmentary, more tenuous form of narration. But poetry will also move from the precise creation of perfect images and yield to a more passionate, less exclusive attitude to reality. The problems which Malte Laurids Brigge faced – the meaning of love and death, and the relationship between art and life – haunted Rilke after the completion of that book (or, rather, the termination of the notebooks). That which Rilke realised as his task was nothing less than the radical re-interpretation of existence, a poetic reappraisal of traditional concepts and ways of feeling. Rilke's poetry after 1910 is radically new in that it can no longer rely upon a traditional, universally accepted picture of reality; it creates its own world, trusting that the reader, if not immediately comprehending, will be moved by the power and sincerity of the poet's incantation to come to an independent discovery of the new ways of thought and feeling. The *Duineser Elegien*, begun in the early days of 1912, are not examples of a deliberately willed work-process such as Rilke had admired in Cézanne and Rodin, but a rush of lyrical intensity, a hymn-like pathos far removed from the 'French' perfection of the *Neue Gedichte* and resembling more the confessional poetry of Hölderlin or Klopstock. Yet the *Duineser Elegien* are also a modern document, a portrayal not only of man's ontological insufficiency but also of a crisis wrought by inauthentic living, thoughtless technology and the vulgarities of the twentieth-century Vanity Fair. It is a neat coincidence that the *Duineser Elegien* were completed in the same year (1922) in which *The Waste Land* was published. Both are major poetic statements; Rilke's, perhaps, is more elusive and difficult in its personal symbolism – Angel, the unrequited lovers and the young dead. The *Duineser Elegien* are as tentative and hesitant as *Malte Laurids Brigge* in their positing and their reservations: the Angel is no absolute against which man measures his achievements for the scale is a sliding one, and man's position *vis-à-vis* this standard vacillates according to Rilke's prevailing attitudes. The *Elegien* were conceived and written over a period of ten years, during which time the First World War totally destroyed the fabric of European civilisation: the darkest elegy, the fourth, written in Munich during the war itself, seems unable to bless or praise despite the emphasis on affirmation which Rilke felt was the task of the poet. The *Elegien* alternate between an awareness of man's fallenness and a tremulous hope with the poet constantly aware of the need to wrest wonder and significance from the most humble and transient of objects. Eschewing Eliot's Christian (or Buddhist) dimension Rilke creates his own mythological world which culminates in the luminous landscape of the dead. The famous letter to his Polish translator (November 1925) describes the great task of reinterpretation which he attempted in the elegies and also tells of the advent of the *Sonette an Orpheus*, stressing the similar concerns and preoccupations of the two cycles: that Orphic principle, the identification of artistic subjectivtity and objective reality, is the poet's goal. The testament of Rilke's latest poems, however, the awareness of the remoteness of the Orphic powers and the vulnerability of human existence, demonstrate a knowledge of fragmentation despite the holistic vision adumbrated by the visionary of Duino.

Rilke, Thomas Mann and Gerhart Hauptmann are writers who achieved world status: Thomas Mann and Gerhart Hauptmann would, with Hermann Hesse, be awarded the Nobel prize for literature. Hesse achieved early fame with the melancholy lyricism of his *Romantische Lieder* (1898) and the diluted romanticism of his *Bildungsroman Peter Camenzind* (1904); *Unterm Rad* (1906) endeared Hesse to many adolescent readers with its anti-intellectualism and sympathy for those who fail and who reject the adult world. Hesse's later work, particularly *Der Steppenwolf* (1927), will ensure a very wide readership; the novels before the First World War, for example *Gertrud* (1910) and *Rosshalde* (1913), deal with problems of artistry and marriage in an undemanding manner; the psychoanalytical preoccupations of *Demian* (1919) and the pseudo-orientalism of *Siddhartha* (1922) are pretentious rather than intriguing. *Klein und Wagner* (1919) with its theme of flight from order to disorder, from North to South, is a pale imitation of *Der Tod in Venedig*, whilst *Eine Kinderseele*, a portrayal of the relationship between child and parental authority, lacks the nervous subtlety of Kafka's *Brief an den Vater*, written the same year, 1919. The mawkish sentimentality of *Narziß und Goldmund* (1930) confirms the suspicion that Hesse rarely succeeded in shaking off the elegiac *Schwärmerei* of his youth (the poet Ernst Stadler commented shrewdly on his lack of incision and passion); the fame derived mainly from the ill-digested psychology and anti-materialism of his day, and a writing easy to assimilate and intellectually unsophisticated. To return to *Der Steppenwolf*: this novel endeared Hesse to countless readers who saw in him the psychologist most able to analyse the problems of the fragmented self. Harry Haller, the 'Steppenwolf' of the title, must learn that the rigid polarity between 'man' and 'wolf' is unhelpful: in a 'magic theatre' he experiences a drug-induced phantasmagoria where the self is experienced as a kaleidoscope of different aspects. Haller must learn to 'laugh', and Mozart is extolled as that artist who effortlessly combines the sublime with the human. A similar novelist is Jakob Wassermann, whose books were widely read at this time: *Caspar Hauser* (1908) is a memorable attack on the torpor and indifference of provincial society, and *Das Gänsemännchen* (1913) gives again a most perceptive picture of the stultifying narrowness of a German town in which the musician Daniel Nothafft is driven into a shrill and bitter self-assertion. Heinrich Mann's *Professor Unrat* (1905) may have proved the model for these novels of narrow-minded vindictiveness: although Heinrich Mann's fame rests squarely on his later work, that novel, and also *Im Schlaraffenland* (1900), should not be overlooked, the latter being a satirical attack on the pretensions of the *haute bourgeoisie* in Berlin at the turn of the century.

The years leading up to, and during, the First World War saw the consolidation of the literary merits of Rilke, Hofmannsthal, George, Thomas Mann, Gerhart Hauptmann and the writers of Expressionism to be described later; perhaps the most extraordinary, certainly the most fascinating German writer is Franz Kafka. As Rilke gave the German language a new suppleness and precision, so Kafka created a sober and elegant prose style, a lucidity which conceals extraordinary and frequently disturbing shadows. He sought a form of writing without convolutions and excrescences, and his reservations concerning the excesses of much Expressionist writing stem from this fastidiousness. He has somehow become the spokesman of modern Europe, a claim which would doubtless have amused, even embarrassed, him; his private agonies have become part of the stock-in-trade of readers the world over. The writer of *Angst*, of bureaucratic confusion, of nameless terrors, of fear or frustration, the explorer of sub-rational darkness where powerful figures of authority hold sway, of trials and castles – this is the Kafka of the popular imagination: his irony, oblique humour and self-deprecating modesty should also be remembered. Much has been made of his Prague background, his sense of alienation as a non-orthodox Jew living within the German-speaking minority of the Czech capital of the Kingdom of Bohemia within Austro-Hungary; his legal training (and Jewish exegetical practice) led to a competence in the portrayal of tortuous self-analysis and labyrinthine self-exculpation. The theme of isolation imposed by literature he shares with Thomas Mann; the portrayal of the tensions between father and son was a central concern of the Expressionists, as will become apparent; there are echoes of Dostoyevsky and Dickens. But Kafka made very much his own the droll and disturbing analysis of normality, an analysis which, frequently based on a metaphor, possesses an inconsequential, dreamlike logic; he seldom indulged in mystification for its own sake. He is also a master in the parabolic and aphoristic, failing perhaps as a novelist because he is no great organiser of experience and unwilling to sustain a narrative thread for long.

His first publications were the eight small vignettes *Betrachtungen*, appearing in 1908 in *Hyperion* (in the same year Carl Einstein's *Verwandlungen* appeared in that journal and shared with Kafka a capricious awareness of the absurd). The impressionistic nature of the sketches does not have the pellucid quality of Kafka's later prose, and it is only with extreme reluctance that, encouraged by Max Brod, he let the *Betrachtungen* be published in extended form by Ernst Rowohlt. The literary breakthrough is achieved by *Das Urteil*, written during the night of 22–23 September 1912, a short story that amazed Kafka by its force, precision and mystery. The purely personal element (the awareness of the impossibility of a permanent relationship with his fiancée) gives way to a wider statement: before the giant figure of the father and the vivid, reproachful memory of the friend (the lonely introvert) the brash protagonist succumbs. Kafka knew that his way was to be one of loneliness and dedication to art; the avid reader of the memoirs of Flaubert and Grillparzer would acknowledge the demands of literature and their manifest incompatibility with domestic normality. *Die Verwandlung* (1915) is an acknowledged masterpiece, probably one of the greatest short stories in the German language. Kafka had read, and indeed reviewed, the work of Heinrich von Kleist, and the precision and economy of his finest writing is indeed reminiscent of Kleist's prose fiction, as the writer Kurt Tucholsky had noted. The opening paragraph is the most famous in modern German literature: the reader's reaction is one of shock, bafflement and also amusement. No explanation is given for this metamorphosis: an image is presented, a metaphor treated as an actual fact. The protagonist's servility, total lack of valid human relationships and blind, scurrying industriousness are externalised into insect shape; the refusal to live in the fullest, widest sense, and the pusillanimous readiness to accept the demands of professional and family life are, Kafka sees, the greatest sin. The reader is tempted to consider the relationship between Kafka and his own family, or the inauthentic existence of so many in modern society; the story is also, like *Der Tod in Venedig*, one of degradation. But the *Galgenhumor* should not be overlooked, the sheer lack of commensuration between situation and response, and the absurd, even farcical nature of talking all too seriously about such a fantastic situation should always be admitted. Kafka proposed that this story, together with *Das Urteil* and *Der Heizer* (*Der Verschollene*) should be published together under the title *Die Söhne: Der Heizer*, later to become incorporated into the novel *Amerika*, has much of Robert Walser in it, a writer whom Kafka greatly esteemed, and whose novel *Jakob von Gunten* (1909) he may have had in mind when portraying the 'guileless fool' and his adventures.

Amerika, *Der Proceß* and *Das Schloß* are attempts at a longer narrative form which are not entirely successful, and Kafka may well have sensed this when he gave instructions that his work, with a few exceptions, should be destroyed. *Der Proceß* is certainly the most famous of the three. The thirty-year-old protagonist (Kafka's own age when he started writing the novel) is 'arrested' by those aspects of himself which he had hitherto ignored, by externalizations of certain tendencies which achieve an independent life. His involvement in a legal battle is his obsession with his own ratiocination: his undoubted intellect, his arrogance and his furtive sexuality assert themselves and prevent the emergence of a loving, generous character. Josef K. is his own worst enemy; occasionally a glimpse of the truth dawns on him and he is almost ready to admit his guilt, but selfishness invariably prevails. He turns to the lawyer Huld, the secretary cum nurse Leni and the painter Titorelli in his attempts at self-exculpation; it is the prison chaplain who advises self-scrutiny. The famous parable *Vor dem Gesetz* (*Before the Law*) demonstrates that it is man who prevents himself from reaching the truth, that man is not thwarted by malevolent demons but by that which is human, all-to-human. Josef K's rejection of Huld, who represents excessive, labyrinthine exegesis, and of Leni's sexuality, is a progressive step, but Kafka is ruthless: the execution is as meaningless, and embarrassing as Josef K.'s life had been. The reference to the 'highest judges', and the glimpse of the figure at the window with outstretched arms hint at the possible existence of a divine realm, but Kafka's Gnostic meditations on man's shortcomings did not allow him to believe in the necessary impingement of this realm on human affairs. *Das Schloß*, like *Der Proceß*, is unfinished, and shares many of the shortcomings of that novel – tedium, an inability to translate an inner state into sustained external narration and a manic self-obsession lit only infrequently by shafts of humour. Certain images, clear, disquieting and redolent of menace, do remain in the mind, however: the castle itself (or rather a huddle of broken buildings) surrounded by crows, the road that gets nowhere, the snowbound wastes. *Das Schloß* is concerned with the attempt to break the citadel of the ego, to come to terms with the self. The landsurveyor K. has to map out, or define, the boundaries of self; his assistants are grotesque parodies of his own preoccupations and desires. His abasement is necessary, and he must 'go to school' to gain self-knowledge. The novel is a stunted *Bildungsroman*:

unfinished and perhaps unfinishable it shows the reader a real world of bureaucratic confusion and telephone exchanges, insolent officials and dulled, ignorant villages against a background now precise, now blurred. And the Castle, resembling more and more an obsessed, deranged mind, loses significance: the attempt to live is of greater importance. Had the novel been completed K. may have been integrated into life – but this is mere speculation. Both novels may be flawed. But Kafka is best remembered for his remarkable short stories (not only *Das Urteil* and *Die Verwandlung* but also *In der Strafkolonie*, *Ein Landarzt* and the later *Josephine die Sängerin*, *Ein Hungerkünstler* and *Der Bau*) and his penetrating aphorisms. He is not a writer to be listed alongside Dante and Shakespeare (as Auden claimed), nor is he Edmund Wilson's 'self-doubting soul, trampled under', but a modern classic, one who sought to open men's eyes to the puzzling and elusive qualities of life, to provide startling images and situations which deflate and unsettle, but also amuse. And the skill and elegance of his writing were achieved despite sickness, loneliness and feelings of inadequacy: as the pertinent image of the nut-cracker in *Josephine die Sängerin* illustrates, the one who was perhaps less able to live than the rest of his fellows is the one who provides the most telling information.

Kafka's writing spans the period 1910–24, dates which conventionally have been held to encompass the years of Expressionism, a movement to which Kafka's writing runs parallel and which it touches at certain points despite his strictures and reservations. This chapter began by looking at various writers to determine their modernity and their European, even world, status; it will now turn to that particularly German contribution to modernism, that 'gash of fire across the world' to which so many fertile (and febrile) talents contributed. Chapter 1 of this book drew attention to two tendencies, the Naturalist–impressionist which concentrated on surface reality, or social and political problems, and the aesthetic or Neo-romantic attitude which was one of flight from the world towards the creation of artificial paradises: both failed to satisfy on a profound level. The former tendency remained too close to the surface of things and, in its frequent emphasis on social amelioration, was felt to be stultifying and drab; the latter tendency, with its emphasis on the rarefied and the refined, became ultra-precious, decadent and jejune. The Naturalist's descriptions of social conditions will give way to the expression of a subjective vision regardless of mimesis, and the concern for human life, for man crushed by pitiless machinery became far more intense than mere social reporting; likewise the emphasis upon inner vision, and on the fertile powers of the imagination would far exceed the symbolist cult of the soul. More vital emotions, more dynamic powers of description were extolled, as was an intense subjectivity which had no reluctance in destroying the conventional picture of reality in order that the expression be more powerful. And if distortion and aggressive expression of emotion were found in earlier works of art, then these were extolled as being forerunners of the new outlook, to which was given the name Expressionism.

The term, apparently derived from painting, has rarely been used with precision. Associated with intensity of expression is the tendency to dissolve traditional form, to abstract both colours and metaphors and use various anti-Naturalist devices, and here the term 'Expressionist' was also used to describe modernist techniques in general: not unlike Imagism, the word was used to denote an anti-mimetic employment of autotelic metaphors. The movement towards modern techniques such as simultaneity, collage-effects and startling, even absurd, imagery may have little to do with fervour and passion, but the term 'Expressionist' has perforce to describe both phenomena. In Germany particularly the sense of revolt implied in the new movement was associated with a vitalism which often found political outlets on both the Left and the Right; the word 'Expressionist' came to be applied to a desire to alter radically the meaning of art, man and society (Goebbels announced in his novel *Michael* that 'we men of today are all Expressionists'). A spiritual regeneration was also adumbrated, intense but often diffuse. It is no wonder that the term has been increasingly modified, qualified and also rejected because of its lack of precision: to group such writers as Jakob van Hoddis, Franz Werfel, Georg Kaiser and Hanns Johst under this blanket term is hardly satisfactory and when the names Carl Sternheim, Frank Wedekind and even Alfred Mombert are claimed as being 'Expressionist' then the critic must needs despair.

A further problem concerns the applicability of the term 'Expressionist' to writers not necessarily German, that is, the desirability of using the word to describe authors such as Strindberg, Dostoyevsky, Whitman and others who expressed with passionate intensity extreme subjective states. Playwrights such as Reinhard Sorge and Walter Hasenclever learned much from Strindberg's

Stationendramen with their pseudo-religious portrayal of purifica-
tion and regeneration. Both the dramatic techniques used by
Strindberg (the characters as emanations of a soul) and the ultimate message of the later plays (the need for self-transcendence)
will later dominate the German stage: Strindberg is of great importance in any study concerning the roots of those anti-Naturalistic
tendencies which appeared at the turn of the century. The predilection for extreme psychic states, ecstatic or desperate, came to be
identified with these tendencies and also termed Expressionistic;
here Dostoyevsky is of importance. The Naturalists had admired
him for his portrayals of poverty and social outcasts, but the new
generation greeted him as the explorer of pathological conditions
and the psychologist of crime: here a thinker like Moeller van den
Bruck found the perfect mouthpiece for his own reactionary pronouncements. Dostoevsky's portrayal of suffering and passion
from which a spiritual rebirth might ensue fascinated readers
grown tired of both the mechanical nature of Naturalism and of
sterile aestheticism.

What might be called the rhapsodic utopianism of much German
Expressionist writing was already present in the work of Walt
Whitman, a poet whose writing had a profound effect on the young
writers in Germany. Arno Holz's *Revolution der Lyrik* was pallid
indeed when compared with Whitman's powerful affirmation and
his hymn-like grandeur which Johannes Schlaf later propagated
and translated. (The Belgian Émile Verhaeren was also greeted by
Schlaf and Stefan Zweig, who praised particularly the collection *Les
forces tumultueuses* of 1902.) Whitman's praise of the creative potential of the New World also strikingly anticipates the emphasis on
the modern which played an important part in the new outlook and
would reach its climax in Marinetti's *Futurist Manifesto* of 1909
where the age of the machine is extolled, the destruction of muse-
ums and art-galleries is advocated and the moonlight is 'murdered': war is waged on the old and the moribund. It becomes
apparent that the movement away from Naturalism and symbolism towards a more intense subjectivity, and the rejection of
mimesis in favour of abstraction and distortion are European
phenomena. A disturbing vitalism breaks to the surface, basically
apolitical but later to be associated with an anarchic rejection of
the established order and, as an aftermath of the First World War,
tending towards radical political extremes. The importance of
Nietzsche is again paramount in any discussion of vitalism and the

destruction of social norms: Nietzsche, whose dithyrambic ecstasies reverberated throughout German literature during the first quarter of the twentieth century, as a writer like Gottfried Benn never ceased to proclaim, calling him the 'world-wide giant of the post-Goethean epoch'. Benn will stress the daring pathos of Nietzsche's thought, also the profundity of his psychological insights; others would find the rhapsodic fervour of *Also sprach Zarathustra* a most powerful stimulus. The provocative imagery of this work, the often hectic emphasis on heroism, individualism and frenzy, inspired a whole generation, and the praise of unbridled energy seemed to herald a new beginning. We have noticed (Chapter 1) that the Naturalists had supported Nietzsche's attack on the mundane and the banal, and the aesthetes had quoted with approval his defence of art; the new generation, however, that which may be called the Expressionist generation, saw in his daring apostacy and imperious gestures, his emphasis on idealism and passionate ecstasy, a necessary defiance. The New Man, an ideal frequently upheld by the Expressionists, often bore a startling resemblance to Zarathustra: the inflated hyperbole of much Expressionist writing may also result from an unsuccessful attempt to emulate the style of Nietzsche's masterpiece, and his own lapses into bathos became grossly magnified by lesser writers who strove to embrace the cosmos in their writing, or to exult in unemotional pantheism in the manner of Whitman. But that which has been called Expressionism is a complex mentality, and the description has to cover not only swirling rodomontade but also clipped, paratactic compression not far removed from Anglo-American Imagism. Certain writers expressed the fervour of their vision in a language derived from Nietzsche; others reduced language to a minimum, to the limits of intelligibility to express not an outer reality, but an inner state, frequently one of foreboding, and the nonchalant acceptance of absurdity. Absurdity, together with grotesque anti-bourgeois attitudes, is not far from the surface of Expressionism, and Dada will be the ultimate consequence.

It was Berlin, rather than Vienna, Munich or Prague which seemed, in the early years of the century, to contain the most exciting and the most productive of the new experiments in the arts: whereas the older generation of writers would meet at the house of the publisher Samuel Fischer (the writer Otto Flake describes meeting Gerhart Hauptmann, Thomas Mann, Arthur Schnitzler and Hugo von Hofmannsthal there, as well as politicians such as

Walther Rathenau), the younger writers would prefer the cafés, where readings took place and influential journals were founded. An early circle was *Die neue Gemeinschaft*, mostly anarchists whose members included Erich Mühsam, Peter Hille, Gustav Landauer and Else Lasker-Schüler. In 1909 Kurt Hiller and Erich Loewensohn founded *Der neue Club* and the *Neopathetisches Cabaret* associated with it; the poet Jakob van Hoddis (i.e. Hans Davidson) joined the group and read his poem 'Weltende' at one of the gatherings (it was later published in Franz Pfemfert's journal *Der Demokrat*). The collage effect, the juxtaposition and concatenation of bizarre images presents a picture, but basically expresses the poet's sense of vulnerability and disharmony in the world; formally quite conventional, it nevertheless conveys a disturbing sense of malaise which borders on the grotesque. (The poem may, incidentally, be an ironic reference to the effect caused by Halley's comet in May 1910 but, nevertheless, was felt to be prophetic of the end of 'sense' in art and in the bourgeois world.) The poet J.R. Becher, later to become Minister for the Arts in East Germany, was overwhelmed by it, and with characteristic hyperbole exulted in the impact that the poem made. Other memorable evenings at the *Neopathetisches Cabaret* included Max Brod's reading of Franz Werfel's poetry, and the introduction of the young Georg Heym. Whereas Werfel's poetry exemplifies the Whitmanesque, utopian-pantheistic element of Expressionism, Heym's came more and more to manifest a sense of disaster: his portrayal of the hallucinatory horror of cities and his sombre, chiliastic presentiments of doom express a mythological awareness of human destiny. The poem 'Der Krieg' combines a sense of dread with a feeling of awe for that fearful god who rises from chthonic depths: it exemplifies the Expressionist tendency to see beneath the surface of things to behold a mythical, archetypal vision. The novelist Kasimir Edschmid (i.e. Eduard Schmid) will later, in his famous essay 'Expressionismus in der Dichtung', stress the fact that although the Expressionist may take the same themes as the Naturalist there is a vast difference between the two modes of description: 'So the space inhabited by the Expressionist artist becomes vision. He doesn't look – he sees. He doesn't describe – he experiences. He doesn't reproduce – he forms. He doesn't take – he seeks. There is no longer the chain of facts – factories, houses, sickness, whores, screams, hunger. Now we have the *vision* of these.'

The group which gathered around Herwarth Walden's table in the Café des Westens formed *Der Sturm*, a periodical (later also an art gallery and a theatre) at the very centre of the Expressionist movement; the avantgarde of Berlin and elsewhere flocked to Walden: Alfred Döblin, Carl Einstein and Mynona (i.e. Salomo Friedländer) contributed, as did August Stramm, who sought to reduce language and syntax to an absolute minimum. For Walden, Stramm's work seemed to provide the literary equivalent of Futurist and Cubist paintings: subjective inner states in a form of words which approximate to an abstract picture, where neologisms intensify the sense of alienation from conventional descriptive poetry. Stramm's plays likewise reduce utterances to dramatic essentials: at the end of 1913 Stramm sent Walden his *Sancta Susanna*, which received its first performance in the *Sturmbühne* in October 1918, three years after Stramm's death on the Eastern front. Walden's chief rival in Berlin was Franz Pfemfert who began publishing *Die Aktion* in 1911. Pfemfert was more pragmatic than Walden and his political objectives were more sharply defined (Walden's interest in Communism was a comparatively late development): he fought for the release of Otto Gross and was in close touch with Karl Liebknecht and Rosa Luxemburg. In 1916 he launched his *Aktions-Bücher der Aeternisten* whose first spokesman, Ferdinand Hardekopf (i.e. Stefan Wronski), proclaimed the overtly anti-bourgeois attitudes of the new forms of art. Other important Berlin journals included Alfred Richard Meyer's *Lyrische Flugblätter*: his most important publication was Gottfried Benn's *Morgue und andere Gedichte* (1912). Here was no poeticising of death such as the young Rilke may have advocated, but a cynical awareness of disease by this young doctor in the hospitals of Berlin. After the publication of the *Morgue* poems Benn's work appeared in both the *Sturm* and *Die Aktion*, also in René Schickele's *Die Weißen Blätter*; in this latter journal he published the short sketch *Ithaca* (1914), a work which extolled youth, myth and violence as opposed to petrified academic pedantry and which anticipates Benn's later preoccupation with atavistic ideologies and 'thinking with the blood'. Before the First World War Benn was very much part of the Expressionist scene in Berlin; admired as a poet by both Stadler and Sternheim, as well as being a military doctor, he was a keen observer of the new direction in the arts. In the same year as the *Morgue* poems Pfemfert published in instalments Carl Einstein's *Bebuquin oder die Dilettanten des Wunders*, and Benn praised highly the 'absolute prose' of Einstein's novel, a concept which, together with that of the absolute poem, would come to preoccupy him.

Mention has been made of Ernst Stadler, a poet whose work, like that of Georg Trakl, exemplifies the movement away from Neo-romantic, *Jugendstil* elements to that which may be called predominantly Expressionist poetry. Stadler's review of Heym's *Der ewige Tag* and *Umbra Vitae* made him aware that the time of the Viennese *Kulturlyrik* was passed and that a more positive, affirmative, expressive form of poetry was necessary to convey the 'new pathos'. In 1913 Kurt Wolff published Stadler's mature verse in the Verlag der weißen Bücher; the title Stadler gave to it, *Der Aufbruch*, shows that the world of his earlier collections (*Praeludien*) has been left far behind. Two of his famous poems, 'Form ist Wollust' and 'Fahrt über die Kölner Rheinbrücke bei Nacht' demonstrate a high degree of craftsmanship as well as a yearning for cosmic embrace and exaltation. The excesses of a J.R. Becher are not found in Stadler, whose poem 'Der Spruch' contains the injunction very dear to the heart of the Expressionist generation, the untranslatable motto from Angelus Silesius – 'Mensch, werde wesentlich!' Stadler was killed on the Western Front in 1914; had he lived he would doubtless have joined those Expressionists who hailed this new and transfigured image of man, but the Nietzschean accents would certainly have been tempered by his experiences among the poor in the East End of London and his humanistic desire for communion with all. He is here akin to Franz Werfel, probably the best-known of all Expressionist poets, although not necessarily the best. The appearance of *Der Weltfreund* (1911) and Max Brod's reading of 'An den Leser' made an enormous impact: the four thousand copies of the first edition were sold out in a matter of weeks and Werfel's success was such that it was frequently claimed that the Expressionist movement began with him and with these poems. 'An den Leser' represents the declamatory, rhetorical aspect of the movement, much indebted to Whitman, as are many of the poems of the second collection, *Wir sind*, whose ecstatic tones are difficult to respond to at length. The 'O Mensch!' pathos cannot be sustained on a high level, and rapturous fervour sinks all too readily into the bathetic. As has been stated, the difficulty of subsuming the collage technique of a van Hoddis and the hymnic fervour of a Werfel under the heading 'Expressionist verse' is obviously unsatisfactory: discussions concerning the use of abstract metaphor, autotelic image, simultaneity and parataxis are relevant to certain areas but not to others. The broadest common denominator would seem to be the desire to express a subjective insight, whether it be in terse, urban images or in rhapsodic, cosmic metaphors: the flippant, almost cynical sense of urban malaise found in van Hoddis or Alfred Lichtenstein will lead indirectly to the poetry of *Neue Sachlichkeit* ('New Objectivity').

The links between the arts at this time are a fascinating source of study: as well as being an important innovator in painting, Wassili Kandinsky wrote poems and 'absolute plays', studies in synaesthesia similar to the experiments of a composer like Scriabin. Kandinsky was the mouthpiece of the Munich school of painters known as *Der blaue Reiter*, where Schönberg's music, and his paintings, were held in high esteem. Kandinsky had read a pre-publication extract of Schönberg's essay *Harmonielehre*, and this played a considerable part in the formulation of his own seminal work *Über das Geistige in der Kunst* (1912) where an 'inner necessity' in each art work is advocated and also the need for all the arts to progress towards the abstract status of music. Another important essay from this time is Wilhelm Worringer's *Abstraktion und Einfühlung* (1908), an exploration of the movement away from realism and representation towards the non-Naturalistic and the abstract: 'Einfühlung', or sympathetic representation giving way to 'Abstraktion'. In the theatre another painter, Oskar Kokoschka, prepared the way for a new intensity, a new violence of expression with his *Mörder Hoffnung der Frauen* (1910), a psycho-drama of violent sexual urges whose performance in Vienna led to Kokoschka's dismissal from the School of Applied Arts. Herwarth Walden recognised Kokoschka's talent after the latter left Vienna and moved to Berlin: *Der Sturm* benefited greatly from his work, especially his illustrations. There are echoes in *Mörder Hoffnung der Frauen* of Schönberg's *Erwartung* (1909), a febrile monodrama of presentiment and cruel knowledge, expressed in hectic exaggeration. It should be remembered that Freud's *Die Traumdeutung* had appeared scarcely a decade before this time: sexual tensions and, indeed, violence will play a considerable part in early Expressionist drama. Frank Wedekind looms large here, that 'Gehirnerotiker' (Julius Bab) whose eccentric talents, verging at times on the grotesque, often seem more appropriate to cabaret and Grand Guignol than conventional theatre. (He did, in fact, greatly enjoy cabaret, appearing in the *Elf Scharfrichter* in Munich where he both shocked and delighted the audience with his scurrilous performances.) Wedekind's attack on bourgeois *moeurs* is frequently bracketed with that of later Expressionist dramatists, but his cult of vitalism is manifested in eccentric characters: he could not tolerate the inflated ideals and hollow rhetoric of the 'O Mensch!' dramas but stylistically belongs in the early Expressionist camp with his predilection for the *outré* and the exaggerated. Whereas Max Halbe's *Jugend* (1893) with its psychology of adolescent love has certain things in common with *Frühlings Erwachen* (which appeared in book form in 1891), Wedekind's play, with the absurd caricatures, headless ghost and personification of 'life' belongs very much in the new repertoire. It is the play which is probably Wedekind's best: the torments and confusion of the young people, as well as the hypocrisy and pusillanimous deviousness of the other generation are portrayed with sympathy and precision. The outspoken discussion of sexual problems and the directness of certain scenes led to protracted battles with the censor: Wedekind's insistence on the absolute freedom of the creative artist endeared him to the avantgarde and greatly enhanced his reputation, zealously sought, as a *Bürgerschreck*.

Wedekind greeted the new century in prison on a charge of *lèse-majesté*: during this time he worked on his preposterous, erotic fantasy *Mine Haha oder Über die körperliche Erziehung der jungen Mädchen* (1901), where the limbs and breasts of young girls in their scanty costumes are wittily described. Physical aspects are paramount in this establishment for young ladies, and the mental and moral realms are totally ignored. This is the world of Effie in Wedekind's *Schloss Wetterstein* (1910), but also of his most famous creation. His stays in Paris and London had sharpened his observations of the pimps, swindlers, perverts and prostitutes, as well as of the dark London streets haunted by Jack the Ripper; the artistic *Boheme* of Munich, the corruption of Parisian society and the sordid wretchedness of Whitechapel provided the world through which Lulu moves with disdain and a curious naiveté. The prologue to the first Lulu play, *Erdgeist* (1895), uses a circus technique, later to be endorsed by Brecht: the lion-tamer, with whip and pistol, announces that he will provide the true, wild, beautiful animal and derides the so-called 'heroes' of German theatre (Hauptmann particularly is lampooned). Lulu is both fascinating and revolting and personifies a type of woman both Strindberg and Nietzsche described. Yet her courage and ultimate integrity must be admired: she remains true to herself throughout *Erdgeist* and most of *Die Büchse der Pandora* (1902), a play where the lesbianism of the Gräfin Geschwitz is portrayed with sympathy and compassion. The Lulu plays are marred by discursive longueurs and an undeniable tendency towards exhibitionism: *Erdgeist* is the more successful in its curious mixture of Feydeau farce and Victorian melodrama. The *Marquis von Keith* (1901) is another of his plays which deserve mention, a play which has kept its place in the standard repertoire; Thomas Mann recommended it and especially praised the final scene. Wedekind's talents, however, eccentric and one-sided, did not develop or mature and he remains a flawed and freakish example in early Expressionism. The same could be claimed for Carl Sternheim, who wrote over thirty plays but whose reputation rests largely on a handful of works written in his early years, the famous cycle *Aus dem bürgerlichen Heldenleben*. The deliberate flouting of Wilhelmine taboos is seen in the very title of the play *Die Hose*, i.e. *Knickers* (1911): if Wedekind is the cynical moralist then Sternheim, the modern Molière, is a satirist, aloof and merciless; the attack on red plush, potted plants and bric-à-brac is heightened and sharpened to ruthless precision. Sternheim strove to cut through the genteel in the German language, to expunge sentimentality and platitudes; the foreshortening of language and syntax is highly effective, and both he and Wedekind share a quirkily anti-Naturalistic method, a reduction to types and a deliberate artificiality of language which alienate and also fascinate the reader.

Immediately preceding, and during, the First World War remarkable works appeared on the German stage which portray with increasing violence the emergence of a new type of man. This vision will later be fused with a Utopian ideal, but in the plays of Sorge, Hasenclever, Johst and Kornfeld a desire for self-expression is found, a vital release stemming above all from Nietzsche. If it was the problem of sex which loomed large in Wedekind and Kokoschka, then the theme of the conflict between father and son becomes of prime importance. The younger German playwrights, between 1900 and the war years, portrayed with extraordinary intensity and violence the clash between generations, where incest and murder play a significant role. The father-figure becomes a symbol for authority in many of these plays, and the rebellion against this image reached febrile and strident proportions. Reinhard Sorge's *Der Bettler* (1912) and Walter Hasenclever's *Der Sohn* (1914) are famous examples here, as is Arnolt Bronnen's later *Vatermord* (1922), where the act of murder is perpetrated in a paroxysm of hatred. Further violence is rife in Paul Kornfeld's *Die Verführung* (1913), Hanns Johst's *Der junge Mensch* (1916) and

Anton Wildgans's *Dies Irae* (1918); Alfred Brust and Hans Henny Jahnn should also be mentioned. The great call is for 'Aufbruch', a new beginning, for change at all costs: an incandescent fervour is present which has not yet achieved an overtly political direction, that 'Aktivismus' demanded by a writer like Kurt Hiller. And the most famous German Expressionist playwright, Georg Kaiser, in his vision of the New Man, preferred a portrayal that had mystical, frequently apocalyptic, overtones. Kaiser was utterly obsessed by his task, or mission, and his intense energy and logical schematisation derive from a passionately held conviction – the regeneration of man. The lucid, mathematical precision of his plays contains a zealous fervour, and the staccato *Telegrammstil* becomes the perfect tool to describe the clash of concepts and the dialectical vitality of the resolution. In Kaiser the idea of social reform is only of secondary importance: a Nietzschean self-overcoming, a spiritual regeneration must be achieved before society can be changed. It is false to refer Kaiser's plays solely to conditions prevailing in Germany during and immediately after the war but a certain relevance is undeniable: *Die Bürger von Calais* (1913, first performed 1917) speaks of war, sacrifice and the attainment of moral sublimity. Kaiser's most well-known play is *Von morgens bis mitternachts* (1912): the Expressionist tendency to create types rather than fully-rounded characters, and the theme of self-discovery à la Strindberg are cleverly displayed. The *Gas* trilogy established Kaiser's reputation throughout Europe: *Die Koralle* (staged 1917) portrays capitalist ruthlessness and the need for a new, altruistic vision; *Gas I*, performed a few days after the armistice, illustrates the clash between two *Weltanschauungen*, one pastoral-idyllic and the other materialist-scientific.The play ends on a note of optimism, but *Gas II*, performed two years later, is a portrayal of apocalyptic destruction: the vision of the New Man recedes before the madness of the demagogue. The obsession of Kaiser with certain themes, the almost monomaniacal dedication of many of his characters, the frequent reduction of men to automata, the abstract stage settings, the steel constructions and harsh lighting seem to reflect a predisposition towards cruelty and bleakness which is not altogether dispelled by an ideal which seems a disturbing fusion of Nietzscheanism and Christianity. Perhaps only a Kafka could remain aloof from that which was happening around him: the plays Kaiser wrote between 1917 and 1923 were created while Germany was in the grip of defeat, collapse, disillusion and revolution; the country was tremulous with hopes for the future, yet shot through with brutality and civil strife.

Before the end of the fighting in November 1918 two plays appeared on the German stage (albeit in restricted performances) which showed the senselessness of war and its brutalising effect upon men: Fritz von Unruh's *Ein Geschlecht* (written 1916) and Reinhart Goering's *Seeschlacht* (written 1917). The former play, with the lofty grandeur of its language, looks back to Kleist, but the violence and the extremity of the emotions expressed place von Unruh very much in the Expressionist fold: it is a concentrated outburst of explosive power, dwelling on the proximity of lust and hatred and combines an optimistic humanitarian ideal with a shrill, hectic sadism. *Seeschlacht*, more closely linked to a particular situation (the battle of Jutland), has a gripping, fatalistic quality at times reminiscent of ancient tragedy: the language is clipped and jagged, but swells at times to a rhythmic pathos. Goering portrays men under stress, going ineluctably to their doom and reacting with expressive intensity to their predicament. These, and the plays of Kaiser, have no equal anywhere else in Europe: the collapse of Germany, the establishment under enormous difficulties of the Weimar Republic, the turmoil of violence unleashed on the streets during the fighting between extremist factions, the hectic optimism and the strident call for brotherhood created an atmosphere without parallel. Hopes for the emergence of the New Man, for the spiritual transfiguration of mankind, alternated with a sense of frustration and disillusionment: not only the theatre, but the introduction by Kurt Pinthus to his famous anthology of Expressionist poetry, *Menschheitsdämmerung* (1919), described the almost Messianic aspirations and the tribulations of the time. But the supreme example in the theatre of that fervent expression of hope for the transfiguration and redemption of man is Ernst Toller, whose *Die Wandlung* (1919) is perhaps the finest product of the German theatre at this time. The nightmare visions, the alternation of dream sequences and realistic scenes, the obvious indebtedness to Georg Büchner in the scene with the sadistic medical professor and the mutilated patients, the hero's realisation that he must join the masses, the radical language and final triumph of visionary fervour make this a climax of Expressionist theatre, a supreme example of Expressionist political activism. *Masse Mensch* (1919) is less ecstatic and illustrates the working-out of a conflict between the intellectual and the masses who are not yet ripe for ultimate comprehension: the situation is obviously Toller's own, his involvement in the Soviet Republic in Munich in the winter of 1918–19. Toller's subsequent and growing disillusionment with the progress of Weimar society is seen in *Hoppla, wir leben!* (1927); other works explore the basic problems of pain and suffering, problems which social amelioration cannot resolve. Toller collaborated closely with Erwin Piscator in the 1920s, and the use of film-sequences and documentary material was to be taken up later by Bertolt Brecht. It is true to say that the theatre (as well as painting) would make Expressionism known throughout Europe and even the world: the New York stage of the early 1920s was aware of the new German theatre and emulated many of its achievements, performing Toller, Hasenclever, Wedekind and Werfel (*Spiegelmensch*). German Expressionist cinema should also be mentioned here, the cinema of Robert Wiene (*Das Cabinet des Dr Caligari*), Friedrich Murnau (*Nosferatu*), Paul Wegener (*Der Golem*) and Fritz Lang (*Metropolis*): the preoccupation with madness, tyranny and death, and the haunting use of nightmarish menace providing a unique and chilling experience.

If the theatre and the lyric were in the foregound of avantgarde Expressionism in Germany, then prose fiction seemed to lag behind, apparently lacking the potentiality for immediate, ecstatic expressiveness. But it would be false, as has been shown, to identify the movement purely with declamatory fervour: a close examination would show that the discursive prose form also underwent drastic modification in the early years of this century. Parataxis, ellipsis, dislocation and simultaneity characterise the work of many writers, particularly Carl Einstein, Mynona and Döblin. The common denominator of most of the works mentioned here, in the lyric, drama and prose fiction, is an attitude of revolt, sometimes political (Toller), sometimes mystical (in the poetry of Mombert and the plays of Barlach), sometimes eccentric or grotesque (van Hoddis). The revolt is seen either in the subject-matter (defiance of authority, disregard of sexual taboos) or in stylistic experimentation. It may be claimed that the three movements which superseded Expressionism – Dada, Surrealism and *Neue Sachlichkeit* – were unthinkable without it, the first deriving from the cult of anarchic absurdity, the second from the pursuit of the irrational and the last from the cynical, flippant awareness of modernism. The antics of Arp and Huelsenbeck in Zurich and the later contortions of the 'Oberdada' Johannes Baader in Berlin, the 'Merz' of

Schwitters, the photomontage experiments of Grosz and Herzfelde and the lunatic excesses of *Jedermann sein eigener Fußball* explore an area where absurdity, nihilism and political and sexual provocation uneasily overlap. Febrile and inchoate Expressionism may have become, but the energies released, although diffuse and shortlived, produced unique and astonishing works, some of which represent Germany's most distinctive contribution to twentieth-century art.

This chapter began by looking at the new century and its main artistic preoccupations: doubt in the ability of language to express the new uncertainties; dissatisfaction with *fin-de-siècle* velleities; a search for greater plasticity and precision in poetry; the phenomenon of Kafka; the rise of Expressionism. Writers such as Hugo von Hofmannsthal, Robert Musil, Hermann Hesse, Rilke, George and Heinrich and Thomas Mann will be shown as developing organically from the *Jahrhundertwende* onwards, reaching their maturity in the years of the Weimar Republic and later: this the next chapter will discuss. Expressionism may well have carried the seeds of its own destruction within itself, but its achievements are now recognised, not only in literature, but in painting and in music. We shall now turn to the 1920s and 1930s to assess the major accomplishments in German literature; although it is erroneous, as has been shown, to equate the period of Weimar with the triumph of the avantgarde in Germany and false to see Weimar culture as a radical break with the past, the fourteen or so years under discussion do mark a watershed in literature that has few equals. The era of *Der Zauberberg, Der Steppenwolf, Berlin Alexanderplatz, Die Dreigroschenoper* and the beginnings of *Der Mann ohne Eigenschaften* is indeed a memorable one. The period of epic theatre, of monumental novels, of the late, quintessential utterances of George and Hofmannsthal (Rilke we have already noted), of war novels of international stature is one which equals the wealth of the pre-1914 period, perhaps even surpasses it.

3

The Literature of the Weimar Republic and the First Austrian Republic

Germany's defeat in the First World War and the consequent collapse of the Second Reich resulted in a state of demoralisation and social anomie which was only partially overcome during a period of relative prosperity in the 1920s, before the Great Depression led to further polarisation of political views. In this situation Thomas Mann, Heinrich Mann and Hermann Broch produced a series of novels which provided in one form or another a critical conspectus of the process by which Germany had grown to be a confident imperial power, then metamorphosed into a republic. They show why parliamentary democracy, to which its new rulers were committed, lacked the support of large sections of the community, which looked to more radical alternatives, either to dictatorship of the proletariat on the Soviet model instituted after the October Revolution of 1917, or to the restoration of Germany's former military strength and national self-esteem.

Thomas Mann's *Der Zauberberg* (1924), although set in a Swiss sanatorium during the seven years preceding the First World War and not overtly concerned with politics, must be understood in the context of its author's development during the novel's eleven-year-long gestation from aestheticism through national conservatism, which finds expression in *Gedanken im Kriege* (1914), *Friedrich und die große Koalition* (1915) and above all in *Betrachtungen eines Unpolitischen* (1918), to reluctant acceptance then support of the Weimar Republic, declared in *Von deutscher Republik* (1922). Mann later defined *Der Zauberberg* as a *Bildungsroman* and a *Zeitroman*; however, the theme of education here receives ironical treatment in the person of the central figure Hans Castorp, whose intended brief visit to Davos is extended to seven years when he too becomes ill. He is exposed to a variety of unfamiliar influences which throw his simple view of life and the world into a confusion which is never fully resolved. Time, too, receives no straightforward definition; on the one hand it refers to the flexible sense of time induced by the enforced leisure of the sanatorium under the threat of death; on the other to the fact that the patients form a social microcosm of a Europe about to be plunged into the crisis of the First World War, the outbreak of which ends the novel. Thomas Mann does not give a specifically German definition to the opposing philosophies Castorp absorbs in his encounters with Settembrini, who advocates a west European liberalism with its roots in the enlightenment, and Naphta, who stands for a disciplined hierarchical system. Yet the resemblance of Settembrini's views to those of Heinrich Mann, with whom Thomas had clashed in *Betrachtungen eines Unpolitischen* in defence of a position of 'machtgeschützte Innerlichkeit', suggests that he came to see in Castorp a representative of Germany at the parting of the ways, forced to choose between East and West or adopt a third course. The third course is defined in a dream vision experienced by the hero in the chapter 'Schnee', written early in 1923, as a humanism which can be related to Mann's position in *Von deutscher Republik*. Mann's fears that his new commitment was not shared by many of his compatriots are perhaps reflected in the fact that the vision, placed shortly after the centre of the novel, is quickly forgotten by Castorp, who is drawn into a miasma of more dubious influences before he departs for the war.

Heinrich Mann's *Kaiserreich* trilogy, consisting of *Der Untertan* (1918), *Die Armen* (1917) and *Der Kopf* (1925), is fired throughout by a firm adherence to republicanism, conveyed by means of a satirical exposure of the social and psychological mechanisms by which the authoritarian structure of the Second Reich was perpetuated. Sub-titled 'Geschichte der öffentlichen Seele unter Wilhelm II', *Der Untertan* focuses on the small town of Netzig and the representative figure of Diederich Heßling, whose rise in the social hierarchy is achieved by a mixture of craven submission to the establishment and ruthless elimination of rivals. While in *Die Armen* Heinrich Mann retains this setting while concentrating on the futile efforts of a worker to challenge the corruption of the system by legal means, he directs his attention in *Der Kopf* to the intrigues of the governing élite as he traces the careers of closely linked protagonists, Terra and Mangolf, who represent differing ways in which the ambitious intellectual may accommodate himself to a system immune to reform from outside.

Although Hermann Broch was Austrian, his trilogy *Die Schlafwandler* (1931–2) deserves consideration here as another attempt to define the forces underlying Germany's progress and collapse during the thirty years of Wilhelm II's reign. The salient contrasts between the beginning, middle and end of the period are made evident by the technique of setting each unit of the trilogy in a single year and examining how an individual with the typical features of his social position copes (or fails to cope) with the disintegration of values which in Broch's view lay at the root of the contemporary malaise. The attachment of his figures to attitudes which have a blinkering effect, whether it is the anachronistic Romanticism of the Prussian officer in *Pasenow*, the anarchic disillusionment with accepted norms and sectarian enthusiasm of Esch, or the crudely selfish realism of Huguenau, has its counterpart in similar characterisations in the novels of Broch's fellow Austrians Doderer, Canetti and Musil. His ethical concern cannot be reduced to a simple advocacy of social responsibility, although the trilogy ends with a vision of a new human unity. In the final part of the trilogy Huguenau's *Sachlichkeit*, however morally repellent, is contrasted as a means of coming to terms with the chaos of Germany's defeat with the forms of escapism represented by the alcoholism of Jaretzki, the domestic withdrawal of Hanna Wendling or the idealism of the Salvation Army girl Marie, whose stories receive separate treatment in conjunction with philosophical excurses on 'Zerfall der Werte' designed as commentary on the trilogy as a whole. *Die Schlafwandler* thus develops into a multi-stranded or 'polyhistorical' novel with similarities to the work of Joyce and Proust.

The closing events of *Die Schlafwandler* take place in Alsace as the western front collapses; the novel can thus be linked to a number of novels which take the defeat and the revolution as their themes and approach them from various standpoints and in different styles. They include Theodor Plievier, *Der Kaiser ging, die Generäle blieben* (1932) (documentary), Bernhard Kellermann, *Der neunte November* (1920) (Expressionist), Ernst Glaeser, *Frieden* (1930) (a provincial *Zeitroman* centred on a confused adolescent), and Georg Hermann, *November achtzehn* (1930) (in which the events merely form the background to the personal crisis of a cultivated middle-class figure whose ruminations are conveyed in an impressionistic style which owes much to Fontane). All these, however, pale to insignificance beside Alfred Döblin's *1918. Eine deutsche Revolution*, which, although it was written much later under the influence of its author's conversion to Catholicism and appeared at intervals between 1939 and 1950, demands inclusion here on account of the range and thoroughness of its treatment. It shares with *Die Schlafwandler* a multi-stranded narration of concurrent plots, but concentrates on the soldier and grammar-school teacher Friedrich Becker, who in book 1 (*Bürger und Soldaten*), which covers two weeks in November 1918, is portrayed recovering from wounds in a hospital in Alsace. In book 2 (*Verratenes Volk*), which lasts from 2 November to 7 December, Döblin broadens his account to include the activities of the Rat der Volksbeauftragten under Friedrich Ebert, the Spartakusbund under Wilhelm Liebknecht and Rosa Luxemburg, and the General Staff in Kassel. Book 3 (*Heimkehr der Fronttruppen*) adds references to Woodrow Wilson's peace efforts, while book 4 (*Karl und Rosa*) concentrates on the imprisonment of the leading Spartacists in 1915 and from mid-December to mid-January 1918–19, and their fatal decision to unleash a badly prepared uprising, presented by Döblin as doomed to failure. This vast panoramic novel is much more than a historical reconstruction based on a study of sources. Its religious dimension finds expression in Friedrich Becker's visions of the mystic Johannes Tauler and in his decision after his brief and accidental participation in the Spartakus uprising to become a wandering preacher. Furthermore, Döblin drew on his psychiatric expertise to portray the leading revolutionaries as pathological figures, subject to hallucinations, as exemplified by Rosa Luxemburg's prison conversations with the spirit of her former lover Hans, and delusions of grandeur, as in Karl Liebknecht's identification with Milton's Satan. At the same time Ebert's pact with the military is interpreted as a betrayal of the people, so that the reader is left with the impression that the revolution is a fateful process in which no politician possesses the knowledge of what is right or the power to implement it.

Not only the revolution, but the war which preceded it demanded literary evocation, touching as it did on the experience of a whole generation of men forced to come to terms with a conflict in which a yawning gulf had become apparent between the imperative of personal survival and the demands of national interest. Although Ernst Jünger's diary *In Stahlgewittern* appeared as early as 1920, the war novel of the Weimar Republic, whether written from a right-wing nationalist or left-wing humanitarian point of view, is a phenomenon of the years 1927–31 and reflects the coincidental polarisation of political forces. (Mention should also be made of works which deal with the conflict at sea, culminating in the inconclusive battle of Jutland: Plievier, *Des Kaisers Kulis*, 1929; Goering, *Seeschlacht*, 1917 and *Scapa Flow*, 1919.) The war novels of the right (Schauwecker, *Aufbruch der Nation*, 1929; Wehner, *Sieben vor Verdun*, 1930; Beumelburg, *Die Gruppe Bösemüller*, 1930, and many others; Zöberlein, *Glaube an Deutschland*, 1931; and Dwinger, the trilogy *Die deutsche Passion*, 1929–32) owe much to Jünger and share his view of modern mechanised warfare as a testimony to nature's capacity to release instincts which, we are to believe, cleanse the individual of isolating egotism. The novels of the left, on the other hand (Arnold Zweig, *Der Streit um den Sergeanten Grischa*, the first and best of a cycle of six novels written in the course of thirty years and given the collective title *Der große Krieg der weißen Männer*, and Renn, *Krieg*, both 1927; Remarque, *Im Westen nichts Neues*, Scharrer, *Vaterlandslose Gesellen*, Frey, *Die Pflasterkästen*, all 1929; Köppen, *Heeresbericht*, 1930), besides possessing greater authenticity (claimed also by the right), challenge this view. Arnold Zweig's *Grischa*, in which a Russian soldier, although innocent, is executed on spying charges, traces the process by which an intellectual gains insight through contact with higher ranks into a case in which *raison d'état* takes precedence over humanity. The bestseller *Im Westen nichts Neues* emphasises the futility of war, in which survival is a matter of chance, contrasts the squalor and suffering of the trenches with the jingoism of the home front, portrays traditional notions of heroism as anachronistic and gives value only to the comradeship of shared fear and privation.

Alfred Döblin's *Berlin Alexanderplatz. Die Geschichte vom Franz Biberkopf* (1929) is now recognised as the archetypal metropolitan novel of the twentieth century, although its skeletal plot, conveyed with remarkable fidelity in twelve of the thirteen parts of Rainer Werner Fassbinder's television film, is a squalid tale of an ex-convict who tries to go straight, alone or with others' help, but is sucked into the Berlin underworld until the murder of his mistress and his physical and mental breakdown lead to a transformation of his personality and prospects. Döblin, however, fleshes out these bare bones with a mass of disparate material consisting largely of the sights and sounds of the metropolis, conveyed by means of a montage technique which has its counterpart in the collages characteristic of the art of the 1920s. Numerous voices make themselves heard, none of which can be clearly identified with Döblin's authorial self, although he occasionally adopts the mask of a didactic narrator, who comes particularly to the fore in the introductory summaries to the nine books. Allegorical and mythical figures are introduced, and there is a profusion of Classical and biblical references and quotations, which in juxtaposition with the crass Naturalism of speech (Berlin dialect) and action (violent crime), produce an effect of extraordinary density and momentum. The example of James Joyce, whose *Ulysses* Döblin read before completion of the novel, and the medical knowledge he gained as a psychiatrist in a mental hospital and as a GP in one of Berlin's poorest districts, contribute much to the portrayal of Franz, from the moment he leaves prison and fragments of the urban scene crowd in on his confused senses, to the point when he emerges from a deep coma. The ending, in which the didactic narrator counselling clear-eyed individual responsibility clashes with the collective voice of the metropolis which appears to represent mass euphoria, may indicate Döblin's ambivalent position, characteristic of the intellectual in the Weimar Republic, responding to the demands of the individual conscience yet aware of the need for solidarity with the like-minded.

A similar ambivalence emerges from Lion Feuchtwanger's *Erfolg* (1930), especially in its treatment of the role of art. Here again personal, moral and political crises are made to coincide in a multi-stranded novel, in which the director of a Munich art gallery is imprisoned for flouting conservative norms in his choice of works for exhibition, a rabble-rouser attempts to take over the government (an incident modelled on Hitler's Munich putsch of 1923), and Jacques Tüverlin, a writer-figure close to Feuchtwanger, as he witnesses these events and develops his relationship with a woman working for the imprisoned man's release, is brought to revise his view of art, advocating in the end an engagement for the victims of a corrupt judicial system, while refusing adherence to the Marxist aesthetic of Pröckl, an engineer modelled on Brecht. Feuchtwanger's narrative style aims at a distancing effect, as if he were writing a historical novel in the year 2000. Such a point of view may be linked to his position, comparable in its ambivalence to that of Döblin, between the ivory tower and a commitment definable in political terms. Under the pressure of later events he was to move ever closer to the latter.

Erfolg is merely the most substantial and, in its treatment of the theme of justice and the role of the artist, the most intellectually far-reaching of a number of novels which, set in Berlin or the provinces, reflect the social developments of the time, especially as these affect the personal and professional lives of workers, petty bourgeois and (often displaced) intellectuals. Of these Erich Kästner's *Fabian* and Hans Fallada's *Kleiner Mann, was nun?* share a bleak view of the prospects of a decent life for those with minimum ambitions when mass unemployment, after the Wall Street crash and the consequent withdrawal of American loans on which the shaky Weimar Republic economy depended, proved in Germany to be even more devastating than elsewhere. *Fabian* (1931), subtitled 'Geschichte eines Moralisten', presents the distorting mirror of satire to a period of social anomie in order to warn against the passivity of its principal characters, who despite the best intentions fail to halt the course towards political extremism or challenge the commercial rat-race and its corruption of personal relations. The morality of the individual needs force and direction if it is to be effective; such is the implication of the final episode, in which Fabian drowns in the attempt to save a child who has fallen into a river (and swims to the bank). *Kleiner Mann, was nun?* (1932) traces the vicissitudes of the marriage of Pinneberg, a white-collar worker, and Lämmchen, a working-class girl, as his position as a department-store assistant is undermined by the recession and his employers resort to increasingly dubious practices in order to reduce staff. When he is eventually dismissed the family is forced to the margins of society despite the wife's resolute efforts to maintain morale and basic comforts. Significantly, their predicament is alleviated temporarily by contact with characters whose financial security is dependent on business of a shady nature. The enforced proletarianisation of a man without the psychological prop of working-class consciousness is indicated by the final episode, in which Pinneberg is beaten by a policeman who takes him to be a member of a workers' demonstration; as he lies in the gutter the question of the title remains unanswered. The fate of the unemployed is also the theme of Remarque's *Drei Kameraden* (1938) and Leonhard Frank's *Von drei Millionen drei* (1932), while the problems of white-collar workers and dependent professional people, who since the First World War had come to form a large and distinct social group (the subject of Siegfried Kracauer's classic social analysis *Die Angestellten*, 1930), receive comparable treatment in novels by Hermann Kesten, Martin Kessel, Marieluise Fleißer and Irmgard Keun.

The detachment apparent in the narrative style of these works as in the attitudes of their protagonists in a cut-throat society can be defined as the main feature of *Neue Sachlichkeit* (new objectivity, realism, matter-of-factness). For all its deficiencies as a catch-all concept it encapsulates the trends and tendencies of metropolitan art in the later years of the Weimar Republic; their vulgarisation formed a heady mixture of Americanism, media-awareness, permissiveness and growing technological sophistication which finds an echo in more recent developments.

In other fiction a sharper criticism and a clearer political commitment emerge. Leonhard Frank's *Im letzten Wagen* (1925), in which a railway carriage is accidentally detached from the rest of a train and hurtles backwards downhill, and the passengers are overwhelmed by otherwise dormant primitive instincts, may be interpreted as an allegory of the economic and political crisis of the Weimar Republic's last years, while his *Der Bürger* (1924) traces the career of an average middle-class man who after initial doubts and attachment to a female Socialist agitator abandons frustrating political work and marries into wealth, only to suffer depression and loss of identity until attendance at a political meeting addressed by his old love prompts him to change course yet again. Johannes R. Becher, in whose early Expressionist poems the dynamism of an inchoate rebelliousness finds expression in pretentious imagery, became the most active Communist littérateur of the Weimar years, leading figure in the Bund proletarisch-revolutionärer Schriftsteller and author of the banned novel *Levisite oder Der einzige gerechte Krieg* (1926), a dystopia in which poison gas is unleashed against the workers as the proletarian revolution takes on world-wide dimensions.

Other fiction inspired by adherence to the extreme left includes Franz Jung's *Proletarier* (1921), directed against class-based justice, *Die rote Woche* (1921) on a week-long localised workers' uprising, *Arbeitsfriede* (1922) on the collective struggle to ensure the survival of a workers' settlement as a harbinger of a future Communist state, and *Die Eroberung der Maschinen* (1923), in which these themes are combined. The Malik-Verlag of Wieland Herzfelde became the main outlet of literature for and about the proletariat and included works based on direct experience of the sporadic workers' agitation which marked the early years of the Weimar

Republic, including the Ruhr strike against the Kapp putsch in 1920 (Karl Grünberg, *Brennende Ruhr*, 1929; Hans Marchwitza, *Sturm auf Essen*, 1930, and *Schlacht vor Kohle*, 1931), further unrest in Central Germany in 1921 (Otto Gotsche, *Märzstürme*, 1933) and a mass demonstration and street battle with the police on 1 May 1929 in Berlin (Klaus Neukrantz, *Barrikaden am Wedding*, 1931). The most representative accounts of working-class life from a Communist point of view are found in Willi Bredel's *Machinenfabrik N & K* and *Rosenhofstraße* (both 1931), set in Hamburg. Some of these appeared in the Malik-Verlag's Rote 1-Mark Roman series, which aimed to contribute to a working-class consciousness by means of a Socialist realism which, via canonic interpretation in the Soviet Union during the 1930s, eventually formed one of the foundations of cultural policy in the early years of the GDR.

Political agitation on the right found expression in a number of novels and plays with a strong autobiographical and documentary element inspired by the activities of the Freikorps (para-military groups consisting largely of demobilised soldiers unwilling or unable to find a niche in civilian life) in frontier conflicts in eastern Europe and Carinthia, Austria, the suppression of the 1919 revolutions in Berlin and Munich, and the protest against the French occupation of the Ruhr in 1923 after Germany's failure to maintain reparations payments. Of these, Arnolt Bronnen's *O.S.* (1929) and *Roßbach* (1930) and Ernst von Salomon's *Die Geächteten* (1930) are by men who continued to make their literary mark during eventful and wayward careers until after the Second World War. The Schwarze Reichswehr, which became a focus for these groups, received a critical portrayal in the novel *Verratene Jungen* by Peter Martin Lampel (1929) and the play *Sladek der schwarze Reichswehrmann* by Ödön von Horváth (1929).

It has become customary, at least in Germany, to see in a preoccupation with myth a mark of irrationalism which might easily be related and harnessed to an ideology based on the instinctual promptings of blood and soil and a racist interpretation of the concept of the *Volksseele*. However, mythical and legendary themes and figures abound not only in the work of those approved by the Nazis (as exemplified by the idiosyncratic adaptation of elements of Germanic myth in Hermann Burte's *Wiltfeber, der ewige Deutsche*, 1912), but also in that of major writers who achieved an international status which in some instances has remained undiminished. The transition of Gerhart Hauptmann from Naturalism via an

unstable blend of vitalism and spirituality which eschews definition in orthodox religious terms to a reworking of legendary
tradition not confined to the German sphere, is paralleled in the
progress of other writers, many now forgotten, whose resort to
legend was motivated partly by the brief revival of Romantic
themes shortly after the turn of the century, partly by the challenge
of recasting such material in a form which would address contemporary problems, and partly by the conviction that the figures they
aimed to revive represented archetypes of timeless significance or,
especially if they were German, would strike a popular chord. The
appeal of such figures, whether King Arthur and Merlin, Buddha,
Mohammed, the larger-than-life heroes and heroines of the
Nibelungenlied, Parzival, Tristan and Isolde, Wieland der Schmied,
Till Eulenspiegel or the Baron von Münchhausen, cuts across the
divisions between literary groups and continues sporadically to
the present. A hunger for myth specific to the 1920s can be associated with the failure of religious orthodoxy or scientific materialism to satisfy a highly educated middle class; the impact of
Nietzsche, although it became steadily more diffuse and underwent agglomoration with other trends, played its part, as did the
pessimism underlying the cyclical view of history in Oswald
Spengler's *Der Untergang des Abendlands*. The religions of India and
the Far East were as likely to leave their mark as the myths of
ancient Greece and Germany. The ambivalent response which
could be evoked by these interests is exemplified by Gerhart
Hauptmann's *Die Insel der Großen Mutter* (1924), which combines
utopia and parody in an account of a matriarchal republic established on a desert island by a group of shipwrecked women accompanied by one boy.

Paul Ernst, Walter von Molo and Bernd von Heiseler, although
they deal with historical themes in a variety of national settings,
show a predilection for great figures of the German past, especially
Martin Luther and the kings and generals associated with the rise
of Prussia. While national conservative overtones prompted by
a wish to bolster morale after defeat are sometimes evident here,
other authors, including Bruno Frank in *Tage des Königs* (1920), on
Frederick the Great, aim to demythologise their subjects through
the application of modern psychological insights.

The relation to myth of Alfred Döblin and Hans Henny Jahnn
is more complex. The case of Döblin can be considered only in
the context of a modernism based on the view that new forms

were necessary to grasp an unfamiliar reality that neither scientific positivism nor traditional cosmologies could accommodate. The mythical references in *Berlin Alexanderplatz* have already been referred to. His other works of this period are an attempt to discover beneath the chaotic surface of events the guiding forces of nature and human behaviour with the help of oriental religion and an idiosyncratic biologism eventually set out in *Das Ich über der Natur* (1928). *Die drei Sprünge des Wang-lun* (1915) on an uprising in China in which millions were massacred, evoked in a spirit of oriental fatalism, and *Wallenstein* (1920) on the Thirty Years War (an event comparable in its impact on Germany to the First World War and its aftermath) show Döblin developing a style which originated in his response to Italian Futurism in order to present mass movements with sensational vividness and dynamism but without resort to individualistic psychology. The principal protagonists in *Wallenstein*, the title figure and the emperor Ferdinand, come to represent alternative reactions of activity and passivity (which can be related to the contrast of east and west, Buddha and Nietzsche, which underlies the action of Feuchtwanger's *Warren Hastings* and *Jud Süß*, as well as parts of *Erfolg*) to an impersonal process which has a momentum of its own and which Döblin later conveyed in the futuristic fantasy *Berge, Meere und Giganten* (1924).

Jahnn remained almost totally detached from the literary trends of his time, although Expressionist features, such as the themes of redemption and renewal, are evident, and his mastery of inner monologue, by which the problematic aspects of his characters' psyche are revealed, owes much to Joyce, whose *Ulysses* he knew. However, his long periods of emigration (in which political pressures played an insignificant part), first in Norway, later on the Danish island of Bornholm, and the ancillary occupations of organ-building and animal hormone research, make it impossible to relate him to the positions of conservative and radical, right and left, characteristic of the Weimar Republic. The strong utopian strain of Jahnn's first major fiction *Perrudja* (1929) can be associated with the small artistic community of Ugrino which he founded in 1920; envisaged as the nucleus of a society which would turn its back on war, it soon foundered on financial problems. It also brings him close to Hauptmann, whose dreams of an island paradise are however partly ironised in *Die Insel der Großen Mutter* and whose challenge to sexual norms which finds expression here and in *Der Ketzer von Soana* (1918) is taken much further by Jahnn, who does not shrink from the presentation of homoerotic and animal sodomy and incest (the last of which is a theme treated by several other writers of this period). Jahnn's work is based on a creation myth influenced by the ancient Babylonian epic *Gilgamesh*, which pre-dates the Old Testament conception of a watchful and jealous God. In Jahnn's strange Nordic world man and nature are one; this fundamental vitalistic tenet forms the background not only to the excesses and eccentric acts of his protagonists (including also the embalming of corpses and apparently unmotivated sadism) but also to his opposition to the atom-bomb, against which he later campaigned vigorously. In their regression to archaic forms of consciousness Jahnn's characters can be related to some of D.H. Lawrence's later creations whose impulses are governed by the blood, yet it would be a mistake to associate Jahnn with the *Blut und Boden* literature of the Third Reich, which became the vehicle of a doctrine of racial purity and hegemony imposed by a totally militarised state. An episode in *Perrudja* reflects once again the dream of a utopian refuge; here a few chosen ones withdraw to an island after victory in a war against a society based on exploitation and corruption. Jahnn later claimed that the portrayal of this war, planned for an unwritten second volume, proved impossible in the face of events between 1933 and Hiroshima. The even more monumental *Fluß ohne Ufer* (1949–50, 1961), conceived as a trilogy, but left incomplete at Jahnn's death, is marked by a more sombre apocalyptic mood; in it the central figure, Gustav Anias Horn, composes a symphony, 'Das Unausweichliche', inspired by his awareness of a fate against which the individual is impotent. In the fragmentary last part of the novel, 'Epilog', sexual love in all its manifestations becomes a challenge to a merciless nature rather than the assertion of an ecstatic identification with it.

Although the Austrians have the reputation of reacting to crises with equanimity, the disintegration of the Austro-Hungarian Empire had a traumatic effect on the citizens of what became the first Austrian Republic, inducing reactions comparable to those in Germany. A complicating factor was the presence of small national minorities in Austria and the other successor states, which had been established partly to satisfy the political aspirations of the larger national groups in the *Vielvölkerstaat*. Czechoslovakia in particular contained a large German minority whose concentration in the Sudetenland frontier area had a destabilising effect, leading ultimately to its accession to Nazi Germany and the dismembership of a model democratic republic which had pursued a temporarily successful integration policy. More significant for the fate of literature was the existence of an established and prosperous German-speaking Jewish group in Prague and Vienna whose contribution to the cultural life of Central Europe and to international modernism in most of the arts has only recently been fully appreciated. Vienna also acted as a magnet to those from the more remote areas of the old empire and from the Balkan lands beyond who were keen to make a career in literature, journalism and the arts.

Arthur Schnitzler remained faithful to the themes he had varied in drama and fiction from the beginning of his career: the entropy of passion under the influence of social prejudice, time and the threat of death, without developing his insight into anti-Semitism (apparent in *Professor Bernhardi*) to take account of its later more virulent form. However, *Fräulein Else* (1924) and *Traumnovelle* (1926) represent a radical application of Freudian psychology to the inner monologue pioneered in *Leutnant Gustl* (1900), while the impact of the outbreak of the First World War at the end of *Komödie der Verführung* (1924) recalls the same theme in Shaw's *Heartbreak House*.

Franz Werfel combined a vestigial attachment to Judaism with a growing attraction to Catholicism, the latter more and more in evidence as he progressed from the portrayal of an assimilated milieu, as in the school novel *Der Abituriententag* (1928), to *Barbara oder Die Frömmigkeit* (1929), which traces the impact of war and revolution on its protagonist, especially in his contact with figures representing a Viennese form of anarchistic Bohemianism, in parallel with his relation to the title-figure, a family maid who becomes a mother surrogate. The portrayal of her simple devoutness looks forward to the stronger focus on naive piety in *Der veruntreute Himmel* (1939), which culminates in a papal blessing on its heroine, and *Das Lied von Bernadette* (1941), on the saint of Lourdes. In the early works, political action, where it appears as a theme, is viewed with suspicion, but in *Die vierzig Tage des Musa Dagh* (1933), on the enforced resettlement of the Armenian minority in Turkey and its partially successful resistance to a policy of extermination, it is justified.

Max Brod, remembered now as friend and editor of Kafka, showed remarkable versatility as a novelist, moral philosopher, composer, opera librettist and translator. His novels of Prague life, centring on school conflicts and sexuality, as in *Stefan Rott oder das Jahr der Entscheidung* (1931), resemble those of Werfel, but in his treatment in fiction of historical and religious topics (in the trilogy *Tycho Brahes Weg zu Gott*, 1916, *Rëubeni, Fürst der Juden*, 1925 and *Galilei in Gefangenschaft* , 1948; and in *Der Meister*, 1952, an admiring portrayal of Jesus from a liberal Jewish point of view), as in the philosophical writings (*Heidentum, Christentum, Judentum*, 1921; and *Diesseits und Jenseits*, 2 volumes, 1946–7), he considers the problem of Jewish identity and the relation of religion and science at a profounder level than his contemporaries.

Stefan Zweig, after the anti-war play *Jeremias* (1917), concentrated on shorter fiction, in which he usually focused on the predicament of a single character, the victim either of anonymous political forces or more often of an individual obsession. His portrayal of the twilight of the Austro-Hungarian monarchy in his sole novel *Ungeduld des Herzens* (1939) prompts comparison with the best work of Joseph Roth, the novel *Radetzkymarsch* (1932), the story of four generations of the Trotta family between the battle of Solferino (1859) and the death of the Emperor Franz Joseph (1916), in which an awareness of the hollowness of the Habsburg ethos in the declining years of the monarchy (and of the deficiencies of those who pay lip-service to it) is balanced by nostalgia for its multinational ideals. (In the sequel *Die Kapuzinergruft* (1938) this balance is undermined by a sense of fate prompted by the drift to Nazism, vividly conveyed in the final chapter as the narrator, another Trotta, witnesses Hitler's annexation of Austria in a mood of impotent resignation.) Roth's earlier novels are more detached and concern the disorientation of the soldier returning from the First World War (*Das Spinnennetz*, 1923; *Hotel Savoy*, 1924; *Zipper und sein Vater*, and *Die Rebellion*, both 1924) and Jewish themes (*Hiob*, 1930), while *Die Flucht ohne Ende* (1927) and *Der stumme Prophet* (written 1929, published 1969) testify to a growing disenchantment with the Russian Revolution and party politics.

Similar themes and attitudes, without the Jewish component, emerge in the early novels of Heimito von Doderer, whose experiences as a prisoner-of-war in Russia are reflected in *Das Geheimnis des Reichs* (1930) (and much later in *Der Grenzwald*, 1967). His principal achievement consists of the monumental novels *Die Strudlhofstiege* (1951) and *Die Dämonen* (1956), which with the shorter *Die erleuchteten Fenster* (1950) form a trilogy, most of which was conceived and written before the Second World War. Marked by a complex interweaving of plots and disruption of normal narrative sequence, these novels urge that the tyranny of ideology or 'zweite Wirklichkeit' (second reality) be replaced by a realism and individualism defined as 'Menschwerdung' (humanisation). Ideology is broadly defined so that it can include personal obsessions (the 'Dämonen' of one title) as well as slogans and clichés which blind their victims to a complex reality or offer illusory solutions to the problems it presents. The burning of the Palace of Justice in Vienna on 15 July 1927 during a workers' demonstration against a case of judicial malpractice, a key event in *Die Dämonen*, signals for Doderer 'die Cannae der österreichischen Freiheit' and is interpreted by him as an ideological reaction. However, the nebulous definitions given to ideology and the second reality and the profusion of phenomena which they cover make it difficult to distinguish sensible pragmatism from a conservative advocacy of traditional norms in Doderer's work.

Elias Canetti, in his much more sharply focused study of obsession (exemplified by the scholarly mania of the sinologist Kien and the equally blinkered preoccupations of those who surround and exploit him) in *Die Blendung* (1935–6), carries more conviction while sharing Doderer's view of 'Menschwerdung' and the factors which prevent it and implicitly comparing the conflagration of Kien's library with the fate of the Palace of Justice, which he had personally witnessed.

Broch's later fiction set in a contemporary urban milieu, *Die Schuldlosen* (1950), a cycle of stories set in the years 1913, 1923 and 1933, some of which were written before the Second World War, presents a similar connection between the private and the public realms by portraying figures who are unpolitical and therefore in a conventional sense 'guiltless' (hence the title) while at the same time indicating that apathy and thoughtlessness lead indirectly to consequences as far-reaching as a culpable act. Although Nazism is only a shadowy presence in some of the stories, it is clear that Broch sees it in the context of the 'Wertzerfall' (disintegration of values) he had analysed in *Die Schlafwandler*. Equally striking are the Freudian elements in the personal relationships portrayed.

These are given further elaboration in the novels of Ernst Weiß, in which the male protagonists struggle desperately and in most instances vainly to break free of stifling sometimes Oedipal love–hate ties to parents and wives, to whose exploitative manipulations they react with almost masochistic guilt (*Georg Letham, Arzt und Mörder*, 1931; *Der arme Verschwender*, 1936). Like Döblin and Gottfried Benn, Weiß was a doctor with his roots in Expressionism; in his transition from the regressive fantasies of his early work to psychological realism he draws on his medical and psychiatric experience, which bears fruit in *Der Augenzeuge* (1963), on the fateful encounter in a military hospital at the end of the First World War of a doctor with the young Hitler, whose psychosomatic blindness he cures, only to become his quarry when his rise to power requires that all trace of this episode be eliminated.

Robert Musil's *Der Mann ohne Eigenschaften* (volume 1, 1930, volume 2, 1933, volume 3, on which the author was still working when he died in 1942, appeared the following year) is acknowledged as the summa and apogee of most of the trends of inter-war Austrian literature and as a fundamental text of European modernism. Its nucleus is the appointment of Ulrich, the man without qualities, of high intelligence, independent means and experience in various professions, as secretary to the 'Parallelaktion', a plan instigated by a cross-section of the high society of Kakanien (Musil's term derived from the abbreviation k. und k. for the Austro-Hungarian Empire) in August 1913 to celebrate the seventieth anniversary of the Emperor Franz Joseph's accession to the throne, due to coincide in 1918 with the thirtieth year of Kaiser Wilhelm II's reign. The intervention of the First World War and the defeat and fall of both dynasties shed an ironical light on the whole undertaking and allow Musil manifold opportunities for a satire which concentrates on the constant discrepancy between appearance and reality as the glorification of the dynasty becomes an excuse for the assertion of diverging personal interests. Ulrich, like Törleß in Musil's first novel, remains a detached observer, immune from the clashing ideologies represented by the other characters, whether Leinsdorf (the aristocratic right), Fischel (economic liberalism), Tuzzi (bureaucracy), Diotima (cultural conservatism suspicious of the intellect), Clarisse (an exalted cult of Nietzsche), Walter (aestheticism with Wagnerian overtones), Hans Sepp (nationalism), Feuermaul, modelled on Franz Werfel (perfervid idealism), Meingast, modelled on the windy mystagogue Ludwig Klages (*Lebensphilosophie*), or Arnheim, modelled on the industrialist Walther Rathenau (monopoly capitalism with philanthropic ambitions). Ulrich, precisely because he lacks those features which are the stuff of the conventional novel, becomes in his position *au dessus de la mêlée* the perfect vehicle for the author's speculations on the intellectual currents of his time. Yet even Ulrich is moved to undertake his own search for 'der andere Zustand' or alternative mode of being in the company of his twin sister Agathe, whom he meets for the first time when the 'Parallelaktion' is well under way. The state of 'taghelle Mystik' which they briefly achieve has its source partly in Musil's reading of Martin Buber and can be related to the fusion of rationality and soul on which Ulrich takes his stand, while the plethora of ideologies finds its ultimate consequence in the war to which Kakanien is drifting and the violence embodied in the sex murderer Moosbrugger. The fascination exercised by this figure is shown to have its roots in a deep-seated social malaise. Most of the chapters of the fragmentary last volume (and the numerous surviving drafts for its continuation) illustrate the impossibility of perpetuating the blissful detachment of 'der andere Zustand' or rendering it compatible with the fulfilment implied by the siblings' physical attraction for one another. There are signs, however, that Musil aimed in the end to convey an ideal relationship in which sex played a necessary but secondary role, and Musil's reluctance to end the standstill implied in this unresolved tension either by the separation of the couple or the sexual fulfilment of their relationship explains his failure to complete the novel. Irresolution was an inevitable corollary of Ulrich's 'Möglichkeitssinn' or sense of possibility, his talent for speculation without commitment, diagnosis without therapy, registered in numerous chapters of essayistic elaboration which allow free scope to Musil's intelligence, schooled in the precision of the sciences, yet devoted not to the investigation of the world as it is, but to the exploration of the world that might be.

The Austrian authors here discussed, most of whom were brought up in a secure world (nostalgically evoked by Stefan Zweig in *Die Welt von gestern* (1944)) based on the consensus created by the mutual accommodation of a conservative aristocracy and a liberal middle class, all steered clear of that steady commitment to a definable (and usually left-wing) political standpoint which marks many of their German counterparts at this time; political programmes are in general eschewed in favour of either a cultural or religious ethos, whether monarchism (the later Roth), Catholicism (Werfel) or radical conservatism (Hofmannsthal and Kraus), or a more personal solution of ethical idealism or scepticism with strong mystical overtones (Broch and Musil).

Gerhart Hauptmann's patriotism was not chauvinistic, and when in response to a commission to commemorate the centenary of the Battle of Leipzig he wrote *Festspiel in deutschen Reimen* (1913), he challenged jingoistic expectations. Yet the man who had in 1889 stood at the centre of a movement which broke with nineteenth-century traditions of national self-assurance, moral uplift and innocuous entertainment had by the 1920s become an establishment-figure whose works represented an uneasy fusion of the personal, the transcendental and the traditional. He was thus able to switch at will from plays which in their realistic contemporary settings recall the Naturalism and the *Künstlerdramen* of his youth (*Herbert Engelmann, Dorothea Angermann, Vor Sonnenuntergang*) and more ambitious and diffuse projects which can be linked to an increasing concern with Shakespeare (in *Schluck und Jau, Indipohdi,* and especially *Hamlet in Wittenberg*). The problems specific to the Weimar crisis, class conflict, economic insecurity, the power of the state, national demoralisation, were ignored, except in the picaresque epic poem *Till Eulenspiegel.* Of these plays *Vor Sonnenuntergang* stands out as a deeply felt if verbose evocation of the painful family conflict engendered by the decision of the seventy-year-old much respected Geheimrat Clausen to marry the young Inken Peters, the niece of his gardener. Here Hauptmann takes up the familiar theme of the dissolution of nineteenth-century bourgeois values in which the spiritual and the material formed a harmony, now undermined by the philistinism of the younger members of the family, who fail to live up to the Goethean ideals represented by their names Wolfgang, Egmont, Bettina and Ottilie. Clausen fears too that his apparently successful embodiment of this harmony is a sham, and his love for Inken (which echoes that of the old Goethe for Ulrike von Levetzow) is a desperate attempt to revive it. Conventional in form but marked, like many of Hauptmann's Naturalist plays, by the contrast of a claustrophobic interior and the implied presence of a broader outdoor setting which reflects the turbulent emotions of the protagonist, *Vor Sonnenuntergang* hints at Hauptmann's unease at contemporary political developments without specific reference to events or ideology.

However, Hauptmann's later plays, which like his fiction remained untouched by Expressionism and the war, cannot be considered typical of the drama produced during the Weimar Republic. Its early years are marked by the transition to 'activist'

Expressionism, which responded to the revolutionary situation created by the defeat and the end of the Second Reich. Of the drama of this brief phase, *Masse Mensch* has already been described. Close to it in theme is Lion Feuchtwanger's *Thomas Wendt* (1920) (re-titled in 1936 *Neunzehnhundertachtzehn*), clearly inspired by the collapse of hopes that the political course of the Republic would be determined by the artist-intellectual. Its genre definition – 'dramatischer Roman' – reflects Feuchtwanger's move from the conventional plays of his pre-war youth to the fiction by which he is now remembered and to the co-operation with Brecht on dramas which became a testing-ground for the latter's developing theory of epic theatre. (*Warren Hastings, Gouverneur von Indien*, written in 1916, was revised with Brecht and re-named *Kalkutta, 4. Mai* in 1925, after their first collaboration on a version of Marlowe's *Edward II* in 1923.) Thomas Wendt, like Sonja, the protagonist of *Masse Mensch*, shrinks from the violence necessary to consolidate the revolution and is displaced by the unscrupulous businessman Schulz.

There followed a brief phase of 'black' Expressionism in which the ecstatic idealism of Toller's *Die Wandlung*, von Unruh's *Ein Geschlecht* and Kaiser's *Gas I* is superseded by a disillusionment reflected in a more strained emotionalism which finds an outlet in sexual excess and indiscriminate mayhem, as in Arnolt Bronnen's *Vatermord* (written 1915, performed 1922), *Die Geburt der Jugend* (1922) and *Die Exzesse* (1923). These were followed by plays in a more epic style (*Anarchie in Sillian*, 1924, and *Ostpolzug*, 1926), in the second of which the campaign of Alexander the Great is paralleled by a modern expedition to the Himalayas. Jahnn's play *Pastor Ephraim Magnus* (performed 1923) radically challenges sexual norms in the name of vitalism, while his version of *Medea* (performed 1926) departs from Classical antiquity by drawing on the irrationalism of pre-Classical tradition and by setting the play in a colony. Here the title-figure, a negress, accompanied by a chorus of black slaves, loses not only Jason but also the eternal youth she had enjoyed before their marriage. The murder of her children is motivated not by revenge or the despair of abandonment but by the desire for rejuvenation. Ernst Barlach's plays *Der arme Vetter* (1919), *Die echten Sedemunds* (1920) and *Der blaue Boll* (1924) combine Naturalist settings in rural north Germany with the station structure typical of Expressionism. In the second of these Barlach adds symbolic overtones without resort to the supernatural through the motif of a lion's escape from a circus, but the other plays assert the transcendental dimension through visionary spectacles and Christian (*Der Findling*, 1922) and Old Testament (*Die Sündflut*, 1924) themes. Man's spiritual–sensual double nature takes precedence over social criticism in plots involving figures who, like those of Barlach's wood sculptures, appear subject to elemental forces inside and outside themselves.

By 1920, as a form of parliamentary democracy under what was on paper a model constitution achieved a measure of stability, the Expressionist movement had degenerated into a repetition of hollow gestures lacking philosophical substance and relevance to the contemporary situation. Its authors turned their attention almost unanimously to comedy, a genre which in Germany was without a strong tradition on which they could build. Before the First World War Carl Sternheim had begun a cycle of satirical plays which received the collective title *Aus dem bürgerlichen Heldenleben* (*Die Hose*, 1911, *Der Snob*, 1914, *1913*, 1915), which he now completed with *Das Fossil* (1922). The apparent collapse of the Wilhelmine social hierarchy seemed to deprive Sternheim of his original targets, but he shrewdly noted in the last of these plays the ability of former establishment-figures to survive thanks to an unreconstructed judicial system, while implicitly condemning their stance as anachronistic. The lack of ideological commitment entailed by his concept of 'die eigene Nuance' or quintessential mark of individuality, which was already the touchstone of his view of character, made it possible for him to direct his satirical eye to new fads and fashions which deflected people from self-realisation. The conservative taboos of the Second Reich and the Romantic illusions which were their side-effects are replaced in this clear-eyed view by a liberal consensus which finds expression in women's emancipation and the youth movement; and because these are phenomena characteristic of an industrialised mass society, their effect on the individual is shown to be the same, as in *Die Schule von Uznach oder Neue Sachlichkeit* (1926). For the Expressionists the writing of comedy meant a more radical readjustment, conditioned partly by the competition of the new media and the absence of a middle-class audience during the inflation. Walter Hasenclever, having passed through a phase of Swedenborgian occultism, wrote *Ein besserer Herr* (1926), a satire of 'Sachlichkeit' close to Sternheim, and *Ehen werden im Himmel geschlossen* (1927–8), in which two men and a woman, all of whom have committed suicide, are given the chance to relive their lives under different circumstances. The device of having supernatural figures appear in a comic setting was to be repeated in Walter Mehring's *Die höllische Komödie* (1932) and Odön von Horváth's *Himmelwärts* (1934–5). In *Napoleon greift ein* (1928–9) and *Christoph Kolumbus* (1932, in collaboration with Kurt Tucholsky) Hasenclever achieves comic or deflating effects by showing how, in the former, the political aims of the Emperor can no longer be realised by 'heroic' means, and in the latter, that the discovery of America was an accident. At the same time the human need to preserve illusions is emphasised by Napoleon's transformation from a waxwork in a museum to an actor playing himself in a film, and by the insistence by Amerigo Vespucci in a conversation with Columbus that 'Wir brauchen Helden, um uns selbst zu bestätigen' ('We need heroes, in order to find confirmation of ourselves'). In the comedies *Der ewige Traum* (1922), *Palme oder Der Gekränkte* (1924) and *Kilian oder Die gelbe Rose* (1926) Paul Kornfeld supplied variations on the theme of the clash of Expressionist ideals with the demands of the real world in which the latter are ultimately endorsed and the Expressionist redeemer becomes a maladjusted outsider. Georg Kaiser turned to the realism of an identifiable time and place, as in *Nebeneinander* (1923) . Its three parallel plots involve a pawnbroker who with his daughter sets out to deliver a letter found in a pawned suit and poisons himself when he fails to find the addressee, an opportunistic speculator attached to the film industry (a figure typical of *Neue Sachlichkeit*), and the girl he abandons. When she returns to her country roots her disappointment is manifest, and her fate, conventional marriage to a nationalist student, can be compared to that of Horváth's later female protagonists. As in *Von morgens bis mitternachts* (1916) Kaiser laments the impossibility of successfully challenging impersonal, above all economic forces, here epitomised by the chaos of inflation. However, in *Nebeneinander*, as in Kaiser's other works of the1920s – e.g. *Kolportage* (1924), *Mississippi* (1930), *Zwei Krawatten* (1930), culminating in the musical *Der Silbersee* (1933) in which he collaborated with Kurt Weill – the martyr figure characteristic of Kaiser's Expressionist plays, if still present, has ceased to be the vehicle for the proclamation of ideals, while the type represented by the speculator is now even more firmly in control.

This disillusionment finds quintessential expression in Toller's *Hoppla, wir leben!* (1927), which begins in 1919 after the failure of a revolt and traces the fate of several revolutionaries who are then imprisoned. Wilhelm Kilman, who gains a reprieve, becomes a minister in a government implicitly identified with the SPD coalition under Ebert and viewed as a pragmatic compromise with the right. Other prisoners remain faithful to their ideals but are forced into piecemeal work for their slow advancement. The central figure, Karl Thomas, having been diagnosed insane, is released from an asylum years later to find himself, like Rip van Winkle, in a changed world. Having made contact with his former fellow-prisoners and learned of their respective adjustments to a new reality, he becomes a waiter in the Grand Hotel, which in its stage realisation at the première directed by Erwin Piscator became a cross-section of the Weimar Republic's social hierarchy, represented by guests and employees assigned to different rooms on several tiers. Arrested for the murder of Kilman, in fact committed by a nationalist student, Thomas returns to prison where he kills himself just before the true culprit is discovered. Like Kaiser, Toller continues to sympathise with Expressionist ideals but doubts whether they can be realised; he goes beyond Kaiser by presenting a panorama of contemporary society (evident also in the episode of a presidential election). The rhetoric of a protagonist who is made to share the author's experience (Toller's imprisonment from 1919 to 1924 for his part in the Munich Räterepublik) is juxtaposed with a style of reportage typical of *Neue Sachlichkeit*, so that the audience is both moved by his fate and made aware of his problematic position.

A similarly wide-ranging and realistic assessment of an earlier society (the Second Reich) is provided by Carl Zuckmayer in his comic masterpiece *Der Hauptmann von Köpenick* (1931), the authentic story of Wilhelm Voigt, an ex-convict who, determined to secure from an unsympathetic bureaucracy the papers which will enable him to lead an honest life, disguises himself as an army officer and with the help of commandeered troops takes over the town hall where he mistakenly assumes he will find what he is after. This defeat of authority by means of its own weapons is a perfect vehicle for a satire of Wilhelmine militarism, conveyed in an epic manner in a series of episodes which parallel the history of the uniform with the ups and downs of Voigt's unlucky progress through prison, brief employment, doss-house and his sister's flat. The portrayal of milieu and the mastery of dialect and jargon recall Hauptmann's comedies *Der Biberpelz* and *Der rote Hahn*. The play's sub-title, 'ein deutsches Märchen' indicates that while the episode could and did happen, it embodies those hopes which normally remain in the realm of fantasy. As he observes his mirror-image in uniform in the final scene, Voigt sums up his fate in the one word, 'unmöglich', as if to warn his audience that militarism is neither dead nor so easily fooled.

A comedy which presents its critique of the bourgeois in more radical form, Iwan Goll's *Methusalem oder Der ewige Bürger* (1922), owes much to Berlin Dadaism and may be compared in its style, which Goll calls 'Überrealismus' (superrealism), to the contemporary photomontages of John Heartfield. In its portrayal of a family of grotesque 'Spießer', in which at one point the daughter's idealist lover divides into three separate identities before death in a duel and resurrection as an equally conventional member of the family, the play anticipates the theatre of the absurd, and in its use of film in the dream scenes, found also in *Die Unsterblichen* (1920) and *Die Chaplinade* (1920), the technical innovations of Piscator.

The conditions for a revolution in the theatre were provided by the continuation of state patronage under the new regime; in this process Leopold Jessner, Director of the state theatres in Berlin, was a powerful force, supported by the intelligent open-mindedness of the critic Herbert Ihering. However, a more radical alternative theatre developed alongside Jessner's modern reappraisals of such classics as *Hamlet* as a critique of monarchy or Schiller's *Wilhelm Tell* as an apologia of rebellion, in the form of the series of companies formed by Erwin Piscator. The short-lived Proletarisches Theater of 1920–1, which performed agitprop plays by K.A. Wittfogel and Franz Jung, was followed by the takeover of the workers' subscription theatre the Volksbühne. Productions here included Alfons Paquet's *Fahnen* (1924), on the Chicago anarchist trial in 1886, and *Sturmflut* (1926), on the October Revolution, as well as two seminal agitprop reviews, *Revue Roter Rummel* (1924) and *Trotz alledem!* (1925), devised with Felix Gasbarra and commissioned by the Communist Party. Here the technical devices which became Piscator's hallmark were first applied – projections, documentary film clips, segmental division of a half-globe mounted on the revolving stage, scene titles on placards, compères as in cabaret, scenery in constructivist style – and these were further developed in Ehm Welk's *Gewitter über Gotland*, on a popular uprising in medieval Scandinavia, Toller's *Hoppla, wir leben!*, Alexei Tolstoy's *Rasputin* (all 1927). Further productions in the following year were Leo Lania's *Konjunktur* and, in collaboration with Brecht, an adaptation for the stage of Hašek's *The Adventures of the Good Soldier Schweik*, in which live actors and puppets appeared on a treadmill in front of moving projections painted in cartoon style. By 1927 Piscator had formed his own company which performed in several theatres, sometimes under other directors. He over-reached himself with Walter Mehring's *Der Kaufmann von Berlin* (1929), in which stage-machinery of excessive complexity led to an expensive flop and bankruptcy. Thereafter he confined himself to simpler productions with a small collective of plays which formed part of a wave of drama on contemporary social problems, includ-ing abortion (Friedrich Wolf, *Cyankali*, 1928; and Carl Credé, *§ 218* (*Frauen in Not*),   1929) and miscarriages of justice (Hans José Rehfisch/Wilhelm Herzog, *Die Affäre Dreyfus*, 1929), before emi-grating to the Soviet Union in 1932. Piscator's influence is apparent in the activities of numerous Socialist acting groups (Rotes Sprachrohr, Rote Blusen), who were drawn especially to the review form, and in the resemblance to cabaret of the more sophisticated agitprop of Friedrich Wolf and Gustav von Wangenheim, as in the latter's *Die Mausefalle* (1930), on the problems of unemployed white-collar workers. Ferdinand Bruckner used the split stage to good effect in *Die Verbrecher* (1929) in order to demonstrate the social preconditions of crime, and in *Elisabeth von England* (1930), in which the courts of London and Madrid are juxtaposed as the two monarchs pray for victory.

Bertolt Brecht and Piscator shared the belief that the individual was caught up in forces over which he had no control, but rejected the traditional view of tragic fate; both recognised that a new form of drama was necessary in order to identify and demonstrate the nature of these forces. However, while Piscator in his experiments with the resources of the theatre aimed at a mass multi-media spec-tacle designed to activate an audience already convinced, Brecht developed a range of anti-illusionistic techniques or alienation effects in reaction to the unrestrained and undirected emotion of the Expressionists. Both abandoned the well-made play perfected by the Naturalists in favour of epic forms, but Brecht became sus-picious of Piscator's preoccupation with machinery; confusing effect with substance, it distracted the audience instead of stimu-lating critical thought. Brecht's theory of epic theatre receives its first and most cogent formulation in the notes to the musical play *Aufstieg und Fall der Stadt Mahagonny* (1928–9), written some two years after his first close study of Marxism; before that his plays had centred on the anarchic individual who turns his back on society and rejoices in the process of creation and destruction manifest in a godless universe (*Baal*, 1918, performed 1923; *Trommeln in der Nacht*, 1923; *Im Dickicht der Städte*, 1927). The alienation induced by the urban environment in the last of these plays and by membership of a military machine in *Mann ist Mann* (1927) indicates Brecht's awareness of the general trend towards 'Sachlichkeit' characteristic, as we have seen, of the literature of the Weimar Republic towards the end of the decade. His ambivalent response to it is evident in the musical works *Die Dreigroschenoper* (1928) and *Mahagonny*, in which he collaborated with Kurt Weill. The former, an adaptation of John Gay's *The Beggar's Opera*, spiced with ballads derived from Kipling and Villon, was (and has remained) his most popular work; the cheeky identification of bourgeois success and crime is conveyed by a deliberate travesty of conventional opera culminating in a deliciously contrived ending. In *Mahagonny*, however, the critical undertone is stronger, especially in the transition from the 'anything goes' atmosphere of a boom-town to the final scene in which the conflicting slogans voiced in a demonstration of the destitute epitomise the uncertainty of a society about to be plunged into the chaos of mass unemployment. Brecht's determination to come to terms with these changes, as well as his impatience with a commercial theatre and a politically biased public broadcasting service, led to the *Lehrstücke*, experimental plays marked by an austere Marxist didacticism. The most important of these are *Die Maßnahme* (1930), which has remained his most controversial work on account of its refusal to offer an easy solution to the problem of Communist party discipline versus individual initiative prompted by humanitarian feeling, and *Die Mutter* (1932), an adaptation of Maxim Gorki's story of a working-class woman's growing commitment to Communist agitation in pre-revolutionary Russia. Here Brecht comes closest to the more clearly propagandist drama of the left, which partly under the influence of the Bund proletarisch-revolutionärer Schriftsteller derives its impact from simple class confrontations in identifiable historical situations, as in Berta Lask's *Thomas Münzer* (1925) and Friedrich Wolf's *Der arme Konrad* (1932), both based on events of the Peasants' War in early sixteenth-century Germany. In the *Lehrstücke*, on the other hand, Brecht constructs a hypothetical situation as the basis for an exercise in the dialectics which according to his reading of Marx were the only means of giving proper definition to the process of change which from the beginning had fascinated him. The Marxist view of the Great Depression as the crisis of capitalist society demanding a radical, even violent solution is conveyed most directly in Brecht's most ambitious project of the later Weimar years, *Die heilige Johanna der Schlachthöfe* (1931–2), performed at this time only in a shortened radio version. The manipulation of the meat market by Chicago stock-exchange speculators (partly based on Upton Sinclair's *The Jungle*) provides a model for the Marxist theory of the industrial cycle, from which derive the complexities of a plot centred on the confrontation of a Salvation Army girl (and latter-day Joan of Arc) and the captain of industry Pierpoint Mauler. At the end Johanna is forced to the conclusion that the Christian virtues of pity and charity she had advocated (and which she had briefly awakened in her antagonist) are futile palliatives which undermine revolutionary commitment. Equally significant is Brecht's concern to deconstruct the myth of the tragic hero(ine) by means of a parodic treatment of the idealism exemplified by the apotheosis of Joan at the end of Schiller's *Die Jungfrau von Orleans*.

A type of drama which underwent a transformation at the hands of Weimar Republic writers was the *Volksstück*, or folk-play, which had its origin in the work of the Austrians Ferdinand Raimund and Johann Nestroy and their minor predecessors in the late eighteenth and nineteenth centuries. Although Adolf Glaßbrenner, Ludwig Anzengruber and Hans Thoma contributed works of quality to its tradition in the intervening period, it had by the 1920s degenerated to a stereotyped formula later defined by Brecht in his 'Anmerkungen zum Volksstück'. Carl Zuckmayer comes close to the stereotype in *Der fröhliche Weinberg* (1925), which enjoyed huge success, adding a dash of sentimentality in *Katharina Knie* (1929), but these and other plays also owe their appeal to the naive vitality of their protagonists, evident too in Zuckmayer's fiction and embodied by the Robin Hood-figure *Schinderhannes* (1927). Other writers showed a clearer intent to update the *Volksstück* and adapt it to a changed world, so that their work approaches the social problem play considered above. Marieluise Fleißer's *Fegefeuer in Ingolstadt* (1926) and *Pioniere in Ingolstadt* (1929) unmask the domestic repression and suspicion of deviance characteristic of the small-town Bavarian society in which she spent most of her life in a manner which gives particular attention to speech and the position of women, features which she shares with Ödön von Horváth and with the later west German dramatists Kroetz and Sperr, whom she justifiably regarded as her 'sons'. Although Horváth began with a play which exposed the exploitation of workers (*Revolte auf Côte 3018*, 1927, revised as *Die Bergbahn*, 1929), his reputation rests on a series of plays (*Zur schönen Aussicht*, 1926; *Italienische Nacht*, 1930–1; *Geschichten aus dem Wiener Wald*, 1931; *Kasimir und Karoline*, 1932; *Glaube Liebe Hoffnung*, written 1932, performed 1936; and *Die Unbekannte aus der Seine*, 1933) in which under the pressure of economic circumstances, especially unemployment, blinkered petty bourgeois attitudes defined by a peculiar mixture of callousness and escapism undermine the attempt of vulnerable women to achieve a modicum of happiness and independence. In *Italienische Nacht* he concentrates on figures who allow comfort and routine rather than conviction to dictate their reactions to the rise of National Socialism.

Horváth's intention to unmask consciousness by demonstrating how his characters give pseudo-authority to views prompted more often than not by self-interest by resorting to the clichés typical of the semi-educated ('Bildungsjargon'), can be compared to the aim of Karl Kraus in his writings for *Die Fackel*, the satirical magazine which he founded and edited from 1899 until his death in 1936, in which, by means of a sharp analysis of the language of his targets, exemplified by the journalism of contemporary Vienna, he exposes the hypocrisy and duplicity which underlay declarations of moral superiority. The monumental drama *Die letzten Tage der Menschheit* (published 1919, but not performed until 1964), conceived for production over a ten-day period on the planet Mars, is informed by the same purpose. With 220 scenes and a dramatis personae thirteen pages long, the play recalls in its apocalyptic style the medieval dance of death, yet it consists, as Kraus himself claimed, mainly of authentic quotation from a host of major and minor figures whose reactions to the progress of Austria's involvement in the First World War are given cohesion by a framework consisting of conversations between an optimist and 'der Nörgler' (grumbler), who represents the author. As the pandemonium rises to a climax, a debt to medieval allegory, an appropriate vehicle for Kraus's moral engagement, becomes more and more apparent.

Evidence of a similar debt is present in Hugo von Hofmannsthal's *Das große Salzburger Welttheater* (1922) and *Der Turm* (1925, second version 1927), both of which draw on the *autos sacramentales* of Calderón in order to offer a diagnosis and cure of contemporary ills in the spirit of the conservative revolution, an attempt to overcome the spiritual crisis of the First World War by resorting to values associated with Weimar Classicism which he had advocated in numerous essays. In the first of these plays, revolutionary forces, in the person of a beggar, are tamed; in the second the political upheavals of Europe are represented by the conflict which arises when a king incarcerates his own son Sigismund in the belief that he is a threat to his authority. Released from his tower, Sigismund loses his innocence by entering the world of power, proves unable to control the intrigues and manoeuvrings of those who claim to be his allies and is murdered. The appearance of the Kinderkönig, a symbol of the regeneration of man, in his dying moments, is eliminated in the second version; Sigismund, however, appears as less sullied by his contact with the world and eschews violence, a testimony to the spiritual values Hofmannsthal embraced in his last years.

Hofmannsthal's other main achievement during the years after the First World War is the social comedy *Der Schwierige* (1921), in part a nostalgic evocation of a high society under threat from modern forces (here represented by a calculating new servant). The crisis of language which had preoccupied Hofmannsthal since the Chandos letter is given a social dimension by the contrast between the title figure, Hans Karl Bühl, and the characters, charming but propelled by self-interest, who surround him. His 'difficulty' arises from his reluctance to enter the world of intentions and its linguistic superficiality, and from the inabilty of all the others (with the exception of Helene, the woman to whom he eventually becomes engaged) to grasp his enigmatic personality, marked by awareness of a timeless realm related to the pre-lapsarian state Hofmannsthal had earlier defined as 'Praeexistenz'. Yet the play, like some of the libretti Hofmannsthal wrote for operas by Richard Strauß, concerns the acceptance of a social role, here marriage, which, it is hoped, may be maintained without loss of the privileged insight which had enabled Hans Karl to remain barely affected by the comic whirlpool of cross-purposes in the play's central scenes. Despite the differences in setting and mood between the plays in which they appear, Hans Karl and Sigismund are comparable figures.

Although the last works of Rilke and George did not appear until the 1920s, their poetry, which remained barely affected by Expressionism and *Neue Sachlichkeit*, is not typical of the Weimar

Republic. The Expressionists, on the other hand, either changed their style, as in drama, or abandoned poetry altogether, with the single but important exception of Gottfried Benn. Benn's earliest collections, *Morgue und andere Gedichte* (1912), *Söhne* (1913) and *Fleisch* (1917), which, based in part on his experience as a doctor, shocked readers with their descriptions of a cancer ward and decaying corpses in 'Mann und Frau gehn durch die Krebsbaracke' and 'Kleine Aster', appeared in Expressionist periodicals. Since, however, Benn had never shared the faith in the New Man characteristic of some Expressionists, he was not shaken by their disillusionment. His Nietzschean rejection of metaphysical values, his cultivation of an 'art for art's sake' stance which owed nothing to the decorative effeteness of the *fin de siècle*, and his concomitant refusal to countenance the view of art shared by most of his contemporaries that it should present a clear view of social reality in order to demonstrate its deficiencies, led to a willed isolation from other literary trends. In 1933 he mistakenly saw in Nazism the advent of a new human type who would overcome the disorientation attendant on a nihilism which had undermined the potential that poetry had traditionally possessed to celebrate and provide solace. Apart from this episode Benn held consistently to the position that nihilism is a 'Glücksgefühl' and sought to convey it by descending into the unconscious and the timeless realm of myth. In reaction against the cerebralism of the scientific mentality, the subject of the short play *Ithaka* (1914), Benn advocated a regression to pre-rational states, as in 'Gesänge I', or turned to a trance-like evocation of a coastal landscape, as in 'Palau', 'D-Zug' and 'Untergrundbahn'. Benn's dry cynicism and detachment, expressed in a diction which combines metropolitan jargon and the most recondite terminology drawn from numerous foreign languages and academic sources, are made palatable, even seductive, by his mastery of a distinctive elegiac tone conveyed by falling rhythms in short-lined rhyming stanzas.

During the years of the Weimar Republic Brecht was to develop a view of his role diametrically opposed to that of Benn, and by the time they both died in 1956 they had come to represent two extreme alternatives to which succeeding poets might pay allegiance. Yet the positions from which they both started were similar: an awareness that the formal traditions and values of a Classical–Romantic consensus which had provided the foundation for German poetry from the young Goethe to the Expressionists could not be maintained in the context of modernism. One can therefore see a resemblance between the figure of Baal (in Brecht's first play and his poem 'Choral vom großen Baal') and Benn's Dr Werff Rönne, who appears in several early prose and dramatic works: in both an anarchistic rebellion against prevailing norms arises from metaphysical disorientation. Social criticism however is present in Brecht's poetry as early as the 'Legende vom toten Soldaten', inspired by the slaughter of the First World War, and is developed in a wide variety of forms, as in the first collection *Hauspostille* or Book of Devotions for the Home (1927), in which he for the first time consistently adopts the technique of contrafacture of a popular and naive genre for his own purposes. The broadside ballad or broadsheet (*Bänkelsang* or *Moritat*), the hymn, the narrative poem (*Legende* and *Chronik*) and the song with refrain become, partly under the influence of Villon, Rimbaud and Kipling, the vehicles of a relaxed materialism which gradually gains a sharper satirical edge, until the pressure of events during the critical years of the 1920s and 1930s leads to the cultivation of a drier, more rational tone typified by the cycle *Aus einem Lesebuch für Städtebewohner* (1930). The alienation techniques developed in the plays of the same period are also evident in the poems, in the form of abrupt contrasts which imply an argument the reader must reconstruct, as in 'Die Nachtlager'. This feature distinguishes his work from that of his *Neue Sachlichkeit* contemporaries Erich Kästner, Joachim Ringelnatz and Walter Mehring, in whose social vignettes entertainment takes precedence over satire, and also from the Communist poets Becher and Erich Weinert, who place traditional forms in the service of direct exhortation and criticism.

This chapter has sought to indicate the formal variety and thematic range of the literature written during the years of the Weimar Republic and set it against a background of economic instability and political turmoil. While it is right to look back on this time as a period of artistic innovation as seminal in its effects as the turn of the century in Vienna, the writers we now consider to epitomise these trends formed an increasingly embattled minority challenged for the allegiance of readers and audiences by a proto-Fascist strain which gradually gained momentum.

4

The Literature of the Third Reich

The student of modern German literature is necessarily confronted by dates which carry a heavy historical significance: 1871 and the formation of the new, second Reich; the outbreak of war in 1914 and the armistice of November 1918; Hitler's accession to power in 1933; the period of the Second World War, 1939–45; the formation of the two separate Germanies in 1949; the *Wende* of late 1989. This chapter is concerned with those dark years of German history encapsulated by the dates 1933–45, the years of Hitler's triumphs and subsequent defeat, and the literature associated with the Nazi regime and its mentality will be assessed. It would be erroneous, however, to assume that the period in question was a hermetically sealed unit with no precursors and no transitions: novels extolling the greatness of Germany's past, the apparent superiority of the German race and the inherent glory of the German landscape were rife before 1933, and belligerent, chauvinistic attitudes, together with vastly exaggerated claims for the transcendental nobility of the German soul, prepared the way for the even more strident demands of the National Socialists. It will also be necessary to differentiate between antecedents, Nazi literature *per se*, the concept of Inner Emigration and the role of those writers who, publishing in Germany within the Nazi period, survived and continued to write into the early 1960s: the parameters are by no means fixed, and the idea of a sudden beginning in 1933 and of a 'Stunde Null', or zero point, in 1945, is unsatisfactory. The literature of exile is large enough to warrant a separate chapter, and will be considered later.

The military and economic might of Germany after 1871 gave rise to an aggressive chauvinism in many quarters, and Germany's development into Europe's leading industrial nation and undisputed mastery in technological and scientific progress was widely applauded. There were writers, however, who deplored the detrimental effects of massive urbanisation and blight: values which were felt to be essentially 'Germanic' were encroached by concepts which were deemed to be alien, and the growth of a proletariat, plus the rise of capitalism with its Jewish practitioners, seemed to provide a baleful threat to the integrity of the German race. The status of *Heimatdichtung* was much discussed at the turn of the century, and portrayals of that which was natural, elemental and pious abounded, with Germanic (or Nordic) man and woman, close to the natural rhythms of the earth, frequently extolled as archetypal heroes, radiant and healthy, in a sense of earnest dedication. Julius Langbehn's *Rembrandt als Erzieher*, a work of cultural criticism, appeared in 1898 and, reaching over a hundred editions in the space of a few years, did much to encourage the cult of closeness to the soil, a mystical communion with the earth within a specifically North German landscape. Langbehn deplored the sophisticated, over-cerebral and pretentious attitudes he saw among the youth of his day, and sought that which was healthy, earthy and basic: it was the peasant ('Bauer') who is endowed with superior, even mystical, qualities, a man whose blood is not diluted or tainted by decadence but was strong, pure and 'Germanic' in its integrity. A reaction against Naturalism is noticeable here, a rejection of that movement's apparent predilection for urban problems (particularly associated with the squalor of Berlin) and its indebtedness to foreign authors (Zola and Ibsen). The cry of 'Los von Berlin!' was heard: Friedrich Lienhard, in his *Die Vorherrschaft Berlins. Literarische Anregungen* (1900), criticised both Max Halbe and Gerhart Hauptmann for having taken too much from foreign sources. And the emphasis on the provincial, the conservative and the traditional met a responsive reading public: Gustav Frenssen's *Jörn Uhl* (1900) was extremely popular and was enthusiastically reviewed by Rilke, who praised its freshness, power and humanity. Clara Viebig's novels, particularly *Die Wacht am Rhein* (1902) and the stories *Kinder der Eifel* (1897), appealed greatly to an educated, middle-class readership; Wilhelm von Polenz's *Der Büttnerbauer* (1897) should also be noted, a portrayal again of rural permanence and rootedness, a tradition threatened by capitalism, the flight from the land and 'modern' ways of thinking. There is nothing inherently 'fascist' here, nor is there in a work like *Der Wehrwolf* by Hermann Löns (1910), a historical novel set in the turmoil of the Thirty Years War, but a later *Blut und Boden* cult could well arrogate to itself certain phrases and beliefs which might be regarded as precursors, the atavistic aspects of National Socialism seeking all too readily to find confirmation in earlier attitudes. The peasant in earlier writing may well have been harassed by impending industrialisation: later it would become the Jew who is threatening the family home and who comes to represent the invidious poison in the otherwise healthy view of the community. It was the city which increasingly became the place which exemplified modernism, cosmopolitanism and an undeniable Jewish presence, everything, in short, that was 'artfremd', 'zersetzend' and contrary to the 'arteigene Volksgemeinschaft'. The publisher Eugen Diederichs, who had originally published Neo-romantic literature (particularly in its more religious manifestations) increasingly cultivated works which were above all Germanic and anti-rational: he collaborated with writers such as Agnes Miegel, Börries von Münchhausen and Lulu von Strauss and Torney, and also Houston Stewart Chamberlain, author of *Die Grundlagen des Neunzehnten Jahrhunderts* (1899–1901), and Adolf Bartels, most virulent of the anti-Semitic German literary historians. Bartels's most famous novel was *Die Dithmarscher* (1898), which extolled the Low German landscape and *mores* of that region; he achieved popularity in his critical writings with *Die deutsche Dichtung der Gegenwart* (1897) and the attack against Heine (1906). A fascinating, yet also dangerous, concoction of *Volk*, myth, romanticism and anti-Enlightenment was engendered alongside *Heimatdichtung*, and both helped to feed the Nazi *Weltanschauung*.

It was the sense of belligerent superiority in the years leading up to the outbreak of the First World War, combined with an awareness of vulnerability *vis-à-vis* both East and West and an exaggerated fear of capitalism and rapid industrialisation that lent a note of shrillness and abnormal intensity to German nationalism and its literary manifestions: Hermann Burte's *Wiltfeber der ewige Deutsche* (1912) and Artur Dinter's *Die Sünde wider das Blut* (1917) are good examples. The former recounts, in ecstatic terms and imagery derived directly from Nietzsche, the return of Martin Wiltfeber to Germany: concepts such as 'Zeugung' (creation, or procreation), 'Heimat' (home) and 'Der reine Krist' (Christ purified of Jewish taint, and spelt with a Germanic 'K') are couched in capital letters to emphasise their portentous nature. One day in his life is portrayed, from midnight to midnight. The German countryside is ardently portrayed, and German womanhood is extolled (the dark

Magdalene, but even more the fair Ursula von Brittloppen); an aristocratic principle is defended. Martin Wiltfeber, to cheer the young count Heinrich von Susenhart who fears the decline of the fair Nordic race at the hands of 'a mass of racially inferior trash', draws a Swastika in the dust, and its mystical importance is understood. Unable, however, to inspire his fellow countrymen with his vision of 'der reine Krist' (his passage through one day is reminiscent of Zarathustra's attempt to cleanse the people of the market place of dross and complacency) he seeks solace with Ursula von Brittloppen: a violent storm engulfs the house (elemental imagery – the storm as 'dragon' – is abundant) and a flash of lightning incinerates the couple during the act of copulation. Wiltfeber is a 'Heimatsucher', one who seeks eternal German verities and deplores Judaism, the flight from the countryside and egalitarianism (Rousseau is denounced as a 'Selbsterreger' or masturbator, who is responsible for the French Revolution and its perverse doctrines). The book makes a confused impression and is only redeemed by powerful descriptions of the countryside of the Upper Rhine; the pseudo-Nietzscheanism, the cult of Nordic man and the attempt to see Christ as a German hero are less endearing. Artur Dinter's *Die Sünde wider das Blut* (1917) is a singularly repugnant novel, one recounting the career of Dr Hermann Kämpfer (the surname – 'fighter' – is significant) who attempts, in his chemical research, to unlock the secrets of life. His father, a simple farmer, had been ruined by a Jew; Kämpfer, exhausted from overwork, explores a wintry German forest and exults in the beauty of snow and frost (a sentimental flashback recounts the deep fervent happiness of a German Christmas). He falls for an attractive blonde woman in a hotel, and is amazed that her father is a repulsive Jew who had once seduced her mother. Throughout the book Kämpfer seeks to woo the fair Elisabeth and to rid her of her Jewish blood: their child is swarthy and 'simian'. The attempts to extinguish Jewishness takes bizarre forms: the slow movement of Beethoven's ninth symphony, for example, brings out Elisabeth's 'Germanness', whereas the Scherzo wakens her 'Jewish' side (she 'demands champagne'). The second child is also dark, and Elisabeth dies. A child by a simple German girl whom Kämpfer had seduced as a student is taken into his house: his own, half-Jewish son, causes the accident which kills the two boys. A huge tirade seeks to convince the reader of Christ's Germanic origins and the importance of the need to destroy the Old Testament as primitive superstition. Kämpfer

marries a second time; his wife is fair and of pure German blood
but, having been seduced by a Jew as a girl, her body is indelibly
tainted and she can only bear dark, Jewish children. Kämpfer kills
the Jew responsible for this, but his wife kills herself and the child.
Kämpfer is tried for murder, and acquitted: he joins the army and is
killed on Christmas Eve 1914. This farrago of tasteless gibberish
takes Burte's anti-Semitism and Germanic nationalism to sinister
lengths: Dinter appended a pseudo-scholarly account at the end of
the book which gives an ostensibly academic reason for denounc-
ing Judaism and extolling the 'Germanic Christ'.

The German defeat of 1918 and the subsequent loss of territory
added an extra stridency to nationalistic *Heimatdichtung*; in 1926
appeared Hans Grimm's novel *Volk ohne Raum*, a book that enjoyed
enormous popularity and which provided Nazism with one of its
watchwords. Grimm's novel sold more than half a million copies
before the Second World War (and by 1964 more than seven hundred thousand), and exercised a powerful influence, particularly
upon the young and on those unable to cope with the Treaty of
Versailles. Eugen Diederich's wife, the poetess Lulu von Strauss
and Torney, hailed the book as being something not written, but
experienced and suffered, being not literature in the sense com-
monly accepted, but a deed, a spiritual German event, a call to
arms. The terminology chosen by such commentators, the fusion of
the spiritual and the militaristic, is typical of the chauvinistic
groups who refused to acknowledge Germany's defeat and who
sought a revivification of national life through the cultivation of
specifically 'Germanic' values. Grimm's vast novel, well over one
thousand two hundred pages, is blatantly propagandist: his hero,
Cornelius Friebott, is forced to leave his farm in North Germany
and, rejecting life in a Bochum steelworks, emigrates to South
Africa where he volunteers for the Boer War and, after imprisonment by the British on Saint Helena, settles in German Southwest
Africa. After the German collapse in 1918 he escapes to Portuguese
Angola and, in the early 1920s, returns to Germany to awaken his
countrymen to their lack of space and the need to expand. It is only
the novelist Hans Grimm (who appears as a character in the novel)
who understands the true import of his meaning and is determined that Friebott, killed by a stone thrown by a political enemy,
shall not have died in vain. The readers of *Volk ohne Raum* were
told that the Germans were the 'cleanest, most decent, most
honourable, efficient and industrious people on earth'; even a

non-German, a Portuguese officer, laments the demise of German colonial power and attacks British perfidy. The collaboration between the British and the Social Democrats in Germany is repeatedly emphasised, and the Jew likewise is singled out for vilification, the source, apparently, of scabrous attacks upon Germany in the world's press. The novel is over-long and marred by tedious hectoring and repeated demands for *Lebensraum*; the landscape descriptions are slackly written and the characterisation lacks subtlety. The great popularity of the book stems obviously from its simplistic message and desire to boost the confidence of a defeated nation. Grimm, like Burte and Dinter, would not later join the Nazi party, and later stressed that his nationalism was not National Socialism, but the emphasis on expansionist policies and the anti-Semitism expressed in this novel and others would be greeted with enthusiasm by those in power after 1933.

Joseph Goebbels's novel *Michael. Ein deutsches Schicksal in Tagebuchblättern* had nothing like the readership of *Volk ohne Raum*, but is a book which is not without interest. Published in 1929 (its author had also written poetry and plays) it portrays the passage of its eponymous hero through a degraded Germany (i.e. the Weimar Republic). Goebbels, like Hitler an artist-manqué, rejects the modern, that is, the culture of cosmopolitan cities, and longs for essential 'German' values: Michael fulminates against the 'angefaulte Intelligenz', the epicene fashions of the 1920s and the decadence of Munich's Schwabing. The heroine, Hertha Holk, is the archetypal German girl, and Michael praises her simplicity and honesty: like Dinter's hero Hermann Kämpfer he extols blond integrity and has no place for lesser breeds. The rejection of the modern in the arts, however, does not prevent Michael from betraying undeniably Expressionistic tendencies – the enthusiastic admiration for van Gogh, Nietzsche and Dostoyevsky, the castigation of the stultifying limitations of the intellect and the flight into the elemental. 'I feel as though I were no longer living in this world. I rage in ecstasy, in dream, in frenzy. I sense new worlds. Distance grows in me. Give me, oh God, to say what I am suffering!' – such utterances could be found in many a work of Expressionism, as could the following evocation of the mining areas of the Ruhr: 'Grey mist! Smoke! Noise! Screaming! Groans! Flames roar upwards into the skies! Symphony of work! Grandiose work of man!' Michael does, indeed, attempt a definition of Expressionism, claiming that the 'fashionable word of the day' was meaningless: the whole century was Expressionist, and that the men of his time all wished to express, to create new worlds and to mould the external into a new, fervent experience. Goebbels's book has much in common with the short novel by Gustav Sack, *Ein verbummelter Student*, which appeared in 1917; the inflated rhetoric, the yearning for Iceland and the North, the descriptions of industrial landscapes are reproduced in *Michael* almost to the point of plagiarism. Joseph Goebbels found it all too easy to slip into the more excessive diatribes of Expressionistic prose; his later admiration for the painter Nolde caused a certain embarrassment after the rejection of Expressionist painters as degenerate, and his attempts to claim that Expressionism was a typically 'Nordic' phenomenon did not entirely convince. His hero meets his death in the depths of a mine: inspired by van Gogh's example he sought fulfilment in work, having rejected his university studies in Heidelberg and Munich. His apotheosis is achieved therefore in an urban rather than an agricultural milieu (this is reminiscent of Expressionistic *Arbeiterdichtung*), but attempts were also made to describe the Frisian islands and the Bavarian Alps, the storm-girt and the elemental, which were regarded as external correlations to the power of the German soul. The novel is pretentious, the characterisation is wooden and the lapses into bathetic verse are embarrassing (the hero occasionally puts on his helmet, draws his sword and recites the poet Liliencron); it is of interest, however, in the flirtation with Expressionism, its admiration for writers and artists who were not German (Dostoyevsky, van Gogh) and the echoes of German Romanticism and *Sturm und Drang* – the theme of the mine and the description of the funeral which brings to mind that of Goethe's *Werther*.

Expressionism was discussed in Chapter 2, and the writer Hanns Johst was mentioned. He must now be considered as the author of the play *Schlageter*, dedicated to Adolf Hitler ('in loving veneration and unswerving loyalty') and receiving its first performance on Hitler's birthday, 20 April 1933. Albert Leo Schlageter was a volunteer in the *Freikorps* in the Baltic; he took part in the Kapp Putsch in Berlin in 1920 and also fought the Communists in the Ruhr. In 1921 he was involved in skirmishes in Poland and was at the battle of Annaberg. In November 1922 he went to Munich, heard Hitler, met him and became a party member. In 1923 he fought in the Ruhr against the French, was captured, court-martialled and executed on 26 March 1923. He provided the Nazi party with its first martyr and Hitler paid tribute to him at the beginning of *Mein Kampf*. Johst's play was a national event, and the famous German actor and Nazi sympathiser Veit Harlan took one of the leading roles, that of Schlageter's impetuous friend Peter Thiemann (it is he who speaks those notorious lines in Act One – 'Whenever I hear the word "culture" I release the safety-catch on my Browning!'); Hermann Goering's later wife Emmy Sonnemann played Thiemann's sister Alexandra. It was staged at more than a hundred cities in Germany, was broadcast regularly on the radio and became compulsory reading in schools: it is, however, a weak play with little action, verbose peroration and caricatured types (the dedicated hero, the faithful girl, the opportunist Klemm, the Freikorps comrades and the parents). The deliberate echoing of the 'Rütli-Schwur' from Schiller's *Wilhelm Tell* (Act 3) is unconvincing. The ending of the play is, however, of interest in that it looks back to the visionary nature of much Expressionist drama: Alexandra's screaming and Schlageter's pose ('he seems to pull the weight of the entire world behind him') and his last speech, with its extremes of elliptical syntax and punctuation ('Germany!!! Awaken! Catch fire!! Blaze! Burn from one end to the other!!'), looks back to the Johst of *Der junge Mensch* and *Der Einsame*. It is manifestly erroneous to equate Expressionism with left-wing attitudes, and Johst, later president of the Reichsschrifttumskammer (the Literature Section of the Reich's Cultural Advisory Body) and an SS Gruppenführer, demonstrates the essentially ambiguous nature of the movement whose call for the New Man and the destruction of the moribund has, with hindsight, an unsettling and dangerous dimension.

Another erstwhile Expressionist who greeted the Nazi accession to power in 1933, albeit briefly, was Gottfried Benn. This was by no means an aberration, but a natural development of certain tendencies which characterised his poetry from its Expressionist period onward. His primitivism and rejection of *Zivilisation*, his suspicion of reason and fascination with the 'blood', led him to sympathise with the irrationalism and atavistic vitalism of Nazism, and his standpoint is quite clearly put forward in the essay *Der neue Staat und die Intellektuellen* of 1933. Relevant in this context is his *Antwort auf die literarischen Emigranten* of the same year, written in reply to Klaus Mann's letter demanding an explanation for the acceptance of Hitler and the new *Reich*. Benn's thinking is characteristically apolitical, and historical events are viewed *sub specie aeternitatis*, from an almost mystical standpoint: his reply rejects democracy and rationalism, utilitarianism and cosmopolitan culture and praises instead the earth, the people (*das Volk*) and the new biological type that Nazism would bring forth. This reply by Benn was widely broadcast by Goebbels, but tensions between the poet and the Reichsschrifttumskammer became apparent: Benn had been one of the foremost Expressionist poets, and that movement was pronounced degenerate in spite of the close links already discussed. In his *Bekenntnis zum Expressionismus*, written at the end of 1933, Benn strove to defend the movement, seeking antecedents in Kleist's frenzied drama *Penthesilea* and Nietzsche's dithyrambs, but the attack upon him increased in volume and venom. It was Benn who took the 'aristocratic form of inner emigration' (the phrase is his) and rejoined the army, concentrating on a definition of poetry as being an act of defiance in the face of absurdity and nihilism; the concept of the 'absolute poem', created *ex nihilo*, became of increasing importance to him, exemplified in the *Statische Gedichte* which were published in 1948. Benn's essentially apolitical mentality and his blindness to the true nature of Nazism were by no means unique but typical rather of a whole generation of German writers and thinkers who preferred the mythological to the historical, the utopian to the pragmatic and who cherished an instinctive reluctance to consider the realm of politics as being anything other than peripheral and superficial. A writer of similar calibre is Ernst Jünger who, like Benn, remained in Germany after 1933 and rejoined the army. During the First World War Jünger had been frequently wounded and decorated with the highest honours, and in 1920 he described his experiences in *In Stahlgewittern*, a book which went through many revised editions and was reissued in 1942 under the title *Ein Kriegstagebuch*. In contrast to the anti-war novels of Ludwig Renn, Erich Maria Remarque and Arnold Zweig, Jünger's book applauded the excitement of war and greeted the heroism and valour gained in the face of death. With clarity and a fastidious exhilaration Jünger describes the violence and carnage of the front; he nowhere indulges in Expressionistic histrionics or pacifistic platitudes. In *Der Kampf als inneres Erlebnis* (1922) and *Feuer und Blut* Jünger continues to extol the tumult of war, the sense of dedication and courage the conflict bestowed and the transcending of the purely personal in times of need; the *furor teutonicus* is acclaimed as a cleansing force which has no hesitation in expunging the weak and the half-hearted. Later writings (*Die totale Mobilmachung*, 1931 and *Der Arbeiter*, 1932) envisage a worker-state where military virtues hold sway, and it would seem that the author would be eager to welcome the Nazi victory in 1933. Jünger, unlike Benn, however, felt unable to throw in his lot with the new regime, detecting in Hitler an ignorant Austrian criminal who never understood the metaphysics of power and service. The allegorical novel *Auf den Marmorklippen* (1939) contains the theme of resistance, a dangerous one at the time, but the remoteness and the intellectual abstraction of the author's discussion preclude any assumption concerning Jünger's rejection of Hitler. This, and the later *Heliopolis* (1949), fail ultimately as literature because of Jünger's lack of imaginative feeling; the publication of his war diaries *Strahlungen* (1949), which recount his experiences in occupied Paris, betray a neutral stance and an aestheticism which border, at times, on the repugnant.

Once in power, the Nazis made it quite clear what their policy towards literature entailed. A radical cleansing of Jewish, 'decadent', Marxist, un-German elements was to be embarked upon without delay: the notorious Burning of the Books (10 May 1933) demonstrated to the world the intentions of the new masters. The *auto-da-fé* was to take place in all university cities, that in Berlin being the largest. Amidst marches, folksongs and ritual proclamations the finest and most representative works associated above all with the detested Weimar Republic were destroyed. The orators proclaimed that the flames were to consume works

> associated with the class struggle and with materialism, with decadence and moral decay, political irresponsibility and betrayal, the exaggeration of unconscious urges based on the destructive analysis of the psyche, with the un-German journalism of a Jewish-democratic kind, with the literary betrayal of the soldiers of the First World War, with the conceited debasement of the German language and with insolence and presumptuousness.

This burning became, paradoxically, an accolade of excellence, for to have been accepted by the regime must, in the eyes of the writers who fled into exile, become the greatest insult. The writer Oskar Maria Graf, mistaken by the Nazis as a nationalist writer because of his descriptions of Bavarian peasant life, demanded (from the safety of exile) that his works be burned along with those of the great, of Marx and Freud, Heinrich Mann and Erich Kästner, Erich Maria Remarque, Kurt Tucholsky and others. The Dichterakademie now had as it members Hanns Johst, Agnes Miegel, Emil Strauss, Rudolf Binding, Börries von Münchhausen, Erwin Guido Kolbenheyer, Wilhelm Schäfer and Hans Grimm, hardly names to inspire confidence in the new order's intellectual and artistic standards, and the diary of the poet Oskar Loerke is a moving testimony to the sense of spiritual desolation felt by men of good faith in 1933, the sense of loss, waste and disgust at the obligatory denunciations and genuflexions. Loerke's poem 'Winterliches Vogelfüttern', written in January 1936, praises the outsider, Walther von der Vogelweide, who did not accept the jurisdiction of the abbot of Sankt Gallen who fed the birds in winter, but who preferred loneliness and freedom; the meaning is clear.

In November 1933 a Reichskulturkammer was organised by Goebbels to control all aspects of cultural life: the Reichsschrifttumskammer was one of its seven departments (others included the Reichsmusikkammer and the Reichskammer für bildende Kunst). But the essentially fissiparous nature of the Nazi 'monolith' is seen in the proliferation of such organisations as the Reichsstelle zur Förderung des deutschen Schrifttums, under the leadership of Alfred Rosenberg, and the Parteiamtliche Prüfungskommission, bodies which frequently competed against each other and where spheres of competence overlapped. The central concern was to ensure the triumph of German, 'völkisch' art and the extermination of left-wing, Jewish, 'modernist' elements. To be 'modern', in Rosenberg's vituperative speeches, meant to be un-German, degenerate, sub-human, analytic in a 'destructive Jewish' manner and 'bolshevist'; later the abuse intensified, and terms such as 'mestizos, intellectual-syphilitics and bastard drug-addicts' were used. Of those who fled Hanns Johst wrote the following:

> There are, then, writers who say: what's the Party, the Movement, the State got to do with me? I say to all these senile men of yesterday – we can get by marvellously well without you. We couldn't care less about the arrogance of those so-called writers who think they can talk about 'inner fervour' and 'eternal values' and try to avoid committing themselves in a plain and decent fashion to National Socialism and to the German Reich.

Oskar Loerke, as has been shown, gave a different account:

> A shower of hail as I walked in the garden. Loneliness. My friends almost all dead, or a long way away, disappeared. It is forbidden to think, to treat one's fellow men in a human fashion. Wednesday morning there was a meeting of the writer's union – the worthy old neddies are now triumphant, people like Emil Strauss and Hermann Stehr, they really feel worthy and significant now . . . The nationalist gentlemen now feel themselves to be so important and stuck-up: Schäfer, always tending to hysterical outbursts, roaring – a black Alberich. That vindictive, puffed-up, mushy nonentity Kolbenheyer talking for hours . . . The long-standing members were completely passed over – me, Stucken, Molo, Scholz, Benn, Seidel, Halbe.

Benn, it is noticed, despite his initial enthusiasm, was rapidly dropped, later vilified by the new regime and subjected to an odious attack by the journal *Das schwarze Korps*: 'But Mr Benn does not only enjoy stirring his pen in stinking wounds, he also enjoys dipping it into the domain of Eros, and the way he does it justifies his inclusion in the list of those who have been thrown out of the house because of their unnatural, swinish perversions.' The ignorance and brutish ineptitude of such a comment are manifest.

The new order resounded to the poetry of Dietrich Eckart, dedicatee of *Mein Kampf*, and Horst Wessel, pimp and, like Leo Schlageter, a martyr; the poet Hans Baumann provided the well-known song 'Es zittern die morschen Knochen'. The typical themes of those who may be said to have believed in Hitler and his historical mission include the poet's task (Hermann Burte and Heinrich Anacker), the rebirth of the nation (Heinrich Anacker's 'Gegen Versailles' is a good example), fatherland and home (Wolfgang Hercher's 'Deutsch sein!'), the community of the people (Hans Blunck's 'Aufforderung'), marriage and the family (Ruth Storm's 'Deutsches Wiegenlied'), workers and peasants (Karl Bröger's 'Alter Arbeiter'), Hitler as Führer (Baldur von Schirach's 'Das Größte' grudgingly admits that he is mortal), the military life (Herybert Menzel's and Martin Damß's verse) and, of course, war, with innumerable examples. Herybert Menzel's 'Die Schlacht' (1943) attempts to emulate the patriotic fervour of Hölderlin: writers like Kleist and the German Romantics were in vogue, for Goebbels himself had spoken of the 'steely' romanticism' ('stählerne Romantik') of the new era, a combination of hardness and idealism. With modernism deplored, it is not surprising that the sonnet and the ode were frequently found at this time, with romantic fervour and classical restraint strangely juxtaposed. The Austrian poet Josef Weinheber, in his collection *Adel und Untergang* (1934), extols and denounces in a manner consonant with many a Nazi poetaster, although he does not directly mention the momentous events of the times: democracy is rejected, as is the 'decadence' of modern life, and Germanic heroism is worshipped. Although vulgar chauvinism is avoided, Weinheber could and did identify himself with Nazi ideals, yet his formal talents raise him above the level of a Baumann or an Anacker. *Wien wörtlich* (1935) and *Hier ist das Wort* (1944) may be read without embarrassment by those seeking conservatism and an oracular element in twentieth-century poetry.

The novel was less successful during the years 1933 to 1945, the representative works, as has been noticed, having been written earlier; *Hitlerjunge Quex*, by Aloys Schenzinger, had appeared in 1932 and achieved considerable fame in its film version of 1933. Based on the case of Herbert Norkus, a young boy murdered by Communists, the novel tells of Heinrich (or 'Quex') Völker who defies his bullying father, a Communist, and throws in his lot with the Nazis; he is eventually murdered by a group of drunken Bolsheviks. Schenzinger's novel is unusual in that it has an urban setting – the tenement-blocks and streets of Berlin, a milieu not often found in Nazi literature. *Heimatkunst* and *Blut und Boden* novels, continuing the earlier tradition, were more frequent. A novelist like Friedrich Griese well exemplified the *Blut und Boden* school of writing: Griese had achieved a wide readership in 1927 with his novel *Winter* and throughout the 1930s continued to publish prolifically, extolling above all the landscape of Mecklenburg (*Der Ruf des Schicksals. Erzählungen aus dem alten Mecklenburg*, 1934, and *Das ebene Land Mecklenburg*,1935, are good examples). The work of Will Vesper is similar: *Das harte Geschlecht* (1931), a novel of peasant life, anticipates the later concern with *völkisch* situations and traditions. Vesper also edited anthologies of German poetry and fairy-tales; he and Hanns Johst were both chairmen of the Reichsschrifttumskammer. Vesper, *pace* his son Bernward, can scarely be branded a Nazi if the term means a fanatical adherent of Hitler's regime; like many other writers of the time he is patriotic, close to the soil, fiercely proud of Germany's past and her literary

and musical tradition and deliberately anti-urban and conservative. The writer Hans Blunck also belongs in this category, author
of successful historical novels and exponent of Lower German
Heimatdichtung. Blunck, like Griese, published continuously
throughout the 1930s and 1940s and also later: *Die Urvätersaga*
(1933) and *Werdendes Volk* (1934) are good examples of the *Blut und
Boden* cult of Nordic earth and Nordic supremacy. From 1933 to
1935 Blunck was president of the Reichsschrifttumskammer and
highly esteemed by the new order; his Nordic racism, shared also
by Himmler and other prominent Nazis, was deemed to be suspect
during the denazification trials after the end of the war, and
Blunck's attempts at self-exculpation were considered unconvincing (his correspondence with Thomas Mann is enlightening here).
Other *Blut und Boden* novelists include Heinrich Zillich, Karl
Waggerl and Josefa Behrens-Totenohl, writers who had largely
gained their reputations before 1933, wrote during the Nazi period
and continued to publish later. Zillich, born in what is now the
Romanian town of Brasov (then Kronstadt), published his collection of Transylvanian stories *Siebenbürger Flausen* in 1925; he also
edited the literary journal *Klingsor*. His most famous novel is
Zwischen Grenzen und Zeiten (1936), an account of the Germans
(Saxons) of Transylvania and their contacts with the other races of
that exotic melting-pot. The book, despite its chauvinism and the
anti-Semitic elements, is not entirely without sympathy for the various ethnic ingredients of Transylvania; the greatness of the
German people is seen in their awareness of universal ideas and
values which transcend petty self-interest. The protagonist Lutz,
the Transylvanian Saxon, does not emigrate to Germany but stays
in the new Romanian motherland (after 1918) to give that country
what at one time the Germans gave to Austria and to Hungary: a
sense of vision and of dedication. Josefa Behrens (later Behrens-
Totenohl, the addition being the name of her estate in the
Sauerland) is known above all for her novel *Der Femhof* (1934),
a historical novel set in the fourteenth century which tells of the
tragic love between the daughter of a farm-owner and a farm-
hand: Nordic earth is extolled in rhapsodic prose, as are the
rhythms of nature against which this love is enacted. Behrens-
Totenohl published her essay 'Die Frau als Schöpferin und
Erhalterin des Volkstums' in 1938: woman is praised as creator and
preserver of a people's destiny, of that blood which runs from
primitive depths and flows through generations. Poems such as

'Einer Sippe Gesicht' tell of blood, earth, breast and womb in a chthonic, quasi-religious manner, and it is North German soil and history which is deemed the most precious of all. An Austrian example of the *Blut und Boden* manner of writing would be Karl Waggerl, a writer from Salzburg whose *Brot* (1930) is reminiscent of Knut Hamsun. Waggerl excels at portrayals of peasant communities, particularly of the Salzburg countryside: *Das Jahr des Herrn* (1933), later filmed, conveys the darkness as well as the light of Austrian village life in an unsentimental manner. The novel *Schweres Blut* (1931) describes not only those deeply rooted in the soil but also the restless wanderer who can find no home. Other popular books include *Mütter* (1935), an account of Alpine life, *Wagrainer Tagebuch* (1936) and the *Kalendergeschichten* (1937).

The novels listed above, those examples of *Blut und Boden* writing, are generally conservative, backward-looking and provincial, with varying degrees of chauvinism and anti-liberalism; some betray anti-Semitic tendencies. A different group of writers concern themselves with novels which glorify militarism and repudiate the Weimar Republic: these would include Franz Schauwecker, Josef Wehner, Werner Beumelburg, Edwin Erich Dwinger, Ernst von Salomon and Hans Zöberlein. Franz Schauwecker's *Aufbruch der Nation* (1929) praises the German infantryman, his idealism, courage, dedication and ruthless energy in a manner not dissimilar to Ernst Jünger; Werner Beumelburg's *Douaumont* (1923), *Sperrfeuer um Deutschland* (1929) and *Gruppe Bosemüller* likewise extol the heroism of officers and men in the inferno of war, as does Josef Wehner in his *Sieben vor Verdun* (1930). These novels, written before 1933, would obviously be welcomed by the new masters: here was no 'literary betrayal of the soldiers of the First World War' such as, in the view of the Nazis, Erich Maria Remarque had perpetrated with his *Im Westen nichts Neues*, but an exemplary, truthful and noble account of German heroism. Edwin Erich Dwinger's *Die letzten Reiter – Der Zug nach Kurland*, published in 1935, is a bloodthirsty account of the *Freikorps* in the Baltic, a piece of writing which by no means betrays the intelligence and sensitivity of Ernst von Salomon's *Die Geächteten* (1931), a novel with a similar theme which also touches upon the murder of Walther Rathenau. Dwinger was briefly a 'Reichskultursenator'; he received the Dietrich-Eckart prize of the city of Hamburg in 1935 for *Die letzten Reiter* and continued to write war novels up to the German collapse in 1945 (*Der Tod in Polen. Eine volksdeutsche Passion* appeared in

1940) and afterwards. A novelist whose commitment to the Nazi cause was unambiguous was Hans Zöberlein. Zöberlein was active in the liquidation of the Soviet Republic in Munich in 1919 and was an early member of the Nazi party and the SA; for his part in the murders of innocent victims at Penzberg (28 April 1945) he was condemned to death in 1948, a sentence later commuted to life imprisonment. Zöberlein was famous above all for his war novel *Der Glaube an Deutschland. Ein Kriegserleben von Verdun bis zum Umsturz* (1931); in the preface to this book Hitler wrote the following: 'The heights and the depths stand side by side, and everywhere we find the invincible trust of comradeship. We hear the heartbeat of the front, the source of that strength which created our imperishable victories.' In 1937 Zöberlein published *Der Befehl des Gewissens. Ein Roman aus den Wirren der Nachkriegszeit.* This is largely autobiographical, describing the life of one Hans Kraft from front-line soldier, *Freikorps* participant (against the Munich Republic), adherent of the newly formed Nazi party and supporter of the march on the Feldherrnhalle. A maudlin love story is also present, with naked bathing in Bavarian lakes (the Jews, apparently, prefer swimming pools, where Kraft's beloved is sexually molested by them); a quasi-religious ceremony of marriage is celebrated in the open air. Other novels include *Der Druckposten* (1939) and *Der Schrapnellbaum* (1940); Zöberlein also wrote film-scripts, most noticeably *Stoßtruppe 1917*, a reworking of *Der Glaube an Deutschland.*

It is frequently argued that National Socialism failed to produce a literary movement of any value: *Blut und Boden* novels were the offshoot of an older, regional nationalism and the war novels had their precursors in those accounts which proliferated in the Weimar Republic. Poetry was either mediocre or derivative, with classical forms frequently concealing a vacuous message. The atavistic, backward-looking ethos of National Socialism and its rejection of modernism as being symptomatic of spiritual decomposition necessarily precluded vigorous formal experimentation. Probably the most interesting artistic manifestation associated with Nazism was the development of the *Thing* play, a cultic theatre which celebrated the mysteries of *Volk*, struggle and ultimate transcendence. (The word *Thing* meant a public meeting or assembly, a gathering of free men in the open air.) Greek theatre, mediaeval mystery plays and, interestingly, certain aspects of Expressionist theatre (the choric miming and 'Bewegungschor' of Hanns Niedecken-Gebhardt, for example) had shown the way, and the quasi-religious overtones well suited the Nazi desire to demonstrate in cosmic terms the titanic battle between good (the people, Nordic man, the idealist) and evil (the democrat, the Jew, the Marxist). Richard Euringer's *Deutsche Passion* (1933) is one of the first and perhaps the finest representative of the genre, portraying a struggle between the forces of good and evil for the German soul, with an unknown soldier rising from a mass grave with a crown of barbed wire around his head, symbolising a Christ-like leader who has come to save his people. The play was originally written for radio and received its first broadcast on Maundy Thursday, 1933. An example of what such cultic theatre demanded is seen in the performance of Gustav Goes's *Aufbricht Deutschland* (1933) where thousands of marchers (seventeen thousand in the Berlin production) paraded under a forest of banners whilst actors declaimed their words over loudspeakers. Kurt Eggers's *Job der Deutsche* and *Annaberg* (both 1933) should also be noted, as should Kurt Heynicke's *Neurode* and *Der Weg ins Reich* (1935). The climax of the *Thing* theatre was Eberhard Wolfgang Möller's *Frankenberger Würfelspiel* of 1936 which was based upon an event from the Peasant's War. But *Thing* theatre did not last: ambitious plans for vast, open-air theatres built on sites hallowed by pagan, Germanic history came to nothing, and nebulous, pseudo-religious elements were increasingly looked upon with suspicion in many quarters, as were the Neo-expressionist techniques. The huge rallies in Nürnberg and elsewhere became a form of theatre in themselves, and the vast expenditure in time and money demanded by the authors of *Thing* plays were resented. But for three to four years the 'German passion-plays', with their heady fusion of *Faust*, Dornach and the *Ludo de Antichristo*, enacted in the open air, did provide a fascinating experience, the apparent rebirth of idealism and vision with a whole nation seemingly in celebration.

This chapter will now finally look at the concept of 'Inner Emigration' and consider those writers who, as far as possible, refrained from supporting the new order and who devoted themselves to a form of literature which eschewed political ideas or who hinted obliquely at the daily situation. A writer of the stature of Thomas Mann spoke scathingly in his *Die Entstehung des Doktor Faustus* (1949) of 'a body of writers who established themselves with considerable arrogance as representatives of "inner emigration"', writers who formed 'a body of intellectuals' who 'remained true to Germany', 'did not wish to leave her in the lurch', could not 'observe its destiny from comfortable seats abroad' but wished to 'share and suffer it'. It is obvious that Thomas Mann was highly sceptical about the whole idea of inner emigration, whether it be Gottfried Benn's 'aristocratic' form (withdrawal into the army) or not. In May 1945 Thomas Mann broadcast on the subject of German guilt and the disgrace felt by all at the monstrous nature of Nazi crimes; the writer Walter von Molo replied, exhorting Mann to return to his shattered country. Frank Thiess, a writer of popular historical novels whose work had been tolerated by the Nazis, wrote as another reply to Mann an open letter simply entitled 'Innere Emigration' which claimed that those who had remained in Germany were richer in experience, understanding and sympathy than those who fled. The statement in *Die Entstehung des Doktor Faustus* repudiates this, but Mann's reply to Walter von Molo also contains an obvious rejection of Thiess's argument, and a blunt statement leaves no doubt as to Mann's position: 'It may be superstitious, but in my view any books which could be printed at all in Germany between 1933 and 1945 are worse than worthless and not good to touch. The stink of blood and ignominy sticks to them. They should all be pulped.' These provocative words exacerbated the tensions between those writers who had emigrated (see Chapter 5) and those who had remained: Mann, however, was not the only exile to use such hyperbole. The brilliant critic Alfred Kerr, who had written eminent reviews for the *Berliner Tageblatt*, had been castigated by the Nazis and his writings had been burned on 10 May 1933 (the charge being that Kerr had been guilty of 'conceited debasement of our German language'). Kerr went abroad and launched a furious tirade against Gerhart Hauptmann for remaining in Nazi Germany and pusillanimously flying the swastika over his house in Silesia; friendship, wrote Kerr, was no longer possible, for Hauptmann had slavishly acquiesced and accepted the new regime without demur. 'His memory should be buried under thistles, his image lie beneath the dust': with this commination Kerr ended his tirade. Within Germany, however, Hauptmann was attacked for his allegiance to the Jewish publisher Samuel Fischer, and singled out for vituperation for *not* welcoming the Nazi *Weltanschauung*. But Hauptmann, in ever increasing isolation and advancing age (his eightieth birthday was grudgingly noticed in 1942) refused to refrain from writing; his remarkable play *Die Finsternisse*, dating from 1937 and published ten years later, was a moving requiem to his Jewish friend, the Silesian patriot Max Pinkus. This was a play which meditated upon the interaction of life and death and on the omnipresence of suffering and darkness: Hauptmann knew that those who shouted 'Juda perish!' would likewise be destroyed. The work could, obviously, not be performed, but Hauptmann was able to portray the horror of the new Reich by using myth, and that which may be called his greatest poetic achievement during those dark years was the *Atriden* cycle, an astonishing work for a writer in his eighties. The tone of sombre violence, the themes of madness and destructive frenzy which abound in these plays reach an unbearable intensity which the critic Julius Bab later noticed: *Iphigenie in Aulis*, performed in Vienna in 1944, tells of an evil priest, Kalchis, who perverts whole peoples, whilst *Elektra* (written 1944) contains a description of the place of Agamemnon's murder and of the sterile horror of death and putrefaction with a vocabulary that could be seen to portray another place of extermination – Auschwitz – not two hundred miles east of Hauptmann's home in Agnetendorf. Neither the suicide or death of many friends, nor the destruction of Dresden which he observed from afar, could crush Hauptmann's resourceful and vital spirit; in 1933 he had announced that 'My epoch began in 1870 and ended with the burning of the Reichstag', yet he survived the hectic and murderous madness of the Third Reich and remained creative until his death in 1946.

Another writer whose books were burned in 1933 (the charge included 'decadence and moral decay'), yet who remained to publish, was Erich Kästner: objections were raised to his novel *Fabian* (1931), a diverting account of low life in Berlin, rather than to *Emil und die Detektive*. Kästner was removed from the Reichsschrifttumskammer yet continued to write children's stories and also film-scripts. It is frequently forgotten that, nothwithstanding the rigours of 'Gleichschaltung' and the highly organised process of censorship, writers and journals were tolerated who did not follow the party line and who chose to remain aloof from the political events around them. Such authors would include Hans Carossa, Rudolf Alexander Schröder and Werner Bergenruen, traditionalist writers whose conservative stance was regarded by the authorities as harmless and who could demonstrate to the educated middle classes and to the world at large that the Third Reich esteemed and encouraged cultural activities. Werner Bergengruen's *Der Großtyrann und das Gericht* (1935) is an interesting example here.

Stylistically the book looks back to the writing of Conrad Ferdinand Meyer, yet the portrayal of the tyrant who, himself guilty, corrupts a whole society and spreads fear and panic everywhere had an obviously topical resonance at the time of its publication. The novel was, in fact, praised by the Nazi organ *Völkischer Beobachter* as an example of fine, modern writing, the portrayal of the Italian Renaissance being especially commended. Edzard Schaper's novel *Die sterbende Kirche* appeared in the same year, a less sensational account of stoicism and the need for religious faith in dark times. Friedrich Percyval Reck-Malleczewen also deserves mention here, whose study of mass hysteria, *Bockelson. Geschichte eines Massenwahns* (1937), ostensibly dealt with the fanaticism of the anabaptists of Münster in the sixteenth century and the megalomania of their leader. A historicising mask could, then, conceal an awareness of the extraordinary and disturbing nature of the Nazi present, and an aestheticising aloofness demonstrate a tacit rejection of contemporary attitudes. Ernst Jünger's ambiguous stance has already been noted: a more problematic case is that of the writer Ernst Wiechert. Wiechert's *Blut und Boden* writing obviously appealed to the Nazis, as did his backward-looking, anti-liberal attitudes; the autobiographical study *Wälder und Menschen*, however, which appeared in 1936, caused displeasure by its pessimism, individualism and tolerance of writers such as Heine who was anathema to the new regime. In 1938 Wiechert spent two months in Buchenwald concentration camp: the novel *Das einfache Leben* (1939) reached a wide readership with its account of the soldier's homecoming after 1918 and the account of the simple life away from the turmoil of great cities. This was not objectionable to the Nazis, but a public reading of his *Der weiße Büffel oder Von der großen Gerechtigkeit* (published in 1946), an Indian story on the theme of justice, truth and falsehood, was regarded as inflammatory. *Der Totenwald*, again published in 1946, is an account of these times and of his incarceration. Wiechert had also appeared in the Moscow emigré journal *Das Wort*; he is a remarkable phenomenon in any account of conservative writing which, originally given state approval, turned increasingly and courageously to a rejection of National Socialism.

Writers such as Gertrud von Le Fort and Jochen Klepper were able to write under the Third Reich, as was Reinhold Schneider: expression of Christian sentiments was permitted, especially those which extolled the German theological tradition. Literary journals

such as *Hochland* and *Corona*, also *Das Innere Reich* were not pro-
hibited. Recent scholarship has demonstrated that a surprising
amount was published during those twelve years which, if not
openly resisting the Nazi cultural doctrines (although the *Neue
Rundschau* and the *feuilleton* pages of the *Frankfurter Zeitung* came
perilously close), expressed an apolitical indifference. Writers of
the stature of Günther Eich, Peter Huchel, Wolfgang Koeppen and
Maria Luise Kaschnitz produced a body of literature which was by
no means inconsiderable during the Nazi period and established
themselves as writers of substance after 1945. It is also erroneous to
believe that those writers who remained in Germany were hermetically sealed, and had no contact with the outside world; the new
developments in writing elsewhere in Europe were known, and it
was possible to read those authors like Kafka, Proust and the
Expressionists whom the Nazis forebade. Stefan Andres lived for
years in Italy, and travel was only restricted at the outbreak of war.
American writers were widely published until 1942. The war years
obviously meant that non-Nazi literature was difficult to publish,
for paper was reserved for those writers who supported the war
effort. But the earlier concept of the 'Stunde Null', or 'null point' –
that is, the claim that the end of the Second World War represented
a *tabula rasa*, a cultural desert waiting to be fructified – is a superficial one: many writers were waiting in Germany to continue writing, and they frequently moved into the new publishing ventures;
the exiles, when they returned, found a lively literary scene, and
not a vacuum. Many writers of the earlier *Blut und Boden* literature
also continued to write after 1945 although some, like Hans
Blunck, were branded as Nazi 'sympathisers' and fined, in his case
the sum of ten thousand marks. Hence Thomas Mann's condem-
nation of all those works which had been published in Germany
between 1933 and 1945 seems harsh indeed, excusable only when
seen as a rejoinder to the charges levelled against those who had
fled to the haven of Hollywood and the beaches of California. And
his audacious claim that 'German culture is where I am' may be
disregarded as being a statement which, deliberately provocative,
necessarily lacked the knowledge of the literature being produced
in Germany during those years.

Chapter 5 will deal with the writers of exile: this chapter has
sought to look at the different strands of literary activity during the
Nazi period – the conservative, traditionalist forms, frequently of
Blut und Boden provenance, the writers who accepted and glorified

the Nazi State (Johst, Zöberlin and others), the writers of inner emigration and those whose stance is apolitical. The paucity of literature which can be called 'Nazi' is not surprising considering the perverse nature of the *Weltanschauung*; certain experiments in *Thing* theatre, one or two accomplished films, and a sprinkling of poems dealing with war and heroism may perhaps be excluded from the general anathema. Hermann Goering's statement that 'True art is only that which the ordinary man in the street can grasp and understand' is hardly a guarantee for artistic excellence, and the imposition of Hitler's petty-bourgeois criteria, upon architecture and the visual arts above all, but also upon the written word, meant a general stifling of experimentation and the insistence on a state-imposed mediocrity. Those authors who deserve to be read are those of exile and those who quietly wrote, either for themselves or for a group of like-minded non-conformists who ignored the strident hysteria. And it was Gottfried Benn who, after the end of the war, singled out those words from Rilke which, he claimed, meant so much to his generation: 'Who speaks of conquest? To survive is all.'

5

The Literature of the Exile

January 30 1933, when Hitler was appointed Chancellor, marked the beginning of a mass exodus of people unsympathetic to the regime which gathered momentum when the Reichstag fire on 28 February was followed by a wave of arrests. The polarisation of political forces towards the end of the Weimar Republic was to be overcome by the elimination in Germany of one of the poles. The Nazis had already waged a campaign of protest and disruption against the art which directly or indirectly undermined their cause; one small but siginificant example of their measures was the release of white mice in the auditorium when the film of Remarque's *Im Westen nichts Neues* was first screened. They now varied and radicalised their tactics. These included the 'Gleichschaltung' (co-ordination) of the Akademie der Künste, which had a literary section consisting of most of the innovative writers of the Weimar Republic (Thomas and Heinrich Mann, Döblin, Leonhard Frank, Kaiser, Kellermann, Ricarda Huch, Werfel, Wassermann and von Unruh), together with others of more conservative views. The former were induced to resign and were replaced by twenty-two new members with Nazi sympathies (including Hans Friedrich Blunck, Hans Grimm, Erwin Guido Kolbenheyer and Will Vesper). The book-burnings in several university towns on 10 May were merely the most visible manifestation of the new regime's will; other measures included the Nazification of the writers' organisation, censorship, the removal of undesirable literature from bookshops and libraries, expatriation and temporary or permanent imprisonment. There can be no doubt that some of those writers who left at an early date would, had they stayed, have shared the fate of Erich Mühsam, Carl von Ossietzky and Klaus Neukrantz, who were maltreated and murdered in the first concentration camps. All those who could be identified as Jewish or as having Communist sympathies were under threat. The first destinations of these exiles – Brecht, in their name, insisted on this term rather than that of emigrant – were a number of what we would now call front line states: Czechoslovakia, the Netherlands, France, and to a lesser extent Switzerland, Denmark and Sweden. The left-wing Malik-Verlag was re-established in Prague (later in London), the Fischer Verlag (probably the most prestigious publishing house of the Weimar Republic, with Thomas Mann and Gerhart Hauptmann on its list) in Stockholm, while local publishers in Amsterdam (Querido and Allert de Lange) and Zurich (Emil Oprecht) became major outlets for the work of German exiles. Equally important were the magazines, whether already established and re-named (*Die Neue Weltbühne, Das Neue Tagebuch*, both Paris), or new (*Neue deutsche Blätter*, edited in Prague by Communist sympathisers who followed a flexible line from 1933 to 1935, *Die Sammlung*, edited in Amsterdam by Klaus Mann (son of Thomas) during the same period, *Maß und Wert*, edited in Zurich under the aegis of Thomas Mann from 1937 to 1940, and the Moscow publications *Das Wort*, edited by Fritz Erpenbeck with advice from Brecht, Feuchtwanger and Bredel from 1936 to 1939, and *Internationale Literatur*, edited by Becher from 1933 to 1945). *NDB* and *Das Wort* were especially important for the propagation of a left-wing consensus under the banner of the Volksfront (popular front), which eventually found an echo in the policy of the governing coalition in France in 1936–7. Here an alternative writers' organisation had been founded, together with a Deutsche Freiheitsbibliothek (German Freedom Library). The efforts of the exiles to create a common front against Nazism culminated in the First International Congress for the Defence of Culture which met in Paris during 1–25 March 1935, attended by a hundred writers from thirty-eight nations, amongst whom were twenty German exiles, including Ernst Bloch, Alfred Kantorowicz, Brecht, Seghers, Becher, Feuchtwanger, Kisch and, to most sensational effect, Jan Petersen, who, as a member of the underground Bund proletarisch-revolutionärer Schriftsteller still at work in Berlin, wore a mask in order to preserve anonymity. Two later congresses, divided between various venues in Spain and Paris in 1937 and held in Paris in 1938, were more sparsely attended.

The crises of the late 1930s and the beginning of war forced the exiles to move on to states which were, it was hoped, beyond the reach of the Nazis and exercised a liberal immigration policy. The Soviet Union and Mexico became the principal destinations for Communists and fellow travellers, although life in the former was perilous for some in the wake of the Moscow trials and the

Nazi–Soviet pact. It was after the Soviet Union had entered the war that the German exiles (Becher, Friedrich Wolf, Erich Weinert, Bredel, Scharrer) were best able to contribute to the overthrow of Nazism by means of propaganda, mainly in the form of radio broadcasts and contraband literature aimed at German troops on the eastern front, while Mexico became the base of the publishing venture El Libro Libre from 1942 to 1946 and a haven for Anna Seghers. The most prominent writers of the exile eventually settled in the USA, either in New York or Southern California, often after an adventurous journey through German-occupied Vichy France and neutral Spain, or in the case of Brecht, a journey from Scandinavia via the Soviet Union and a crossing of the Pacific. While they were not subject to political pressures before the McCarthy years, survival for these depended on the strength of the reputation they already enjoyed (Thomas Mann) or on their ability to adapt to a new market without surrendering their integrity as artists. Werfel, Remarque and Feuchtwanger made the most successful transition, while H. Mann, Döblin, Broch and Brecht either remained aloof or were forced to depend on hack work for film studios or on scholarships.

The theatre, as the most public of the arts, was affected more severely than fiction by the exile situation, yet it has been calculated that authors produced 724 stage plays, 108 radio plays and 398 film scripts, many of which however were never or only once performed. The Schauspielhaus theatre in Zurich played a key role here; it was the venue not only of the premières of Bruckner's *Die Rassen* and (in German) of Friedrich Wolf's *Professor Mamlock*, but also of Brecht's *Der gute Mensch von Sezuan* (1943), *Mutter Courage und ihre Kinder* (1941) and *Leben des Galilei* (1943), as well as plays by Csokor, Bruno Frank, Curt Goetz, Lasker-Schüler, Horváth, Kaiser, Werfel and Zuckmayer. The exile community in Paris arranged and supported the first performances of Brecht's *Die Gewehre der Frau Carrar* in 1937 and of eight scenes from his *Furcht und Elend des Dritten Reiches* under the title *99%* the following year. In the Soviet Union two of the agitprop groups of the Weimar Republic amalgamated and continued their work as Deutsches Theater Kolonne links, while the plays of Friedrich Wolf, including *Das trojanische Pferd*, premiered in 1936 at the theatre in Engels, capital of the Volga Republic, were successfully performed. In the USA Werfel achieved, first, notoriety with his biblical drama *Der Weg der Verheißung* in 1935 (due to the nightmare conditions in which it was staged), then popularity with *Jacobowsky und der Oberst* in 1944, a comedy of character involving a Jew and a Polish colonel set during the the fall of France in 1940, while Fritz Kortner's collaborations with Dorothy Thompson in *Another Sun* (1937–40) and with Zuckmayer in *Somewhere in France* (1940–1) had little resonance and Brecht's efforts to stage his work to his satisfaction bore fruit only in the performance of *Leben des Galilei* with Charles Laughton in the title role in 1947.

The exile periodicals became a forum for ardent literary debates which turned on the cultural heritage and the writer's present function in the struggle against Fascism. The close connection between these two themes arose from the need to challenge the Nazis' claim that they represented the German culture of the future cleansed from the corrosive influence of forces alien to the *Volk*, and to replace it by work which maintained and built on the best traditions of the past. The controversy between Klaus Mann and Gottfried Benn in 1933 (see Chapter 4) led on to the Expressionism debate, in which Klaus Mann, Alfred Kurella, Georg Lukács, and Ernst Bloch participated and, from the sidelines in contributions which were published much later, also Brecht. Essentially an argument within the left on the possible link between the emotionalism of Expressionist art and the Nazi appeal to irrational instincts, it broadened to include a consideration of the irrational tradition in German thought and its political implications, and became complicated by entanglement with concurrent debates in the Soviet Union on the definition and function of Socialist Realism and with the view adopted by Lukács that its ancestry lay in the critical realism of the nineteenth-century novel. In opposing this position Brecht and Bloch aimed to harness the innovations of modernism, in which Expressionism played a part, to the anti-Fascist cause. The argument proved relevant not only to a critical assessment of exile art but also to the divergent cultural norms established in the two German states after 1945. Brecht was acutely aware of the fact that modernism was under threat both within Germany and from the exile writers, who with the best intentions – to warn readers of the menace of the Third Reich, to inform them about its true character, to draw attention to an alternative Germany and to maintain contact with the resistance, such as it was, inside the German frontiers – resorted to traditional, direct and simple forms in order to achieve maximum impact. (Brecht himself recognised this imperative in much of his work during the 1930s, parts of which were smuggled into Germany under false titles, such as *Practical Guide to First Aid*.) Even when he abandoned hope of reaching German readers, his work was far from being consistently experimental, and he regretted that the plays he wrote between 1938 and his return to Europe, by which he is best remembered, were in formal terms retrograde.

The need for literature to be operative prompted another controversy with an equal bearing on the practice of exile writers. The popularity of the historical novel, especially during the initial years of the exile, has various causes: writers who had already proved themselves in the genre continued to cultivate it or published works begun before 1933 (Feuchtwanger, Stefan Zweig), historical subjects not confined to Germany had a broad appeal indicated already by the international success of Feuchtwanger's *Jud Süß* (1925); nevertheless they were accused by critics of turning away from the burning issues of the present. In defence of the historical novel Feuchtwanger claimed that the distance it created from the present placed in relief the author's view of the world in his own time; by providing examples from the past of the eternal struggle between a reasoning minority and the unenlightened masses, the historical novel could function as a weapon at a time when this antithesis had taken a virulent form. Döblin offered a variation of the same idea, adding that the confusion of the present produced a desire to take one's bearings from the past and to justify oneself by reference to it. As we shall see, the relevance of the material to the present was made more or less explicit in the novels themselves.

However, the two questions uppermost in the minds of the exiles at the start of their activities were: how did the Nazis succeed in eliminating their rivals and gaining acceptance (through the ballot-box) from large sections of the community? and how strong was their power-base in it? These could best be answered by tracing the development of diverging opinions or the consolidation of a single view within a family or a professional milieu over a long period (Brentano, *Theodor Chindler*, 1936; Marchwitza, *Die Kumiaks*, 1934; Döblin, *Pardon wird nicht gegeben*, 1935; Becher, *Abschied*, 1940) or over the crucial months of 1932–3. The best of the so-called *Deutschlandromane*, Feuchtwanger's *Die Geschwister Oppenheim* (later: *Oppermann*) (1933), which sold 257,000 copies within nine months and was translated into fifteen languages, follows the latter course, in an account of how three brothers of a prosperous and highly cultured Berlin Jewish family are forced to change their way of life between November 1932 and the weeks of terror following the Reichstag fire: Martin is forced out of his furniture business, Edgar, an ENT specialist, suffers professional slander and, along with Martin, arrest and maltreatment, and Gustav, a scholar engaged on a biography of Lessing, emigrates. When Gustav returns, intending to gain contact with resistance groups, he is put in a concentration camp and dies shortly after his release, while Martin's son Berthold is driven to suicide after victimisation by his Nazi teacher. The novel indicates how wealth and education are no defence against racism and how they can provide a false sense of security. It shows ideology at work in the classroom in a manner echoed later by Döblin in the final volume of *1918. Eine deutsche Revolution,* in which Friedrich Becker fails to convince his pupils of the priority of Antigone's demands over *raison d'état* in Sophocles' play (although here an enlightened teacher confronts a blinkered class). Although his assessment of the Nazis as a brutalised covetous mass opposed to a cultured but naive élite may be simplistic, it enables Feuchtwanger to place events in the context of a German humanistic tradition.

The underlying structure of the novel – reactions of a small, closely linked number of characters precipitated by the stages of the Nazi seizure of power – is found also in Heinz Liepman's *Das Vaterland* (1933), in which at the end of March 1933 a ship returns to Hamburg after a three-month absence to find Germany transformed, and Franz Carl Weiskopf's *Die Versuchung* (1937, later entitled *Lissy*). Set between December 1931 and March 1933, the second of these begins like *Kleiner Mann, was nun?* but adopts the point of view of Lissy, whose husband becomes a member of the SA (Nazi brownshirts) when he loses his job. Drawn this way and that by all those close to her, whose allegiances cover the entire political spectrum, she eventually joins with her father an illegal group. (A woman from a higher social class undergoes a similar transformation in Balder Olden's *Roman eines Nazi,* 1933). The criticism of the pusillanimity of the SPD (Social Democrats) implied here features more strongly in Oskar Maria Graf's *Der Abgrund* (1936), in the contrast between an SPD town councillor and his son and their respective fates; after the family flees to Austria when Hitler takes power, the father is killed in bed during the February uprising in Vienna in 1934, while the son and his wife, having taken a more active part in the events, escape to Czechoslovakia to

continue the struggle. Ernst Glaeser's *Der letzte Zivilist* (1935), however, offers a gloomier perspective by showing the parallel between
the gradual disillusionment of a rich German–American when he
returns to his ancestral home, and that of the young Hans Diefen-
bach whose adolescent disorientation renders him an easy prey
to Nazi intrigues and rivalries, so that when he is drawn into a
scandal, suicide becomes the only way out. The devastating effects
of unemployment and the vulnerability of its victims to Nazi
promises are central to Seghers' *Die Rettung* (1937) set in a mining
community, while the same author's *Der Kopflohn* (1933), together
with Adam Scharrer's *Maulwürfe* (1933), focus on the peasantry,
the former with greater scepticism regarding the possibility of resistance. Other works are marked by more wishful thinking, especially
those centred on the figure of the disillusioned SA-man (Walter
Schönstedt, *Auf der Flucht erschossen*, 1933), who represented the
possibility of reform within the party or of a transfer of allegiance;
the hopes invested in such scenarios were dashed by the elimination of the 'Socialist' wing of the party under Gregor Strasser and
the Night of the Long Knives in 1934. Yet the portrayal of Nazis
whose adherence to the movement results from misplaced idealism
(as in the title figure of Olden's novel and minor figures present in
novels by Weiskopf, Glaeser, Klaus Mann, Bredel, Scharrer and
Arnold Zweig) continues to be a feature of the *Deutschlandroman* as
striking as the emphasis placed on the crude criminality of other
Nazis, as in Paul Westheim's *Heil Kadlatz!* (1935–6).

Much of the early exile fiction (especially the short stories in a documentary style published in the periodicals by Weiskopf, *Die
Stärkeren*, 1934; Petersen, *Deutsche Episoden*, 1935; *Unsere Straße*,
1936; Bredel, *Der Spitzel*, 1936; and the novels by Bredel *Dein
unbekannter Bruder*, 1937; Liepman, . . . *wird mit dem Tode bestraft*,
1935), in giving due weight to the courage of the illegal opposition
and advocating rapprochement between Communists and
Socialists, overestimated the strength of the anti-Fascist working
class. (The same desire to turn wish into deed is evident in Friedrich
Wolf's plays *Das trojanische Pferd*, 1936, and *Dr. Lilli Wanner*, 1944.)
Readers were however left in no doubt about the terroristic
practices of the regime, as documented in authentic reports of
experiences in the concentration camps Dachau (Hans Beimler),
Oranienburg (Gerhart Seger), Börgermoor (Wolfgang Langhoff)
and Fuhlsbüttel (Bredel's novel *Die Prüfung*, 1935).

Long before the war Nazism was recognised as a phenomenon intent on infiltration and expansion abroad. The return of the Saarland to Germany in January 1935 (opposed by Gustav Regler's *Im Kreuzfeuer* and Theodor Balk's *Hier spricht die Saar*, both 1934) was followed by increasing pressure on Austria, symptomised by the murder of its chancellor Dollfuß in 1934 after the defeat of the February workers' uprising (which forms the background of Seghers' *Der Weg durch den Februar*, 1935, and *Der letzte Weg des Koloman Wallisch*, 1934) had removed the possibility of a common front. However, during the late 1930s the exiles directed their attention to (and participated in) the Spanish Civil War, which became the subject of a vast literature, much of it based on direct experience of the conflict. The Munich crisis and the annexation of the Sudetenland inspired Friedrich Wolf's *Zwei an der Grenze* (1939) and Hans Habe's *Zu spät?* (1939 in English). By this time the hopes held by some exiles that the Nazi regime would be toppled within Germany had given way to pessimism, reflected in works which focus on the vulnerability of the petty bourgeoisie (Graf, *Anton Sittinger*, 1937), the young (Horváth, *Jugend ohne Gott*, 1937, and *Ein Kind unserer Zeit*, 1938), intellectuals (Irmgard Keun, *Nach Mitternacht*, and Bernhard von Brentano, *Prozeß ohne Richter*, both 1937; Klaus Mann, *Mephisto*, written 1936; and novels by Ernst Erich Noth, Martin Haller, Bernhard Diebold and Anna Reiner) and the peasantry in a remote rural community (Broch, *Die Verzauberung*, 1935). The growing scepticism about the future, together with the difficulty of obtaining reliable information about the situation in the Reich, led the exiles to turn their attention to their own precarious position (as in Klaus Mann, *Flucht in den Norden*, 1934; Merz, *Ein Mensch fällt aus Deutschland*, and Graf, *Der Abgrund*, both 1936; Keun, *Kind aller Länder*, 1938; Brecht, *Flüchtlingsgespräche*, written 1940–1; and Remarque, *Liebe deinen Nächsten*, 1941), which became desperate after the fall of France. The trials and tribulations of the exiles at this time, interned by the Vichy regime in the Colombes stadium in Paris or in the camps of Les Milles, Vernet and Gurs, are graphically portrayed in Habe, *Ob tausend fallen* (1941 in English), Feuchtwanger, *Unholdes Frankreich* (1942), Döblin, *Schicksalsreise* (1949), Bruno Frei, *Die Männer von Vernet* (1951), Hasenclever, *Die Rechtslosen* (1963) and Gertrud Isolani, *Stadt ohne Männer* (1945); their efforts to leave France, cross neutral Spain and gain passage from Lisbon to the USA occupy a central place in the memoirs of the exiles and in the novels *Transit*

(1944) by Anna Seghers and *Die Nacht von Lissabon* (1962) by Remarque.

Klaus Mann's *Mephisto* (1936), while clearly based on his acquaintance with the actor Gustaf Gründgens, who was for a time his brother-in-law before rising to the highest artistic position in the German theatre, was not according to its author a *Schlüsselroman* or *roman-à-clef*, but an exposure of one who serves as a model for those whose ambitions and chameleon talents overcome any moral or political scruples they may have had.

The most important novels about life in exile are undoubtedly Klaus Mann's *Der Vulkan* (1939) and Feuchtwanger's *Exil* (1940). Klaus Mann combined a firm commitment to the anti-Fascist cause with a literary allegiance to decadence and the French literature (especially Gide) which sprang from it, and a predilection for vulnerable and deviant figures conditioned by his own homosexuality and suicidal tendencies. The picture he paints of the French exile community could therefore hardly be more different from that of an idealised working-class present in the earlier exile fiction. Yet the determination to retain faith in the future also finds expression, in the decisions made by the motley collection of characters to fight in the International Brigade in Spain, join illegal resistance groups in Germany or influence isolationist opinion in the USA. *Exil*, with which Feuchtwanger completed the trilogy *Der Wartesaal*, begun with *Erfolg* and continued with *Die Geschwister Oppenheim*, has a similar structure, but gives more attention to the role of the artist-intellectual, here represented by the composer Sepp Trautwein, who combats Nazi intrigues aimed at changing the political stance of a German newspaper, *Pariser Nachrichten*, published in Paris, until he is dismissed. His fellow journalists declare their solidarity with the foundation of another publication, and as a result of their efforts and growing international pressure the editor whom Trautwein had originally replaced and whom the Nazis had abducted from Switzerland is released. Trautwein returns to composition, and in his symphony 'Der Wartesaal' ('waiting room') successfully conveys his conception of the period of exile as a time of transition until departure to a better destination is possible. In his passage from an unpolitical position to a clear anti-Fascist commitment Trautwein resembles Tüverlin in *Erfolg*; a new dimension is added however by the discussions with his Communist son Hanns, who eventually departs, like Pröckl, for the Soviet Union, but only after convincing Sepp that a more militant humanism under the banner of the Volksfront represents the only way forward. (The role of Communists in the Volksfront is also a theme of Fritz Erpenbeck's *Emigranten*, 1937.)

The later exile literature is even more heterogeneous, but one can note both the development of already established themes and the introduction of new ones. Anna Seghers' *Das siebte Kreuz* (1942, after parts had appeared in 1939), although written in Mexico, is based on authentic reports smuggled out of Germany and traces the odyssey of Georg Heisler, one of seven prisoners who escape from a concentration camp. While the others are recaptured one by one, he succeeds in reaching the Netherlands, thus frustrating the camp commandant's plan to crucify all the fugitives. Heisler is not a heroic figure and seeks in his numerous meetings with former friends and fellow-workers no more than the minimum assistance needed to ensure survival, yet in some instances these contacts revive a dormant anti-Fascism which testifies to the continued existence of an alternative Germany not confined to the working-class. Other authors indicated the potential for resistance among social groups previously ignored or underestimated: the aristocracy (Bruno Frank, *Der Reisepaß*, 1937), the Bekennende Kirche (Toller's play *Pastor Hall*, 1938), students, especially the Weiße Rose group (Vicki Baum, *Hier stand ein Hotel*, 1943 in English, and Alfred Neumann, *Es waren ihrer sechs*, 1944), and eventually also the officers involved in the attempt to assassinate Hitler on 20 July 1944 (Stephan Hermlin, *Der Leutnant Yorck von Wartenburg*, 1945, and many plays performed after 1945). One novel in particular, Arnold Zweig's *Das Beil von Wandsbek* (1944 in Hebrew) combines a wide social panorama with a thorough analysis of how and why representatives of different social groups (including the Bekennende Kirche) accept or reject the regime. The action covers the year between late August 1937 and the Munich agreement. Four Communists are sentenced to death after false testimony by SA-men, and Hitler on an official visit to Hamburg insists that the sentence is carried out immediately. The illness of the executioner makes it necessary to seek a replacement, who is discovered in the person of Albert Teetjen, a butcher who has fallen on hard times and has accepted Nazism as the small trader's defence against big business. When the identity of the new executioner is passed on to the neighbourhood, Teetjen's shop is boycotted by his customers; faced with financial ruin, social isolation and his wife's suicide, he follows her example. A parallel plot follows the change of heart of two middle-class characters, the doctor Käte Neumeier and the prison governor Dr Koldewey; the former after disappointment with the SPD had been deluded by the Nazi appeal to Socialist sentiment, while the latter under the influence of Nietzsche had seen in Nazism a necessary transition to a patrician order. Their disillusionment leads them to join an officers' conspiracy to assassinate Hitler, which, however, fails. Zweig succeeds in adapting to a new situation the theme of miscarriage of justice which he had treated in the Grischa-novel; both cases were based on fact. He adds a new dimension by combining the sociological analysis present in most other exile novels with an examination of Hitler's pathological personality and of analogous features in the mass of his followers, in which the influence of Freud, with whom Zweig had conducted a lengthy correspondence, is manifest.

Exile literature is not lacking in more sensational treatments of the Nazi phenomenon, in which political commitment, private revenge and romantic interest are closely intertwined, as in the bestsellers of Remarque (*Arc de Triomphe*, 1946, filmed as *Arch of Triumph*, and *Liebe deinen Nächsten*, 1939 in English, filmed as *So ends the Night*) and of Habe (*Ob tausend fallen*, 1941 in English, filmed as *Cross of Lorraine*), or a connection is made between the hypnotic control of the masses exercised by the Nazis and the practice of clairvoyance, as in Feuchtwanger's *Die Brüder Lautensack* (1945). Not even these, however, approach the implausibility of Fritz von Unruh's fantasy *Der nie verlor* (1947 in English), on a monarchist plot to murder Hitler and restore Kaiser Wilhelm II. Such a novel anticipates the kind of political thriller which has a permanent place in the railway and airport bookstalls of Anglo-Saxon countries, but it is the exception rather than the rule amongst German treatments of the Third Reich which, even when they deal with the war, as in Weiskopf's *Himmelfahrts-Kommando* (1944 in English), Remarque's *Zeit zu leben und Zeit zu sterben* (1954) and Plievier's eye-witness account of the turning-point of the war *Stalingrad* (1945), are concerned to avoid cheap effects. The same judgement may be applied to novels concerning the resistance in Czechoslovakia (Stefan Heym, *Der Fall Glasenapp*, 1943 in English; Weiskopf, *Vor einem neuen Tag*, 1941 in English; Winder, *Die Pflicht*, 1949; and Heinrich Mann, *Lidice*, 1943) and France (Feuchtwanger, *Simone*, 1945, and the plays *Geiseln* by Rudolf Leonhard, 1945, and *Die Gesichte der Simone Machard* by Brecht, written 1941–3).

Some exile writers who aimed to uncover the roots of the Nazi mentality in the patriarchal and authoritarian ethos of the Second Reich produced novels which may be defined as hybrids of the *Deutschlandroman* and the historical novel. Wilhelm Speyer's *Das Glück der Andernachs* (1947) portrays an upper-middle-class Jewish family in a positive light; by identifying it with the liberal spirit of the emperor Frederick III, the end of whose short reign in 1888 stifled hopes that the course of German history would be deflected from militarism and imperialism, Speyer draws a contrast with later developments in which the security of such a milieu was progressively undermined. In this process the impact of the First World War on similar figures is highlighted by Arnold Zweig in *Junge Frau von 1914* (1931), but the critique of the Wilhelmine system is sharpened in the same author's *Erziehung vor Verdun* (1935) and the family sagas already mentioned.

To what extent did novelists make good their claim to reflect their own time in the historical novel? Their approach was necessarily very different from that exemplified in the *Deutschlandroman*, yet there are some points of contact. While the second and third parts of Feuchtwanger's *Wartesaal*-trilogy pursue the efforts of the creative artist to come to terms with the imperative of the anti-Fascist struggle, his historical novels of the same period and later are centred on artists and intellectuals in their relations to political power. The connection between these themes is indicated by a conversation at the end of *Die Geschwister Oppenheim* between Gustav Oppenheim, the biographer of Lessing, who has taken steps to emigrate, his nephew Heinrich, forced by victimisation at school to choose between resistance and suicide, and one of Heinrich's school-friends, Pierre Tüverlin. When Pierre dismisses the suggestion of demonstrations against the regime as unrealistic, advocating instead reason and common sense, Gustav asks whether the self-sacrifices of Socrates, Seneca and Christ were futile. In reply Pierre cites the example of Galileo, who recanted his support of the Copernican theory under threat of torture, having come to the conclusion that it is wiser to live for an idea than to die for it, even at the cost of concessions to the powers that be. The particular case of the Italian physicist and astronomer was later taken up by Brecht when he came to write the first version of his play on Galileo towards the end of the decade in Denmark, but it was natural that it should exercise the minds of all victims of Nazism and be adduced in discussion of the strategy and tactics to be observed in the fight against what were rapidly proving overwhelming odds. For Feuchtwanger and others (such as Arnold Zweig, Döblin, Stefan Zweig, Werfel, Broch) the question was further complicated by their position as assimilated Jews, for whom anti-Semitism encouraged a new awareness of their racial origin. Consequently the problem of the Jew in a Gentile society became the principal theme of Feuchtwanger's most substantial contribution to the historical novel at this time, the Josephus-trilogy (*Der jüdische Krieg*, 1932, *Die Söhne*, 1935, *Der Tag wird kommen*, 1945), in which the Jewish historian's accommodation with the Roman Empire in Palestine is progressively abandoned as events induce growing self-criticism. When integration in the name of world citizenship is achieved at the cost of concessions to Roman anti-Semitism and the loss of domestic happiness, he openly declares his allegiance to his Jewish heritage and throws in his lot with a new Jewish rebellion. Josephus had gained Roman citizenship in the first volume of the trilogy by declaring that the victorious general Vespasian (later emperor) was the Messiah; he therefore appears as a renegade who salves his conscience by defining Roman conquest as the fulfilment of a mission to unite the world. The second volume traces his developing awareness that the Roman Empire is based on economic exploitation, which in the third volume is transformed into a reign of terror under the emperor Domitian with clear analogies to the Third Reich. In the end it is not clear whether Josephus's identification with his people and his clear stand against contemporary anti-Semitism in his book *Gegen Apion* are to be interpreted simply as a return to the Jewish fold or as commitment to a militant humanism which allows national and religious liberty. The divisions between the priestly hierarchy, with its extensive land-holdings, and the rebels, who are workers and peasants, suggests that for Feuchtwanger the question of religious identity was secondary to his view that in the context of his time the question of national self-determination was inseparable from the class war.

Feuchtwanger's other historical novel of the exile, *Der falsche Nero* (1936), set in another eastern province of the Roman Empire, allows easier identification of its bearing on the events of the Third Reich. Terenz, a potter with histrionic and rhetorical talent and the double of the emperor Nero, is proclaimed emperor after the latter's death by the Roman ex-senator Varro who hopes thereby to revenge himself on the local administration. The puppet threatens to escape the control of his master, who attempts to retain it by marrying off his daughter to him. The usurper is eventually unmasked by the mistress of the true Nero, but only after he has established a demagogic rule and gained the support of the neighbouring king of Parthia. Terenz and his henchmen are caricatures of Hitler, Göring and Goebbels and the measures he adopts to secure his position correspond to the stages of the Nazi seizure of power. The satirical exposure of the theatricality of mass manipulation by means of historical analogy prompts comparison with Brecht's play *Der aufhaltsame Aufstieg des Arturo Ui*, while the role of Varro points to the view shared with Brecht that Hitler was partly the creature of the industrial élite.

Josephus resembles the protagonists of Feuchtwanger's earlier novels in his wavering between East and West, a comfortable position *au dessus de la mêlée* and commitment to a radical political cause. The central figures of the other major historical novels of the exile are usually presented in a more positive light as the representatives of values opposed to tyranny, reaction and mass hysteria. These include the author of *Don Quixote* in Bruno Frank's *Cervantes* (1934), portrayed as a supporter of the oppressed, whose qualities of courage, imagination and mercy are opposed to the reactionary death-cult of Philip II against the background of a society marked by economic crisis, unemployment, and rearmament, while the insistence of the inquisition that Cervantes submit to a test of racial purity points to a closer analogy with the Third Reich. The title figure of Stefan Zweig's *Triumph und Tragik des Erasmus von Rotterdam* (1934) appears as the first conscious European, friend of peace and advocate of a humanistic ideal, who reacts against fanaticism in all its forms, whether represented by the old church or the reformation of Luther, whose resemblance to Hitler is hinted at by his identification with primitive passion, nationalism and revolution. Erasmus, according to Zweig a veiled self-portrait, embodies the spirit of compromise, which however in the context of the time could be identified as ambivalence. Zweig's critique of totalitarianism emerges more clearly in *Castellio gegen Calvin. Ein Gewissen gegen die Gewalt* (1936); here the account of the Geneva theocracy is marked by deliberate anachronisms drawn from the vocabulary of Nazism, while the fate of Calvin's opponent, who is condemned to the stake, is a further indication of the contemporary bearing. Another 'good European' is the hero of Heinrich Mann's most substantial contribution to the historical genre, the two novels

Die Jugend des Königs Henri Quatre (1935) and *Die Vollendung des Königs Henri Quatre* (1938). Henri's qualities of tolerance, moderation and reason are given expression in his policy of opposition to Habsburg expansionism under the banner of the counter-reformation, his guarantee of religious freedom by the Edict of Nantes and his great plan of a European confederation, translating into action the contemplative scepticism of his mentor Montaigne. Heinrich Mann's didacticism is evident in the portrayal as caricatures of Henri's opponents Catherine de Medici, Philip II and the Jesuits and in passages of commentary which include at the end of each chapter of the first volume 'moralités' composed in Classical French. Here too the transparency of the satirical intent is indicated by the introduction of Nazi slogans in the propaganda supplied by the Goebbels-figure Boucher and by the portrayal of the Duke of Guise as a Führer greeted by the people with raised-arm salute. In giving emphasis to the persecution of Jews and heretics in Renaissance Spain in the trilogy *Sieg der Dämonen* (1936), on Ferdinand and Isabella, *Ich, der König* (1938), on Philip II and *Um die Krone – Der Mohr von Kastilien* (1952) Hermann Kesten followed a similar aim.

The retrospective view of German history encouraged by exile critics in programmatic statements in support of the Volksfront directed attention to the Peasants' War of the sixteenth century, a turning point which had been ignored or misrepresented by earlier non-Marxist historians. It no doubt prompted Gustav Regler to write *Die Saat* (1936), which centres on the peasant leader Joss Fritz, whose conspiratorial activities are seen as a model for the underground work against Nazism and whose co-operation with the runaway priest Martin points to the need for a similar alliance between workers and intellectuals in the present.

A Marxist perspective is more clearly apparent in Brecht's fragmentary novel *Die Geschäfte des Herrn Julius Cäsar* (1957, but written 1938–9), in which the fictional narrator, a Roman lawyer, having undertaken a biography of Caesar, whom he considers one of the greatest men in the history of the world, obtains from a banker the diaries of the emperor's secretary Rarus, which concentrate on his master's business activities. Caesar emerges as a gambler for the highest stakes, who buys his way into office, accumulates vast debts, supports any party whose financial support will enable him to cover them and blackmails those who prove unreliable. The success of his military campaigns in Spain ensures that the state coffers are filled, his debts are repaid and city investments bring in a huge profit. Brecht does more than develop the insights into the capitalist system which underlie *Der Dreigroschenroman* (1934) and *Die heilige Johanna der Schlachthöfe*; by tracing the disillusionment of a narrator initially motivated by adulation he undermines the view that history is made by 'great' personalities evident in earlier biographies and deconstructs the myth of the Führer. Brecht thus combines the Marxist view of history with a sophisticated approach to narrative which owes much to the montage experiments of the 1920s and his own ideas on alienation.

Not all historical novels of the exile were conceived or written as challenges to Nazism; some authors, such as Alfred Neumann in *Struensee* (1935) with a title figure resembling that of Feuchtwanger's *Jud Süß*, and *Neuer Cäsar* (1934), *Kaiserreich* (1936) and *Volksfreunde* (1940), a trilogy on the second French empire, and Joseph Roth in *Die hundert Tage* (1936) on the first Napoleon's return from exile on Elba, adopt a psychological or religious approach to their subjects. The confused amalgam of political, religious and psychological concerns evident in Döblin's *1918* has already been discussed. The same author's *Das Land ohne Tod* (1937–8) follows the European penetration of South America through the centuries, juxtaposing the brutalities of the conquistadores with the prelapsarian simplicity of the native Indians and the efforts of religiously motivated Europeans such as Las Casas and the leaders of the Jesuit republic in Paraguay to protect them. The philosophical foundation of this account emerges only in the closing sections of the second part (*Der blaue Tiger*), which in the edition of 1947–8 were detached to form a third part entitled *Der neue Urwald*, dominated by a fantasy debate between Copernicus, Galileo, Giordano Bruno and a fictional Pole Twardowski on the merits of scientific advance and the human responsibility for its proper application. However, Döblin's broad view of history as an alternation of natural forces marked by movement and stasis, and the religious overtones present in some episodes, do not allow him to treat these themes with the urgency evident in Brecht's *Leben des Galilei*, even in the series of stories, some with a contemporary setting, which close the volume.

Thomas Mann's tetralogy *Joseph und seine Brüder* (*Die Geschichten Jaakobs*, 1933, *Der junge Joseph*, 1934, *Joseph in Ägypten*, 1936, and *Joseph der Ernährer*, 1943), on which he worked, with an interruption of three years for the Goethe novel *Lotte in Weimar* (1939), from 1926 to 1942, may be seen both as a contribution to the debate on myth which had been implicitly present in many of the evocations of myth and legend produced during the Weimar Republic, and as a development of Mann's commitment to a western humanism adumbrated hesitantly in *Der Zauberberg* and his essays of the 1920s. In expanding a few chapters of the Book of Genesis to these monumental proportions he aimed from the beginning to show the relation between myth and power structures and the charisma which often underlies them, as a challenge to the modish anti-intellectualism which resorted to myth in the belief that it expressed an irrational core of the human spirit from which man had become progressively alienated by modern civilisation. The allegiance to this view of Gottfried Benn and the more extreme advocates of *Lebensphilosophie* led them to espouse those elements of Nazism which offered an alternative to the critical spirit associated with *Neue Sachlichkeit*. The progress of the Joseph project well into the years of exile, after its author had declared himself decisively against the regime in 1936, allowed him to harness his critical approach to myth to a clear anti-Fascism. In the end Mann recognises the place of myth in the religious quest of Joseph's forefathers; the tradition they represent constitutes a resource on which he can draw in order to resist the temptation of Potiphar's wife, who represents dark irrational forces, and provide a rational solution to the social problem of famine. Joseph is a privileged figure with special powers (as an interpreter of dreams) and a charisma which has mythical dimensions; yet he emerges as a provider with a clear resemblance to the F.D. Roosevelt of the New Deal, while as a supporter of resistance to the robber kings who threaten Egypt, he contrasts with the decadent figure of the pharaoh Echnaton who can be equated with the pusillanimity of appeasement.

The connection between these themes and Broch's lyrical novel *Der Tod des Vergil* (1945), which begins with the arrival of the mortally ill poet in Brindisi after a sea journey from Greece, may not be immediately apparent. However, the discussions with the emperor Augustus prompted by the decision to burn the almost complete *Aeneid* turn on the role of the writer in relation to the state. Aware of the propagandistic implications of Augustus' view of his work as testimony to the greatness of the Roman people, Virgil voices his loss of faith in the power of art to restore a sense of community and overcome the primitive emotions exemplified by the mob's adulation of the emperor. As he approaches his end the poet's stream of consciousness expands to a mystical participation in the absolute, that insight into death which Broch sees as the ultimate aim of art and which Virgil had failed to provide in his work. From the standpoint of these transcendental heights Virgil is able to prophesy the realisation of an ideal community, thus adding a utopian political dimension to a novel which in contrast to the other historical novels of the exile has been mainly associated with Joyce's *Ulysses* as a radical extension of the interior monologue. Similar monologues of the moribund are to be found in Bruno Frank's fragment *Chamfort erzählt seinen Tod* (1937) and Heinrich Mann's last novel *Der Atem* (1949).

The utopian dimension, as a reaction to the chaos of the time, is more clearly evident in two futuristic fantasies, Hesse's *Das Glasperlenspiel* (1943) and Werfel's *Stern der Ungeborenen* (1946). The former, set in the third millennium, is divided into three parts: a general introduction to the glass-bead game, a system of semiotics derived from mathematics and music which enables its master to store and play with the entire contents and values of culture, to relate all disciplines and genres to one another in endless combinations and variations; the biography of the *magister ludi* Josef Knecht; and the writings he leaves on his death, which consist of poems and three fictional biographies. The masters of the game are gathered together in Kastalien, a pedagogical province, where they form an intellectual élite cut off from the world. The game originated as a reaction to the intellectual superficiality of the twentieth century, defined as the age of the *Feuilleton*, politics and war. The life of Knecht from the age of twelve takes the form of a model career in Kastalien until, after election as successor to the *magister ludi* Thomas von der Trave (a portrait of Thomas Mann), the sterility and social irrelevance of the game and the parasitical nature of Kastalien prompt him to resign and become an ordinary teacher. During a trip to a mountain lake with a pupil, he drowns. The stories he bequeaths offer variations on the theme of the relation between the active and the contemplative life, which had been one of Hesse's chief preoccupations in his earlier novels. Flight from reality may be justified by its deficiencies, but divorce from it leads to esoteric claustrophobia and vain virtuosity; the question whether reality can be improved by contact with the intellectualism encouraged by the glass-bead game is left unresolved.

Werfel's last work may be described as a mixture of Shaw's *Back to Methusaleh* and Huxley's *Brave New World*. Remaining in California the author time-travels to the year AD 101,945 and a society in which war, disease, the divisions of nationality and language, material want and material desire have been overcome and superseded by a sterile refinement devoid of physical effort and sensual satisfaction. Opposed to this 'astromental' utopia–dystopia is a jungle inhabited by more primitive peoples untainted by this effete civilisation, who unleash a war which destroys it. The author's guide succeeds in rescuing the Isochronion, the totem of the astromental epoch, from a fire, but dies from the burns he sustains, having renounced the astromental way of death – reversal of the genetic process – which would have extinguished pain and consciousness. The new era is symbolised by the spiritual regime of a Catholic and a Jew, a testimony to Werfel's dual religious allegiance and to his belief that even the most advanced utopia cannot guarantee man's moral progress; the mark of Cain, evidenced by war, will remain along with the religions which come to terms with it.

The drama of the exile, like the fiction, deals either with the contemporary situation in Germany, life in exile or historical subjects. Bruckner's *Die Rassen*, first performed on November 1933, and Friedrich Wolf's *Professor Mamlock*, the most often produced exile drama, can be linked to *Die Geschwister Oppenheim* in their aim to bring to the attention of audiences abroad Nazi anti-Semitism. In the first, set in a university milieu, its effects on four medical students are traced from March to April 1933. Bruckner avoids conventional Naturalism by devising scenes of great atmospheric density with intense dialogues and visionary outbursts in Expressionist style in order to convey the psychological pressures on his characters, their misplaced idealism and their vulnerability. Although the action is melodramatic, the portrayal of the main protagonist Karlanner shows awareness of the problems of conscience confronting the more sensitive of the characters. The particular thrust of Nazi propaganda aimed at the intellectual middle-class – German music, philosophy and discipline versus democracy, materialism, liberalism, republicanism, pacifism, with which the Jews and the Weimar Republic are seen as tainted – is a major element in what is a debate about the identity of the nation.

Wolf's play is more traditional in structure and dominated by the title role, a Jewish doctor with a leading position in a Berlin hospital, who like the corresponding figures in *Die Geschwister Oppenheim* fails to recognise the danger represented by Nazi racial measures until he and his working associates are directly affected. Even after his humiliation at the hands of the SA – a card identifying him as a Jew is hung round his neck – he assumes he will be spared dismissal on account of his war service. However, when a Jewish male nurse is to be sacked he openly supports him and shoots himself when forced to sign a document concocted to incriminate him. The plot is complicated by the decision of his son to join a Communist resistance group after Mamlock, still blind to the full meaning of the Nazi takeover, orders him to stop political activity or leave home. By creating a figure with which the audience could readily sympathise Wolf succeeded in delivering the necessary warning, but at the cost of ignoring the deeper causes of support for the new regime.

Gustav von Wangenheim, who had transformed the agitprop play in the last years of the Weimar Republic, provided in *Helden im Keller* (1934) an exposure of Nazi strong-arm tactics by the ingenious method of setting it in a local SA headquarters where prisoners – invisible to the audience – are being tortured in the cellar. Their presence is indicated by a flashing light, a signal to the SA-men to sing so that their victims' cries may not reach the outside world. The SA-men are presented as a motley bunch; the dissatisfaction expressed by some is a sign that the author shared the view found elsewhere in early exile works that the new regime would be undermined by mass defections. Johannes Wüsten's *Bessie Bosch* (1936) is the product of a period when this view had proved to be unfounded; the play aims to boost morale against all the odds, by portraying in the title figure a woman who, when she receives the news from a Communist party official that her husband has been executed, overcomes her grief with the thought that his sacrifice has not been in vain but will spur on his comrades. This one-act play, in its structure and message, looks forward to the most carefully contrived and theatrically effective of the dramatic works devoted to exposing, warning and encouraging, Brecht's *Furcht und Elend des Dritten Reiches* (first published complete in 1945). By dividing the play into twenty-four distinct episodes with a prologue, linking verses and ironical titles Brecht retains an epic structure; in other respects, however, he departs from the practice, evident in his other exile plays, of providing a model, whether fable, allegory or legend, by means of which the audience would not be distracted by the physical detail and psychological realism of Naturalism from focusing on the issue. The scenes, although according to Brecht drawn from eye-witness accounts and newspaper reports, form a carefully ordered sequence ranging in date from 30 January 1933 (Hitler's appointment as Chancellor) to 12 March 1938 (the annexation of Austria). They also offer a wide range of regional, social and working milieux, so that a panorama of German society emerges. The longer scenes, especially 'Die jüdische Frau' and 'Rechtsfindung', allow scope for the elaboration of complex problems of conscience. Brecht concentrates on the terrorism and the lies of the regime, the former engendering an all pervasive fear which divides families and undermines professional integrity, the latter providing opportunities for numerous ironic contrasts typical of Brecht the dialectician. Some of the later scenes convey the hope that the delusions of propaganda will lose their effect and that committed opponents will remain steadfast.

In a few later exile plays the theme of resistance is more in evidence, whether that of the church in Germany, as in Toller's *Pastor Hall* (1938), or in occupied Norway, as in Bruckner's *Denn seine Zeit ist kurz* (written 1942–3). Lampel's *Nazi-Dämmerung* (1945) is set in the Reich Chancellery shortly before the Russian capture of Berlin; the imminent collapse of the Third Reich prompts the assembled SS-men to reassess their attitudes to it and their motives for supporting it, a theme given much weightier treatment in Zuckmayer's highly successful *Des Teufels General* (1946), based on the historical figure of the air force general Ernst Udet. The portrayal of him as an attractive personality brings the play close to offering an apology for the many *Mitläufer* (fellow travellers) who supported the regime without any commitment to its ideology. Other plays deal with the Night of the Long Knives (Max Zweig, *Die deutsche Bartholomäusnacht*, 1940), the 'Reichskristallnacht' or pogrom of 1938 (Frank/Halbert, *Kraft durch Feuer*, 1939), the annexation of Austria (von Wangenheim, *Friedensstörer*, 1938; Zinner, *Caféhaus Payer*, 1945; Blume, *Abschied von Wien*, 1938; Wolf, *Das Schiff an der Donau*, 1955) and the Russian campaign (Becher, *Schlacht vor Moskau*, 1942; and the end of Brecht's *Schweyk im zweiten Weltkrieg*, 1944). The problems of life in exile are the subject of Lampel's *Mensch ohne Paß!* (1936) and Wolf's *Die letzte Probe* (1946).

While the historical fiction of the exile features the artist-intellectual who is brought under the pressure of events and the influence of committed revolutionaries to abandon an unpolitical stance, two historical dramas of the period trace a movement in the reverse direction. The title-figure in Wolf's *Beaumarchais* (1946) makes a fortune and reneges on the commitment implied in the attack on aristocratic privilege of his creation Figaro; when the revolution begins he leaves his luxurious town house where the people have built barricades from his books. These however will one day have a different function, to instruct and entertain a new class. Beaumarchais is a man of divided aspirations at the junction of two epochs, according to Wolf; the same can be said of the title-figure of *Leben des Galilei*, but Brecht added a further dimension by the changes he made to his text in response to the news of Hiroshima. By sharpening Galileo's self-criticism in the penultimate scene he modified his earlier view, conditioned by the impotence and disunity of the exiles, that small concessions were justified in order to ensure survival until a time when resistance to authority could be effective. In 1945 the responsibility of the scientist to maintain control over the use made of his discoveries takes precedence over the tactics of clandestine work. Brecht had however become increasingly preoccupied over a long period with the role of the intellectual in relation to the state and made it the subject of the so-called *Tui*-complex, consisting of a fragmentary novel and the play *Turandot*, which was conceived during the exile, although not performed until 1953. The term 'Tui' is derived from the word 'intellectual' and denotes those who sell their talents to government regardless of its political complexion. In the novel and the play the Tuis appear as mandarin figures in a Chinese context, but there are numerous transparently disguised references in both to the situation in Germany before, during and even after the Third Reich. Furthermore, Brecht's other historical drama of the exile, *Mutter Courage und ihre Kinder*, sub-titled 'Eine Chronik aus dem dreißigjährigen Krieg', can be related to the theme of commitment and betrayal. The title figure, although she is neither a politician nor an intellectual, believes that she and her children can survive the war and profit from it; instead her activities contribute to its destructive capacity to which her children fall victim one after the other. The last of these deaths, however, follows the decision by Mutter Courage's daughter Kattrin to warn the inhabitants of a town under threat of surprise attack by beating a drum in growing awareness that the besiegers will kill her. There is a clear contrast established between the stand she takes and her mother's policy of muddling through.

The exile dramatists continued a long tradition of plays centred on Napoleon with Bruckner's *Napoleon der Erste* (1936), Kaiser's *Napoleon in New Orleans* (1937–41), Arnold Zweig's *Bonaparte in Jaffa* (1934), Kesser's *Talleyrand und Napoleon* (1938) and Mostar's *Putsch in Paris* (written 1934), of which the last offers the clearest analogy to the Nazi regime and, in the near-success of a military coup, a model for its potential destruction. Bruckner's *Heroische Komödie* (1939–42) presents the relationship between Napoleon's most determined critic, Madame de Stael, and Benjamin Constant, whose ambivalent attitude towards his mistress arises from his awareness that the energy of her commitment to the downfall of Napoleon is fired by vanity. The uncertainties of life in exile are reflected in the feeling that their activities find no resonance, that they are merely actors in a comedy before an indifferent audience. In the same author's *Simon Bolivar* (1945), however, the liberator of South America advocates the view that idealism will prove ineffective against a ruthless enemy unless it is accompanied by a power vested in an exceptional personality who may override the claims of the collective – a problem related to Brecht's theme in *Der gute Mensch von Sezuan* (1938–41) and *Der kaukasische Kreidekreis* (1944–5), the survival of goodness in an evil world.

Two plays on the subject of anti-Semitism present an interesting contrast to the plays of Bruckner and Wolf which initiated the drama of exile. In *Die Rundköpfe und die Spitzköpfe* (written 1931–5) Brecht conveys his theory that Nazi anti-Semitism is a measure devised to conceal the machinations of a conservative élite concerned to consolidate its power. Combining the didactic elements of the *Lehrstück* with the parable structure which he was to develop with increasing sophistication, Brecht presents Hitler as Iberin, the catspaw of a ruling clique, who by dividing society into round heads and pointed heads distracts attention from the fundamental division between those with and those without property and thus undermines popular militancy; when he has performed his function he is dispensed with. In *Konflikt in Assyrien* (1938), Walter Hasenclever adapts the Old Testament story of Esther, the Jewish queen of Assyria, who outwits the prime minister Haman after he has gained dictatorial powers by engineering a crisis and casting the Jews in the role of scapegoat. The happy ending, in which Haman is banished, makes light of the problem and reduces the conflict to the level of court intrigue.

Other authors were more successful in giving a contemporary slant to comedy. Toller, in *Nie wieder Friede!* (1936), presents war hysteria in a mini-state within the framework of a Faustian wager in heaven between Napoleon and St Francis on the prospects for peace, while Wangenheim's *Stürmisches Wiegenlied* (1937) satirises eugenic theories. Brecht's *Schweyk im zweiten Weltkrieg* (1943) preserves the spirit of the title-figure in Jaroslav Hašek's *The Good Soldier Schweik* while providing a true reflection of the new conditions in which he is forced to display his subversive naivety. The same author's *Der aufhaltsame Aufstieg des Arturo Ui* (written 1941) provides a satirical portrait of Hitler and his henchmen marked by a double alienation effect which aims to reduce them to size as personalities without trivialising the consequences of their actions: their progress to power between the years 1932 and 1938 is compared to the criminal activities of Chicago gangsters, while the 'grand style' of blank verse is intended to recall the battles and intrigues of Shakespeare's history plays. Brecht here combines a more developed insight into the economic factors underlying the Nazi takeover than was evident in *Die Rundköpfe und die Spitzköpfe* with a shrewd assessment of the contribution of Hitler's histrionic talent to the mass psychology of his movement. Werfel's *Jacobowsky und der Oberst* (1941–2) derives its comedy from the contrast between the two title figures; despite the tensions between them they remain inseparable, and their rescue by a British submarine after a protracted odyssey across occupied France points to a socially harmonious future. Other comedies, such as Hasenclever's *Münchhausen* (1934) and Horváth's later works, lack any pointed reference to contemporary politics, although the latter's *Figaro läßt sich scheiden* (1937) shows psychological insight into the personal problems arising from exile. In *Herr Puntila und sein Knecht Matti* (1940) Brecht follows his own prescription for the revival of the *Volksstück* by adapting some of its stereotypes and farcical elements to the relationship of master and servant on a Finnish estate, here presented as the outwardly idyllic archetype of an exploitative social structure. The later plays of Georg Kaiser range from the semi-autobiographical *Klawitter* (1939–40) to works which draw on Classical mythology (*Zweimal Amphitryon*, 1943; *Pygmalion*, 1943–4; and *Bellerophon*, 1944), while *Der Soldat Tanaka*

(1940) and *Das Floß der Medusa* (1945) are directly inspired by the Second World War.

When one surveys the poetry of the exile one notes the same emphases: on warning, assertion of an alternative, experience of exile, together with the cultivation of such traditional lyrical themes as love, nature, commemoration of friends, each of which is given a special intensification in the context of the diaspora of the poets. These formed a less homogeneous group than the novelists and dramatists and their emigration took them further, not only to France (Mehring, Goll, Wolfenstein), the USA (Brecht, Viertel, Werfel), Britain (Kerr, Herrmann-Neisse, Kramer) and the Soviet Union (Becher, Weinert), but also to South America (Arendt, Zech), Israel (Lasker-Schüler) and even New Zealand (Wolfskehl). Those who had maintained a public role in the Weimar Republic as contributors to the development of critical cabaret and review (Tucholsky, Mehring) were eventually forced to abandon or modify it, yet there was still scope for the poetry of agitation and counter-propaganda, exemplified by the work of Rudolf Leonhard and Weinert and above all by Brecht's collections *Lieder. Gedichte. Chöre* (1934) and *Svendborger Gedichte* (1939), especially the six 'Hitler-Chorÿle' in the former and the 'Deutsche Satiren' and 'Deutsche Kriegsfibel' in the latter. These poems, placed directly in the service of the anti-Fascist struggle, make masterful use of parody and epigram; while Brecht occasionally joins other poets (Kerr, Werfel, Kaiser) in attacking Hitler directly by means of caricature (as in 'Das Lied vom Anstreicher Hitler'), he avoids their tendency to demonise or debunk by means of scatological imagery, aiming instead in most instances to convey the full extent of the social transformation engineered by the Nazis and its ultimate purpose – war. His 'Studien' (poems on Kant, Schiller, Kleist and Nietzsche), together with the 'Sonett vom Erbe', reflect the need to take a critical look at the German cultural tradition in the light of the Nazi misappropriation of it. This concern was shared by other exile poets, especially Becher, whose attempts by means of formal imitation (sonnet, ode and elegy), spiritual discipleship (of Goethe, Heine and Hölderlin) and evocation of German landscape to conform to a representative image of the poet, can be seen as an exercise aimed at raising personal morale as well as overcoming the narrowness of Communist literary allegiances in the spirit of the popular front policy. Homesickness was naturally a common motif in the work of other exile poets, especially Herrmann-Neisse, and it received a further complication in the reflections of Jews such as Lasker-Schüler, Goll and Wolfskehl as to where their true home might lie. (Indeed, certain younger Jewish exiles – Nelly Sachs, Paul Celan, Erich Fried and Rose Ausländer – chose to remain abroad permanently or until long after 1945.) In their homeless state they tended to transcend political circumstances by conceiving the exile in timeless, existential, even mythical terms and by identifying with Odysseus, Ahasverus, Job and, in the case of Goll, John Lackland. The exile lyric has been criticised for its formal conservatism, corresponding to the regression from modernism evident in fiction and drama. Political polemic and personal lament were easily accommodated to traditional forms; only when they were fused, as in the later exile poems of Brecht, does one encounter the development of a new form, here rhymeless verse with irregular rhythms, by means of which a more complex state of mind could be conveyed, as in 'Schlechte Zeit für Lyrik' and 'Gedanken über die Dauer des Exils'.

It will be clear that the German and Austrian exiles considered in this chapter resemble neither the expatriate authors – one thinks of Joyce, Lawrence and Hemingway – typical of English and American literature of the twentieth century, nor indeed the few German writers who in earlier years had left their country on a spiritual quest, such as Hesse, or in search of an exotic environment, such as Dauthendey. The shifting contours of their work arise from the banal but easily forgotten fact that they were unable to foresee precisely while they were writing the process by which the Nazi domination of Europe would be overcome, the political form the future German nation would take and what part the Germans themselves would play in its establishment. These uncertainties contributed to the continuing alienation of several prominent writers – such as Brecht, Döblin and Thomas Mann – from Germany when return became possible in 1945. The relation of the public to exile literature proved uneasy, especially in the Federal Republic during the Adenauer era. It can be claimed that its heritage was fully assimilated only after the process of self-examination undertaken in many areas of national life during the late 1960s and early 1970s had run its course. It was then that a work appeared which by assembling and combining on a monumental scale themes and motifs of German anti-Fascist literature brought to light a submerged tradition which the reading public was at last ready to digest and incorporate into its developing post-war culture. *Die Ästhetik des Widerstands*, by Peter Weiss (1975, 1978, 1981) can be defined as the long-delayed culmination and end point of the literature considered in this chapter.

6

The Literature of the Federal Republic of Germany and the Second Austrian Republic until 1968

When hostilities ceased on 8 May 1945 Germany's devastation was reflected in the state of its intellectual life – a situation which fostered the belief in a 'Stunde Null' or 'year zero' – a *tabula rasa* which permitted a totally fresh start. This view has however been revised recently by critics on the grounds that while the relatively small amount of writing which had a direct bearing on the Third Reich (marching songs, panegyrics to the Führer, etc.) was immediately forgotten, a much larger body of literature by authors who had made fewer concessions to Nazi ideology continued to be read. Many of these remained active, having merely modified their stance. There had been few works produced during the Third Reich which reflected the course of events according to the conventions of realism, and those who had cultivated *Blut und Boden* literature, colonial literature, literature on the fate of the *Auslandsdeutsche* (German minorities abroad) and historical novels and dramas on heroic figures from Germany's past, could point in exoneration to a pre-Nazi tradition in all these genres. Furthermore, much work without ideological bias had and continued to have a broad appeal to a middle-class reading public which looked to its authors, many now barely remembered (Wilhelm Schäfer, Hans Carossa, Erich Kästner, Bernd von Heiseler, Friedrich G. Jünger, Walter von Molo, Frank Thiess), for a certain high-minded escapism or light relief.

The writers of the inner emigration, who rightly saw themselves

120

as an embattled minority in their own country, emerged from the Third Reich with works which explored it and its aftermath in spiritual terms, either through a clear Christian commitment (Elisabeth Langgässer, Ernst Wiechert, Reinhold Schneider, Bergengruen, Gertrud von Le Fort, Schaper, Rudolf Alexander Schröder, Goes) or by recourse to a philosophy, which, as in Hesse's *Das Glasperlenspiel*, diagnosed the contemporary malaise and provided solace by drawing on the accumulated 'Bildungsgut' of a centuries-old European (and Asian) tradition. Ernst Jünger was able to maintain his aristocratically aloof stance (established in *Auf den Marmorklippen*) in *Heliopolis* (1949), a work which in the form of a similar utopia/dystopia invited allegorical interpretation along the lines of his tract *Der Friede* (1945). Such a withdrawal from contamination with the forces which had brought Germany to destruction finds its counterpart in Gottfried Benn's prose of the post-war period. For Benn at this time nihilism may no longer have been 'ein Glücksgefühl', but it was not abandoned.

Other writers, who had begun their careers during the Third Reich without making more than minimal concessions to prevailing ideology, developed a form of magic realism – or fiction in which fabulous or fantastic events are included in a narrative which otherwise conforms to realistic conventions – with a strong allegorical dimension, in which the individualism of a central figure (sometimes a 'Heimkehrer' or soldier returning after defeat to the chaos of his homeland) is seen as the only viable position in the face of those who remain unrepentant, turn back to Christian or humanist values now felt to be vulnerable or unfounded, espouse another ideology (usually Communism) or throw in their lot with the materialism which was eventually to prove the driving force of the economic miracle. Alienation from the past and the potential future, and unease in a present clearly transitional, are the prevailing moods of Gerd Gaiser's *Eine Stimme hebt an* (1950) and *Schlußball* (1958), in which conventional realism is modified by alternating narrative perspectives assigned to the principal characters (a technique developed later by Böll and Hein), and they are even more in evidence in the work of Hans Erich Nossack, especially in *Der Untergang* (1948) and *Nekyia* (1947). The same awareness of a spiritual abyss, here defined as rejection of Christianity, is manifest in the doomed family portrayed in Döblin's *Hamlet oder Die lange Nacht nimmt ein Ende* (1956), although as a former exile he belongs to another group.

Other members of the 'lost generation' gradually or suddenly overcame the desperate vacuum represented by defeat and disorientation by espousing philosophies such as existentialism, which, although its roots were German (Jaspers, Heidegger), had been made both acceptable and accessible in France by its development and adaptation to fiction in the work of Sartre and Camus. Alfred Andersch and Nossack each experienced a traumatic turning-point in their lives during the Second World War, the former when he decided to desert on the Italian front, the latter when he observed the fire-bombing of Hamburg in 1943, in which all his manuscripts, the fruit of several years' clandestine work, were destroyed. Each responded in a different way, Andersch by moving towards a realism based on a positive engagement, marked by social awareness and commitment, Nossack by a solitary exploration of a private world, which, like Hermann Kasack's *Die Stadt hinter dem Strom* (1947), exists under the shadow of death but possesses a supernatural dimension. (A similar view emerges from the situations described in more realistic terms in the novels of Jens Rehn and Heinz Risse.) Walter Jens's first novel *Nein – die Welt der Angeklagten* (1950), a dystopia on the struggle of the individual against a totalitarian state with three categories of subject – accused, witnesses and judges – represents despite the acknowledged debt to Kafka a comparable reaction to the Third Reich and its aftermath. The progress of the university teacher Walter Sturm through this three-tier hierarchy to the position of designated successor to the highest judge, who alone is able to penetrate the state's formidable bureaucracy, makes the novel less pessimistic and less socially specific than Orwell's almost contemporary *1984*, while his decision to refuse the succession can be defined as an act of moral commitment, even if the system remains intact.

In all these works the reality of the Third Reich is present only, if at all, in coded form, although the need for codes, which had prompted Ernst Jünger in *Auf den Marmorklippen* (1939) to disguise the leading Nazis as 'Mauretanier' under a chief forester, in order to avoid censorship and worse, no longer applied. Stefan Andres produced in the trilogy *Die Sintflut* (*Das Tier aus der Tiefe*, 1949; *Die Arche*, 1951; *Der graue Regenbogen*, 1959) the most elaborate and cumbersome allegorical treatment of Germany's fate, while Ilse Aichinger, who as a 'Mischling' had been threatened by Nazi racial policy, examined in *Die größere Hoffnung* (1948) the predicament of a half-Jewish girl desperately in search of an exit visa for America by means of highly charged metaphors in order to convey the existential act of commitment on which the other novels of this period also usually turn.

The existentialist novel that draws upon myth can of course be interpreted as a post-war version of German inwardness and metaphysical striving, yet it also represents a new departure, even more evident in the early work of Arno Schmidt. He, however, develops a highly idiosyncratic blend of cool description of the effects of war and cosmic catastrophe, focusing on a narrow rural environment, and exact portrayal of the mental life of the narrator, which consists of fantasy and speculation inspired by study of the more eccentric neglected authors of the past. Schmidt's immense learning is drawn from two sources: an international modernism whose roots were virtually obliterated by Nazism in Germany, and a rationalism which owes much to the eighteenth century and to Freud and trains its gaze on individual psychology and its bearing on linguistic expression in a spirit of detached curiosity.

However, it is not Schmidt's innovations which most readily spring to mind in connection with the phrase 'Stunde Null', which retains a measure of validity despite recent debates and controversies. It can be associated with the term 'Kahlschlag' ('clearing of terrain'), devised by Wolfgang Weyrauch in the afterword to the anthology *Tausend Gramm* (1949) to define the need felt by contemporary writers to drive through the thicket of jargon and verbiage which had either formed the language of propaganda or blinded its dupes to its true significance, to start afresh with a vocabulary cleansed and simplified. In the case of Weyrauch such a purge of the writer's resources could lead to a refined and stilted style, but others, in particular Wolfgang Borchert, Schnurre, Bender and above all Böll, gained more from this prescription, because their aim was fidelity to their own experience as unwilling recruits to the army of the Third Reich, suffering the guilt, ignominy, victimisation and squalor of the closing phases of the war.

None of these offered extensive works of fiction providing a panoramic view of the war or even of a single campaign (like Theodor Plievier in *Stalingrad*, 1945); instead they cultivated the episode and the vignette and found a suitable model in the American short story with its concentration, spare concrete style and pointed climax. Yet the hard laconicism of Hemingway was only one aspect of a strategy which aimed to come to terms with an experience regarded as utterly futile and degrading, in which the credulous idealism of youth had been cynically manipulated. Humanitarian impulses emerge not because war represents a true test of their presence in the individual but despite war's inexhaustible potential for stifling them. The short story thus conveys a dual impression: the cryptic style of Schnurre and Weyrauch laced with contemporary slang does not always focus narrowly on a slice of life representative of the immediate post-war situation; occasionally mere surface realism is avoided or a predictable naturalism is undermined. The stories of Wolfgang Borchert are further evidence of the need felt by writers seared by the experience of the war to avoid the indulgence in emotional cliché and propagandist abstraction to which the conformist literature of the preceding years had degenerated and at the same time to convey either through characterisation or symbolism some sense of basic human values. The result, more apparent in his sole play *Draußen vor der Tür*, is a paradoxical juxtaposition of soberly presented concrete detail and strong emotional appeal made through a poetic vocabulary which recalls Expressionism and received justification in the posthumously published 'Unser Manifest'. Here, as well as in Böll's 'Bekenntnis zur Trümmerliteratur' and the shorter fiction of Borchert and Böll, individual responses are portrayed in a manner which goes beyond a verism indebted to American models and the documentary literature of the Weimar Republic, the influence of which bore more substantial fruit in the longer prose writings of Walter Kolbenhoff (*Von unserem Fleisch und Blut*, 1946, *Heimkehr in die Fremde*, 1949) and Hans Werner Richter (*Die Geschlagenen*, 1949, *Sie fielen aus Gottes Hand*, 1951).

Richter and Alfred Andersch had played a crucial role as editors of the literary periodical *Der Ruf*, which had its origin during the lengthy period spent by both men as prisoners of war in the USA. Refounded in Munich in 1946 after their repatriation, *Der Ruf* appeared in seventeen issues until the following March, when the American occupation authorities deprived the editors of their licence on the grounds that it was 'nihilistic', in fact because the democratic Socialism within a European framework they advocated was interpreted as a challenge to allied decisions on the political future of Germany. Although the magazine was later able to resume publication under other editors, Andersch and Richter decided to start another, to be called *Der Skorpion* and devoted to literature, and a meeting of potential contributors was held at a country house in Upper Bavaria in September 1947. Although the plan to publish a new periodical came to nothing, a second meeting in the same year led to the establishment of a ritual which undoubtedly directed the course of literature in the Federal Republic for more than twenty years. The annual meetings of what became known as the Gruppe 47 gradually swelled in number of participants and eventually became national (and international) media events; however, although proceedings were formalised to the extent that readings by invited authors were one by one subjected to spontaneous criticism by the assembled guests (without right of reply by the reader), and a prize was occasionally awarded, the group never became an institution with a written constitution or conditions of membership. Admission was at the invitation of Richter, who acted as Chairman until the group's dissolution in 1968, when a planned meeting in Prague was forestalled by the invasion of Czechoslovakia by other members of the Warsaw Pact. After a commemorative gathering in 1977 the group was able to reassemble in the Czech capital in 1990 as a witness to the breakdown of barriers between East and West. To Richter this long-postponed realisation of a frustrated enterprise must have seemed like the fulfilment of some of the ideas advocated by *Der Ruf*'s original contributors, of whom the most prominent, along with Richter and Kolbenhoff, was undoubtedly Alfred Andersch.

Andersch was, like the writers associated with the 'Kahlschlag' and *Trümmerliteratur*, conscious of the need for renewal, but the terms he adopted in his main theoretical statement, the essay 'Deutsche Literatur in der Entscheidung', read at the second meeting of Gruppe 47, show that his view of it was based on a knowledge of contemporary literary developments in other parts of western Europe (Italian neo-realism and French existentialism) which encouraged a broader view and a deeper sense that a critical turning-point had been reached. As a member of a slightly older generation who had gravitated from a national-conservative home and school background to office in the Communist youth movement, brief imprisonment in Dachau and withdrawal to a cultivation of 'Innerlichkeit' more tentative than that of the inner emigration, Andersch pointed to his own desertion in the summer of 1944 on the Italian front as a model for similar crucial decisions made by his fictional protagonists. He thus made clear to his readers how the predicament of an individual is intertwined with the larger forces of history. Firm action can have repercussions which challenge a fatalism tempered only by the solace of religion or some desperate belief in the timeless values of 'Bildung'. *Die Kirschen der Freiheit* (1952), sub-titled 'Ein Bericht' (report), is an autobiographical account of Andersch's experience during the Third Reich and a meditation on the nature of freedom and its relation to art. When in *Sansibar oder der letzte Grund* (1957) five disparate figures succeed in eluding their Nazi persecutors in 1937, their actions transform them and assist others. One of them, a priest, rescues a work of art (a sculpture, based on a work by Ernst Barlach, representing a reading monk and by extension a critical spirit which does not trust prevailing ideologies) and thus establishes an implicit connection between the function of art and the struggle of man against political or existential fate. Andersch remained aware of the limits of the individual's power even when the plunge into freedom had been made; in his most substantial novel, *Winterspelt* (1974), he showed how the attempt of a German major to hand over an entire battalion to the advancing Americans is forestalled by the start of the Ardennes offensive and thus ends in failure without any effect on the course of the war. Two other figures, however, the major's girl-friend and a veteran Communist, are brought to revise their position to one of anti-Fascism without overt party allegiance. Here too art, in the form of a painting by Paul Klee, becomes a symbol of the survival of the free human spirit. Andersch's influence on later writers (e.g. Uwe Johnson, Peter Weiss and Christa Wolf) testifies to the long-term validity of a realism which focuses on the development of a single character under extreme circumstances. He emerges as a crucial transitional figure, who ensured that the bleak resignation which is a feature of the work of Gaiser, the late Benn, Nossack and others could be seen as not the only option.

Wolfgang Koeppen, contemporary with Andersch, showed less determination to emerge from the chrysalis of the artist isolated by an unsettled temperament and a refusal to countenance the superficial accommodations to a new political reality everywhere evident in the early years of the Federal Republic. Yet he has gained a respect equal to if not greater than that enjoyed by Andersch thanks to his readiness to apply the innovations of literary modernism manifest in his narrative sophistication, richly metaphoric language and skilful harnessing of myth to explanation of character in history, the last a feature which brings him close to Thomas Mann. This reputation is based almost entirely on three novels published in quick succession, all imbued with an awareness of the fragility of Germany's position as an infant democracy in the early phase of the Cold War. Set in Munich during a single day in 1948, *Tauben im Gras* (1951) traces the activities of about thirty persons of different class, colour and nationality. Their quest for a stable identity is undermined by memories of the past and fear of the future as they succumb to the pressures of the metropolitan competition for wealth and the illusory satisfactions it brings. The fragmented narrative, divided into short sections consisting of inner monologue, dialogue and impressionistic montage, reflects the diffuse and vacuous consciousness of the drifting characters and recalls the urban chaos conveyed in the novels of Joyce, Dos Passos and Döblin; however, the disparate elements are held together by the brooding presence of a narrator who maintains a distance from reality by means of an associative technique which combines concrete details to produce a barely focused panoramic effect. Koeppen's next novel, *Das Treibhaus* (1953), achieves greater critical force by concentrating on the disillusionment of a Social Democrat member of the Bundestag in the early summer of 1953, against the background of the debates preceding the Federal Republic's rearmament and integration into the western alliance. The title ('greenhouse') is a metaphor for both the climatic conditions in Bonn and a political atmosphere forcing the development of potentially uncontrollable political and economic forces in the new state. In despair at the failure of the Federal Republic to reject the past, Keetenheuve, the journalist and emigrant turned MP, commits suicide two days after his arrival in Bonn. Koeppen's third novel, *Der Tod in Rom* (1954), provides a deeper exploration of the theme of restoration and failure to come to terms with the past by means of the schematic opposition of mind and power, art and politics, in the members of conflicting generations within two representative German families, an approach developed by Böll to a greater level of sophistication in *Billard um halb zehn*.

Böll came to the *Zeitroman* (the novel of contemporary social life) only after he had dealt with the war in novels which show little advance on the short stories. *Der Zug war pünktlich* (1949) adopts the narrow focus of a group of soldiers returning to the front after leave, while the episodic *Wo warst du, Adam?* (1951) merely links a number of vignettes in order to condemn war from the standpoint of a Christian ethic, thus exemplifying what the author defined in his Frankfurt lectures as an 'Ästhetik des Humanen'. *Das*

Vermächtnis (written 1947–8 but not published until 1982) marks a transition to the actuality of post-war Germany by demonstrating its failure to face up to the wrongs committed during the Third Reich. A former soldier reveals in a letter to the brother of his commander how the latter, assumed to be missing in battle, had been shot in a fit of anger by an officer of still higher rank who, his crime having remained undiscovered, has since prospered as a lawyer.

The portrayal of the early years of the Federal Republic in the satirical stories collected in *Dr Murkes gesammeltes Schweigen* (1958) and in the novels *Und sagte kein einziges Wort, Haus ohne Hüter* and *Das Brot der frühen Jahre* achieve their effects by a similar contrast of 'winners' and 'losers', conformists and drop-outs. In the satires, human beings are identified with their paid functions in a working environment marked by hectic and wasteful routine, against which is directed the silent protest of Dr Murke, who strings together sections of tape consisting of the brief interruptions to the manic chatter he must edit for broadcasting. This subversion takes more open form in *Ende einer Dienstfahrt* (1966), in which a soldier in the Bundeswehr misappropriates an army jeep and with the help of his father publicly burns it as a gesture against the mindless waste of the military machine; however, the authorities blunt the force of the protest by acquitting the culprits on a plea that their act represents a new form of art. The other *Zeitromane* are more searching explorations of the side-effects of post-war reconstruction and the success ethos which accompanied the economic miracle, vitiated in the eyes of some by the black–white opposition of sensitive melancholics unable to forget the sufferings of the past and robust opportunists who refuse to remember, which was eventually to receive symbolic expression in the lambs and buffaloes of *Billard um halb zehn*. Böll's perspective is throughout informed by a Catholicism which makes humane concessions to the sensual needs of men and women and is critical of an institutionalised church in which, as in *Und sagte kein einziges Wort* (1953), the upper ranks of a rigid hierarchy form part of an establishment preoccupied by power, self-publicity and wealth. In *Haus ohne Hüter* (1954) social prejudice is shown to affect attitudes to two war widows of differing class origins and economic circumstances; the one forced by poverty to depend on a series of temporary bread-winners suffers greater moral opprobrium than the other. In *Das Brot der frühen Jahre* (1955) the demands of love force a change of heart on a man whose get-rich-quick mentality, encouraged by the economic miracle, had been conditioned by the need to overcome the memory of child-hood deprivation.

The end of the 1950s marked no significant turning-point in the political history of the Federal Republic – the Adenauer era was to continue until the first Chancellor's retirement in 1963, while the construction of the Berlin Wall in 1961 merely set the seal on the political and economic division of the country which had deep-ened since the foundation of the two German states in 1949. However, 1959 saw the appearance of three major novels, Böll's *Billard um halb zehn* and the first substantial works by two new-comers to the literary scene, *Die Blechtrommel* by Günter Grass and *Mutmaßungen über Jakob* by Uwe Johnson. These three authors were each to provide a series of fictional works which taken together offer a panoramic view of a country undergoing radical transfor-mation. 'Panoramic' can be understood in three senses: in temporal terms (the works of Böll and Grass trace the lives of fictional fig-ures who experience their formative years during the Third Reich); in spatial terms (the works of Grass and Johnson are set in territo-ries lost to Poland after 1945, in the GDR and in the Federal Republic); in social terms (the works of all three novelists cover a wide range of social classes, political allegiances and professional activities).

Billard um halb zehn (1959) and *Ansichten eines Clowns* (1963) develop on a larger scale and on a higher level of narrative com-plexity the themes and preoccupations of Böll's social-domestic novels of the 1950s. The first of these longer novels juxtaposes three generations of a Rhineland family of architects and conveys the impact of events on the different political and professional posi-tions of its members in a series of retrospective monologues (and one-sided dialogues) occasioned by the gathering on 6 September 1958 to celebrate the eightieth birthday of grandfather Heinrich Fähmel. The abbey he had built in 1908 has been blown up in the closing phase of the Second World War by his son Robert, the cen-tral figure of the novel, ostensibly on the orders of his commanding general, in fact because in his view the monks had entered into an unholy alliance with the Nazis, a motivation he conceals not only from his father, but also from his son Joseph, who is involved in its reconstruction. Although Robert had opposed the Nazis and emigrated, it is not easy to assign the Fähmels to either of the two categories, lambs and buffaloes, which form the framework of Böll's conception of character in history (except Heinrich's wife, whose confinement to a mental institution, a family move to secure her from Nazi 'justice' after she had outspokenly criticised the regime, is continued at her own wish as a protest against Germany's failure to renew itself). The Fähmels' examination of their past lives leads them to resist the temptation to join the buffaloes and instead to act as protectors of the vulnerable lambs who appear in the guise of the hotel boy who is Robert's daily billiards partner and Schrella who had fled Nazi persecution and returns after a twenty-two-year absence. Böll went on to offer a further variation on the figure of the drop-out, although the clown Hans Schnier in the next novel resembles more the holy fool than the bohemian rebel who is a more familiar protagonist of alternative values in German fiction; as such he points forward to the central female figures of Böll's later novels. While on one level *Ansichten eines Clowns* approaches from a fresh angle the problem of Christian morality in sexual relations evident in *Haus ohne Hüter* – Schnier's career founders when his mistress leaves him to marry a Catholic figure-head – it attains a political dimension through its exploration of his role as clown whose performances satirise contemporary society from the point of view of one who has no recognised place in it; the unsettling but limited effect of Schnier's marginality is implicitly compared to that of the intellectual before the politicisation of art and the accompanying debates in the late sixties.

A similar function can be attributed to Oskar Matzerath, the semi-autobiographical narrator of *Die Blechtrommel* (1959), with which Grass achieved at once a national (and international) prominence. Oskar belongs to a long picaresque tradition through his marginal position in a society from which he has felt alienated from birth. The shabby compromises in social and personal life and the desperate search for illusory satisfactions in religious and political ritual are rejected by Oskar when at the age of three he makes an apparently accidental fall down the stairs to the cellar of his home the occasion for a decision to halt further physical growth, while the manic beating of a series of tin drums and the unnatural power of his voice give him an outlet for forms of a subversion otherwise forbidden. However, Grass demonstrates that Oskar, unlike the uncompromising Hans Schnier, nevertheless makes concessions to prevailing trends which render his position ambivalent, whether as a performer in a travelling theatre entertaining the troops of the Third Reich, or as an artist, artist's model and jazz musician in the early years of the Federal Republic. By presenting a character whose development is in a sense complete at his birth, Grass challenges the long German tradition of the *Bildungsroman*, which focuses on the modifications to the inner life of its hero brought about by new experiences and contact with maturer figures ever ready with sage advice. Instead Oskar represents a consciousness in which the deficiencies of his surroundings are reflected in a distorted form necessary to reveal a truth normally obscured by ideological abstractions and emotional clichés. The surreal quality of certain episodes recalls the desire of some of the 'Kahlschlag' writers to go beyond the photographic vignette, to convey by means of suggestive fantasy their horror at what has been unquestioningly accepted. Oskar, who in an early chapter disrupts a Nazi mass meeting by playing his drum while hiding beneath the terrace of a stadium, is assured by his dwarf mentor Bebra that his place is 'wenn nicht auf der Bühne, dann unter der Bühne, aber niemals vor der Tribüne' (if not on stage then under it, but never with the audience). Indeed whatever he does in order to survive he retains an incorruptible detachment from the emotional indulgences of his contemporaries, whether these consist of the mass enthusiasm of the Nazi rally or the artificially induced weeping in the Zwiebelkeller night club, which encapsulates the *mauvaise foi* of a society unable to confront with both mind and heart the catastrophe of the Third Reich or go beyond a superficial adjustment to a new reality. Yet Oskar's impotence and failure of commitment (as well as his psychological peculiarities, as he transfers his obsessions from tin drums to the nurse who lives in a neighbouring flat) make a dubious role model for the responsible citizen. Grass has made Oskar a vehicle for the initial stages of his own debate with himself on the role of the artist-intellectual in society, a preoccupation already noted in the work of major writers of the Weimar Republic and the exile. Although Grass's approach to fiction lacks the earnest candour of Andersch, his position in *Die Blechtrommel*, as one whose hostility to political ideology and escapist religiosity drew him to the existentialism of Camus, is comparable.

In the following works, *Katz und Maus* (1961) and *Hundejahre* (1963), Grass elaborates his view of German history in the mid twentieth century as a process demanding constant adjustment to new material and ideological conditions from its victims. In the first, Joachim Mahlke compensates for the inferiority complex induced by his outsize Adam's apple by performing feats which will ensure the admiration of his peer-group at school and later that of society at large during the war. When after being awarded the highest medal for bravery he returns to his school with the desire to address its pupils his aim is to follow the example of the officer from whom he had earlier stolen the same decoration. When his former headmaster refuses him this opportunity to appear as a hero, thus frustrating the evident wish to identify with an officially approved role model, he deserts and withdraws to his hideaway on a partially submerged Polish warship, never to reappear. In *Hundejahre* the retrospective narrator who is a feature of the entire trilogy is multiplied by three, thus enabling the ever inventive author to further elaborate the contrast of past and present by going beyond the year 1954 (when *Die Blechtrommel* ends) in an exploration of the post-war period, while running the gamut of shorter narrative forms. Fantasy and symbolism develop in profuse and occasionally confusing abundance, as characters undergo metamorphoses of identity in response to the historical process, like the scarecrows manufactured by Eddi Amsel, whose relation to his blood-brother forms the single guiding thread through the novel. Although Grass's direct political involvement (e.g. in general election campaigns on behalf of the Social Democratic Party) is not reflected in his fiction before the appearance of *Örtlich betäubt* in 1969, the progress of the Danzig trilogy indicated that while Grass continued to separate clearly his activities as artist and politically aware citizen, he came to see them as inspired by the same commitments, which went beyond the existentialist gesture of revolt which had no doubt contributed to the conception of Oskar.

Uwe Johnson's roots lay in Mecklenburg, in the north of the GDR, from which he moved to West Berlin after the failure to secure publication of his earliest novel *Ingrid Babendererde* (which eventually appeared in 1985) and the much more significant *Mutmaßungen über Jakob* (1959), in which the apparently accidental death of the railwayman Jakob Abs prompts an exploration of his life and contacts. The mystery of whether he committed suicide remains unsolved, but the pursuit of an elusive truth leads to the dissolution of a conventional plot into a mosaic of episodes, interviews, narratorial speculations with conflicting implications, shifting narrative perspectives and time levels, the whole marked by a reluctance to see into the minds of the small number of characters or present an all-embracing picture of reality. Johnson refused to accept the label of 'Dichter der beiden Deutschlands' (author of the two Germanys), sensing perhaps in this definition political overtones which he felt to be irrelevant. The inadequacies of those perspectives which had attained the status of norms in the two parts of a divided Germany emerged in the following novels. In *Das dritte Buch über Achim* (1961) a west German journalist fails in his attempt to write a truthful book intended to challenge the stereotypes present in the two previous biographies of an East German cycling champion, and in *Zwei Ansichten* (1965), a more conventionally narrated novel, the relationship between a West German photographer and an East German nurse founders. Although the couple are reunited after a professionally organised escape through the Berlin Wall, Johnson avoids any romantic sensationalism by emphasising the emotional distance concomitant with the two 'Ansichten' (views/opinions) of life arising from their respective social conditioning.

Andersch's novels of this period develop the earlier themes of flight, yearning for freedom and a life directed by positive commitment in a totally different milieu. In *Die Rote* (1960) Franziska Scheler breaks out of the shallow routine of a marriage circumscribed by bourgeois prosperity and vacuous cosmopolitanism, undergoes a change of heart during a winter stay in Venice and becomes a factory worker and the companion of a musician and veteran of the Spanish Civil War. The title figure of *Efraim* (1967), a Jewish émigré, appears at first, like Koeppen's Keetenheuve, to be a totally resigned and disillusioned observer who abandons his profession (journalist for a London newspaper) after the failure of his marriage; however, confronted by the reality of Berlin after the construction of the Wall at a time when East–West tensions place West German democracy under acute strain he comes to terms with his failures and reaches a political position defined by the radical liberalism without party affiliation espoused by the author.

Martin Walser, who began with the short stories collected in *Ein Flugzeug über dem Haus* (1955) and the novel *Ehen in Philippsburg* (1957), developed a distinctive fictional setting in *Halbzeit* (1960). This voluminous novel appears at first sight, like its predecessor, to be no more than the German counterpart to the semi-satirical exposures of class prejudice in British novels published at about the same time, in which anti-heroes either ruthlessly play for the highest stakes (Joe Lambton in John Braine's *Room at the Top*) or waver between desperate conformity and private protest (the title-figure in Kingsley Amis's *Lucky Jim*). The title of Walser's novel ('half time'), which with *Das Einhorn* (1966) and *Der Sturz* (1973) forms the Kristlein trilogy, points to the mid-life career crisis of its 'hero' Anselm Kristlein and also to the awareness present in all these works of 1959–60 that post-war Germany, divided but claustro-phobically stable, had reached a turning-point which might pre-cede a questioning of structures and a modification of entrenched positions. Kristlein is however in no sense a man who foresees the necessity of such changes; unlike Oskar Matzerath in Grass's *Die Blechtrommel*, whose eccentric and distanced position is main-tained throughout a life of picaresque small-scale accommoda-tions, or Robert Fähmel in Böll's *Billard um halb zehn*, whose profession and social base allow him to adopt a stance of comfort-able aloofness, he is a conformist and an opportunist, whose ill-nesses at the beginning and the end of the novel are symptoms of his failure to fulfil self-imposed norms. Kristlein's consciousness dominates the novel, but Walser's mastery of irony enables the reader to distinguish between the perspective of the central figure and the author's own position. Kristlein's endless flow of verbiage and jargon, along with his talent for mimicry and chameleon-like metamorphosis, is a strategy which ensures that he is able to succeed – up to a point. His life is in fact totally absorbed by his working-hours identity; his various jobs as travelling salesman, advertising expert and finally trainee in the art of artificially reduc-ing the life of products require him constantly to adapt to changing consumer needs and modify the techniques of persuasion aimed at satisfying them, a pattern which also influences his numerous erotic adventures. At the same time his mobility and access to various social strata in West Germany at the time of the economic miracle endow him with a panoramic view of society. There is an implicit connection made between the desperate attempts to influ-ence potential customers and the role of the writer, whose social awareness cannot easily be translated into a means of changing the attitudes of his readers. Indeed the trilogy was completed only after Walser had passed through a crisis of confidence in the power of fiction to shape lives, already adumbrated in *Halbzeit* and *Das Einhorn*, made a central concern of the shorter pieces *Fiction* (1970) and *Die Gallistl'sche Krankheit* (1972) and shared by several established authors during the period of politicisation in the late 1960s. *Der Sturz* shows Kristlein as administrator of a sanatorium trying to reconcile the needs of the patients with the demands of his employers, who become the victims of an American takeover; eventually he breaks out of this last stressful situation in a frantic journey across the Alps but cannot shake off a mood of suicidal desperation. Kristlein is to the end harnessed to a system from which he hopes to profit and thereby purchase a freedom which remains a chimera.

The *Zeitroman* of the 1950s and 1960s combines the aim of encompassing a broad view of an increasingly complex and diffuse social structure with an awareness that precisely this complexity and diffuseness preclude the application of traditional techniques in order to achieve this aim. The crisis of the novel, evident already at the beginning of modernism and approached with different strategies by Musil, Broch, Döblin and Thomas Mann, to name only German and Austrian writers, becomes more and more acute, and leads to an interest in the innovations of William Faulkner and the practitioners of the French *nouveau roman*, whose influence has been descried even in the work of the relatively conventional and distinctly untheoretical Heinrich Böll. Böll, Gaiser, Andersch, Johnson and Grass all adopt the device of multiple perspectives, each with a partial and fragmentary view of reality, while the presiding consciousness of an omniscient narrator is absent or merely implicit in those novels which, like the first two parts of the Danzig trilogy and the complete Kristlein trilogy, adopt the perspective of the central figure or a fictional narrator close to him.

However, these writers did not doubt the possibility of approaching reality, at least indirectly, by means of a language in which they had faith as an instrument for the discovery of truth and the expression of man's relation to it. They merely wished to avoid the simplistic reproduction of reportage and the symbolic heightening of subjective experience by means of unfettered fantasy, including the escapism of Kitsch and the surreal elements of magic realism and metaphysically grounded dystopias (Kasack, Nossack, Ernst Jünger, the early Jens). Although the single narrator is often abandoned, the figures who substitute for him possess a definable character which influences their view of the world, except Anselm Kristlein, whose willing subjection to forces he can neither control nor evade leads to a damaged identity without clear contours.

This, in the main socially induced, identity crisis is explored in quasi-existential terms in the early novels of Max Frisch in the belief that definition of a human being in terms of nationality, profession and marital status represents a constriction on the potential freedom of a fluid identity; the escape from social roles is not feared as an irreversible progress into isolation, disorientation and dissolution; indeed, the existential limbo is partly welcomed as a precondition of genuine self-realisation, which may consist of the deliberate choice of constantly shifting identities. However, can this creative metamorphosis be achieved without severing all personal relationships and taking flight into delusion? Frisch's fiction explores these questions without reaching final conclusions. The social roles adopted by Kristlein alienate him from self-fulfilment yet he can never abandon them; the central figure of *Stiller* (1954) voluntarily rejects all social roles, yet discovers that the construction of alternative fantasy identities as a substitute for inborn (and therefore not socially conditioned) deficiencies, must end in failure. In *Homo Faber* (1957) the limitations of a severely constricted but voluntarily chosen identity are overcome by exposure to unfamiliar dimensions of experience, while in *Mein Name sei Gantenbein* (1964) belief in the fluidity of personal identity is made the occasion for an elaborate game with the reader involving a series of arbitrarily constructed fictional creations. Frisch's exploration of the theme of identity looks forward to the 'new subjectivity' of the 1970s and 1980s, yet there is a crucial difference. Frisch sees the lives of real persons as a series of episodes which a number of available or possible identities can be made to match, and the arbitrary nature of an individual's conception of himself endows life with a fictional quality. The authors of 'new subjectivity', some of whom are mentioned in the last chapter, on the other hand aim at reaching unadorned truth about themselves through the process of writing.

The first impression conveyed by the experimental writing of the 1950s and 1960s is one of bewildering variety; its only common factor is a profound concern with the relation of language to concrete and psychological reality. The early prose of Peter Weiss, *Der Schatten des Körpers des Kutschers* (1961, written 1952) and *Das Gespräch der drei Gehenden* (1963), is marked by a desire to achieve a firm standpoint by the painstaking microscopic investigation of reality in the manner of the *nouveau roman*. His next texts, however, *Abschied von den Eltern* (1961) and *Fluchtpunkt* (1962), consist of rambling autobiographical meditations on his emergence from repressed childhood, his experience of exile and his growing self-understanding as an artist and writer. Jürgen Becker's prose miniatures *Felder* (1964), *Ränder* (1968) and *Umgebungen* (1970), which are composed, especially the second, in a strict formal pattern, aim to register with maximum fidelity the author's impressions of his surroundings, the urban landscape and its hinterland. These movements of consciousness through reality and their transformations into language are juxtaposed with the threadbare clichés and debased verbiage by which reality is obscured, in accordance with the author's aim by means of the freshness of his observations and critical reflections to eliminate the dross, even to activate a similar consciousness in his readers. A similar impatience with the traditional role of the writer as a creator of fictions inspires Wolfgang Hildesheimer in *Zeiten in Cornwall* (1971), *Tynset* (1965) and *Masante* (1973) to combine accounts of journeys to exotic locations (a remote part of Norway and the African desert) with meditations on the author's predicament as one who under the pressure of events – Hildesheimer, like Weiss, spent the years of the Third Reich in exile – has lost any sense of orientation and plunged into a melancholy for which literary analogies (Hamlet) are ready to hand. The travels to places which he had known when he saw a clear way forward (Cornwall), which in their emptiness offer no distraction from self-exploration, are intended to provide an appropriate background to the discovery of a true self which however remains elusive.

Arno Schmidt continued during the 1950s and 1960s to develop his own peculiar brand of psychological realism. Here the registration of the author's surroundings – usually a rural retreat in the north German plain where the author-protagonist's hermit existence is occasionally interrupted by visits from equally eccentric figures – takes second place to his stream of consciousness, nourished by an inexhaustible supply of curious literary lore and inspired by the contemporary political situation to flights of fantasy into utopian sci-fi worlds. In *Die Gelehrtenrepublik* (1957) the few survivors of a Third World War form in 2008 a writers' colony on the artificial island IRAS (International Republic of Artists and Scientists), which becomes a microcosm of East–West ideological division, while in *KAFF, auch Mare Crisium* (1960) a research team finds itself marooned in a lunar crater. Schmidt's wayward cultivation of an unstable amalgam of picaresque novel, satirical dystopia, science fiction and erotic fantasy provides ample evidence of his radical experimentalism, and his place among those writers preoccupied by the link between consciousness, language and reality is assured by the development of his etym-theory and its application in practice in the monumental *Zettel's Traum* (1970), in which depth psychology provides the key to a stream of consciousness conveyed by the elaborate play with phonemes, morphemes and syntagms, a technique which owes much to James Joyce. Schmidt thus shares with the other experimenters a concern with detailed registration, in which the epic flow is replaced by a mosaic of fragments and the traditional narrator is dismissed in favour of an all-embracing consciousness exploding with disparate ideas and observations.

From this point it is only a short step to the verbal experiments of Helmut Heißenbüttel in *Das Textbuch* (1970) and to the similar efforts of the Wiener Gruppe, Ernst Jandl and the early Peter Handke. Heißenbüttel's 'texts' appear to be no more than verbal collages comparable to the ready-mades and fragments of visual debris found in the work of the Dadaists and the photomontages of *Neue Sachlichkeit*. Here the author draws the ultimate conclusion from the general awareness that a unified view of the world is no longer within the grasp of a single human subject. The world becomes a series of projects, a second reality produced in many different minds and thus only available through the medium of language, or rather of several languages. The 'texts' and the novel *D'Alemberts Ende* (1970) thus consist of montages of quotations from every conceivable source, which in the case of the 'texts' are aligned and contrasted without punctuation and therefore without the binding sense of a statement by a single subject. The model of subject–predicate–object is rejected as a structure determining consciousness according to an interpretation of the world without inherent validity.

Peter Handke in his early plays (especially *Publikumsbe-schimpfung*, 1966, and *Kaspar*, 1968), the prose collected in *Die Innenwelt der Außenwelt der Innenwelt* (1969) and the essays of *Ich bin ein Bewohner des Elfenbeinturms* (1972) occupies a position between the autonomous artistry of Heißenbüttel and the photo-graphic realism and political edge of the documentary writers. Language as normally used is seen as an inescapable manipulative system to which every person is exposed from birth. Any alterna-tive cannot be conveyed by conventional realism or by politically inspired commitment. Yet the political dimension of language can be revealed and made open to revision and rejection and what is taken for granted as a reality demanding acceptance exposed as a human construct. By pointing in his first anti-play to the artificiality of theatrical practice Handke makes the audience aware of their role in a ritual which normally blinds them to the distinction between illusion and reality. Once they are conscious of this distinction in the theatre they may be brought to think of the 'reality' outside the theatre as a series of fictions imposed on them by forces claiming a monopoly of truth.

There is a resemblance here to Brecht's dramaturgy with its emphasis on alienation effects devised to prompt in the audience reflections on alternatives to a deficient reality. Handke however based his early experiments on the work of the Wiener Gruppe (Achleitner, Artmann, Bayer, Rühm and Wiener), which was closer to Heißenbüttel and the European avant-garde represented by Dadaism, Futurism and Surrealism in its development of a provocative performance art running counter to the expectations of an audience accustomed to constructing a sense or 'message' from signals sanctioned by established aesthetic convention. Language is viewed primarily as a base for the creation of special effects, to which techniques drawn from other sources (e.g. the visual arts and the electronic media) also contribute; at the same time the group's members share with the concrete poets (Mon, Gomringer, Jandl) a concern with language as material which can be arranged in patterns according to unfamiliar but definable procedures (permutation, combination, etc.).

The established novelists already considered (with the exception of Walser and Johnson) had been old enough to experience the Third Reich as soldiers or juvenile members of the war machine; only Koeppen had been a (temporary) emigrant. The anti-Fascist writers who had gone into exile delayed their return to Germany or found it difficult to gain a hearing from a German readership which regarded them with a suspicion shared by the older writers who had remained at home and been able to publish between 1933 and 1945. This lack of resonance prevented contact between the exiles and the younger generation of writers who have occupied the main part of this chapter and who developed their own distinctive approach to the Nazi phenomenon. A number of exiles settled in the GDR and willingly accepted the claim of the ruling party that only Socialism and all its consequences for the social structure and economy of the state could guarantee Germany against a resurgence of Nazism. Of the other exiles only Thomas Mann offered in *Doktor Faustus. Das Leben des deutschen Tonsetzers*

Adrian Leverkühn, erzählt von einem Freunde (1947) a diagnosis of Nazism which gained the attention of a wide public. Despite its manifest distinction and depth, the novel caused considerable controversy and failed to inspire younger writers attempting to come to terms with their own experience. Besides, *Doktor Faustus* is much more than Mann's fictional response to the German catastrophe and the question of guilt, although it was entirely in those terms that it was initially interpreted. By combining a *Künstlerroman*, a modern treatment of the Faust theme, a social novel focusing on the educated middle class and an examination of German spiritual and intellectual traditions, Mann presented a summa of themes which had preoccupied him since long before the rise of Nazism. The critics, represented most eloquently by Hans Egon Holthusen in *Die Welt ohne Transzendenz* (1949), were not aware of the extent to which his assessment of Germany's rejection of bourgeois humanism involved a profound self-examination. Mann's narrator, Serenus Zeitblom, links the course of German history with unpolitical 'Innerlichkeit'. The composer Adrian Leverkühn makes a pact with the devil in order to achieve a breakthrough out of cold intellectualism and artistic sterility into the exhilaration of a new creativity; Germany aims at a similar breakthrough out of isolating encirclement into national aggrandisement. Both the artist and the Fascist leader induce an artificial intoxication of mind, will and senses involving the sacrifice of humane moderation and the individual conscience. While Mann had good reason to postulate a fraternal relationship to the Führer in the essay 'Bruder Hitler', the political implications of the novel seemed to its first readers at best well-meaning, at worst contrived, while his refusal to differentiate between the literature of inner emigration and that which received the approval of the Nazis appeared simplistic. In his remaining years Mann was to transfer his attention to the picaresque hero (*Bekenntnisse des Hochstaplers Felix Krull*, 1954) and the holy sinner Gregorius (*Der Erwählte* 1951) in lighter and more self-indulgent treatments of the dubious velleities of the artist.

Germany's theatres went dark in 1944 when Goebbels announced the phase of 'total war'. When they reopened after the capitulation, classics such as Lessing's *Nathan der Weise*, banned on account of its message of religious and racial tolerance, could be performed again, while plays by anti-Fascist writers received their German premières. These included Günther Weisenborn's *Die Illegalen* (1946), on a resistance group modelled on the Rote Kapelle, with which the author had had contact, and Carl Zuckmayer's *Des Teufels General* (1946), in which an air force general based on Ernst Udet makes the ultimate sacrifice when he realises that he has served evil; after confronting a resistance fighter involved in sabotage he commits suicide by crashing his own aircraft. Zuckmayer undoubtedly identified with the vital Harras, who is contrasted not only with the resistance fighter but also with a sinister Gestapo officer; he could therefore be viewed as an alibi figure by the mass of 'Mitläufer' (fellow-travellers) undergoing a change of heart. These plays by older dramatists follow the well-tried conventions of most exile dramas and do not therefore represent a totally new start. Wolfgang Borchert's *Draußen vor der Tür* (broadcast 13 February 1947, performed on stage 21 November 1947, the day after its author's premature death) conveys a clearer perspective on the war, recognised as futile from the beginning and observed from the point of view of a simple recruit. The theme of the demobilised soldier, POW or exile, returning to a devastated home and trying desperately to pick up the pieces of his life, was treated in numerous now-forgotten works (Kolbenhoff, *Heimkehr in die Fremde*, 1949; Gaiser, *Eine Stimme hebt an*, 1950; Leonhard Frank, *Michaels Rückkehr*, 1950). However, Borchert endowed his contribution with an especially personal intensity. A former POW from Siberia arrives in Hamburg, fails a suicide attempt, loses his wife and another woman, is scorned and rejected by his colonel and a cabaret manager, and having encountered God in the shape of a helpless old man is left isolated, disorientated and betrayed, as if Christ's moment of despair on the Cross has been prolonged to eternity. The play's emotional impact arises from Borchert's unequivocal opposition to the war which had led to spells in prison where already serious illness had been exacerbated.

The surreal elements which figure prominently in this play could however appear mannered when applied by one who observed events from the sidelines, as in the Swiss Max Frisch's *Nun singen sie wieder* (1946). In this attempt at a requiem the members of a German execution squad confront in the beyond the crew of a shot-down allied bomber and Nazism appears as a movement inspired by a kind of metaphysical quest, involving crimes committed to force the spirit to emerge from darkness. Frisch comes closer to the reality of the war in *Als der Krieg zu Ende war* (1949), which examines the question of guilt against the background of the occupation of Berlin by the Red Army, while in *Die chinesische Mauer* (1947) a series of historical personalities (including Napoleon, Brutus and Cleopatra) appear in a Chinese setting to demonstrate the need to overcome the centuries-old faith in power in the context of the newly invented atom bomb.

Warnings against a nuclear apocalypse were also delivered by Zuckmayer in *Das kalte Licht* (1955) and Jahnn in *Die Trümmer des Gewissens*, also called *Der staubige Regenbogen* (1961). In the former, tenuously related to the case of Klaus Fuchs, a spy affair is made the occasion for an exploration of the dilemma of the scientist, caught between the desire to pursue pure research and responsibility for the political consequences of his discoveries, a problem which links it to Brecht's *Leben des Galilei* (1943), Dürrenmatt's *Die Physiker* (1962) and Kipphardt's *In der Sache J. Robert Oppenheimer* (1964). Jahnn, on the other hand, eschews the rational approach of these authors in favour of a protest inspired by his idiosyncratic vitalism, the effect of which is vitiated by a combination of discursiveness and melodrama.

Frisch and his compatriot Friedrich Dürrenmatt developed a form of drama which stands between the realism of the well-made play centred on characters inviting empathy from the audience and the Brechtian parable in which a didactic plot takes precedence over the emotional appeal generated by a particular situation. The Schauspielhaus theatre in Zurich, through its performances of exile writers, had ensured a measure of continuity with social drama of the period before the Third Reich and Frisch gained much from personal contact with Brecht when the latter, appalled by the state of the theatre in West Germany, chose to spend some months in Switzerland before settling in East Berlin.

Dürrenmatt, a son of the manse with a lasting interest in philosophy and theology and an awareness of international political tensions accumulated during extensive travels, came to hold a sceptical, but not, as some of his detractors have claimed, nihilistic view of human aspirations as embodied in political institutions and dogmas. Human beings are readily enslaved to ideas realised in power structures, yet progress can only be ensured by the moderating influence of courageous men who voluntarily abandon the power they possess. The world can be turned upside down, but man remains unchanged. Human hybris is all the more dangerous when it is associated with a desire to improve the world.

Dürrenmatt achieved international fame with the plays *Der Besuch der alten Dame* (1956) and *Die Physiker* (1962), neither of which is linked directly to the specific historical situations in which the moral dilemmas which are their themes are most clearly exemplified (cf. Frisch's *Andorra*). The manner in which the citizens of Güllen capitulate to the terms offered them by the multimillionairess Claire Zachanassian when she returns determined to exact revenge on the respected family man Ill, who years before had seduced and abandoned her, can be associated with behaviour patterns which are evident during political and economic crises in any country and throws light on the peculiar mixture of good intentions and greed which characterises human nature in such situations. In *Die Physiker* the atomic scientist Möbius, having discovered a formula which would allow the production of the ultimate weapon, simulates madness so that his knowledge may remain secret. Two agents, from East and West, also pretend to be insane in order to gain access to Möbius and exclusive right to the formula. Despite the efforts of all three to maintain their impostures their plans are frustrated by the 'mad' female director of the asylum who has secured the formula with the intention of blackmailing the world into submission or destroying it. Chance rules and the best-laid schemes come to nothing. The existence of weapons of mass destruction cannot be wished away; it merely puts to a greater test man's ability to organise his affairs rationally. Dürrenmatt's predilection for plots in which the limitations of human nature are exposed against the background of actual or potential apocalypse is also evident in *Porträt eines Planeten* (1970), yet he remained committed to a rational middle way, chastened by the knowledge that the appeal to moral absolutes or even to justice in the abstract can lead to a blind fanaticism which will poison that which it aims to cure.

Frisch's other early plays (*Santa Cruz*, 1944; *Graf Öderland*, 1951; *Don Juan oder Die Liebe zur Geometrie*, 1953) are more personal and relate to his novels in their concern with identity and openness to experience, as well as to many now-forgotten plays by other authors who cultivate a whimsical melancholy against an exotic or fantastic background (Wünsche, *Über den Gartenzaun*, 1962; Waldmann, *Atlantis*, 1963; Dorst, *Gesellschaft im Herbst*, 1960; Hey, *Thymian und Drachentod*, 1956), influenced by Thornton Wilder (*Our Town* and *The Skin of our Teeth*), Jean Anouilh and Jean Giraudoux. (A similar style emerges in radio plays by Ingeborg

Bachmann – *Die Zikaden* (1955), *Der gute Gott von Manhaitan* (1958); and Günter Eich – *Träume* (1953), *Die Mädchen von Viterbo* (1953), which approaches anti-Semitism through two parallel and related plots.) Two further plays by Frisch first performed during this period can be compared to the works of Dürrenmatt already referred to, in their tight dramatic structure, their spare style, their successful combination of uncanny suspense, dramatic irony and effective climax with a pointed message which emerges naturally from the action. *Biedermann und die Brandstifter* (1955) is a 'Lehrstück ohne Lehre' on the complacency and credulity of the petty bourgeois, whose desire for peace and quiet in a private idyll blinds him to the incendiary intentions of two sinister arsenists when they insinuate themselves into his confidence. Eventually the drums of petrol they have stored in his attic are set alight. The play gained force from the lack of reference to specific political developments, so that several interpretations (the vulnerability of the German 'Bürger' to Fascism, the threat of atomic catastrophe, the Communist coup in Czechoslovakia) could be suggested and considered valid. The problem at the centre of *Andorra* (1961) allows more circumscribed definition: its nucleus is the fable 'Der andorranische Jude' which appears in Frisch's *Tagebuch 1946–1949* (1950) in connection with a visit paid to the devastated Germany of the early post-war period. The non-Jew Andri is a refugee from the tyranny of a neighbouring 'black' state and becomes the foster-child of the local teacher; in the eyes of the self-satisfied citizens of his adopted home he conforms to their stereotyped view of the Jew, an identity which he accepts, even when the 'blacks' invade and execute him as a scapegoat. While the play represents a dramatic reworking of a central theme of Frisch's fiction, the impossibility of sustaining an identity independent of others' mental images, Frisch has successfully transformed what had originated as an existential preoccupation into an allegory with political overtones, which could be applied to Germany, Switzerland and other nations and communities. Frisch did not develop further the tentative didacticism of these plays; instead he produced in the 'game' *Biographie* (1967) a dramatic equivalent of *Mein Name sei Gantenbein*, which preceded it by three years. Only Siegfried Lenz combined the 'ortlose Dramaturgie' (drama with non-specific setting) characteristic of these years with a further exploration of the problem of guilt, in *Zeit der Schuldlosen* (1961).

For a brief phase the theatre of the absurd, which originated in

France in the wake of existentialism and is represented by the work of Eugene Ionesco and Samuel Beckett, occupied the attention of writers later to achieve prominence in other genres (Hildesheimer, Grass, Peter Weiss.) It received its theoretical foundation for a German audience in Hildesheimer's *Erlanger Rede über das absurde Theater*. Hildesheimer, one of whose earliest plays, *Die Eroberung der Prinzessin Turandot* (in four versions – for radio (1954), stage (1955, 1961) and television (1963)) can be defined as 'poetic' theatre in the manner of the early Frisch, passed from witty social comedies spiced with a few surreal effects (evident also in his early stories *Lieblose Legenden* (1952, 1961) and the novel *Paradies der falschen Vögel* (1953)) to darker visions of metamorphosis and solipsism in the manner of Ionesco and Beckett, while Grass cultivated a more playfully grotesque mode, as in his best-known pre-documentary play *Die bösen Köche* (1961), in which cooks run amok in search of a secret recipe.

More serious issues were adapted to the historical drama and the supernatural *Märchenstück* by the Austrian dramatists Franz Theodor Csokor (*Die Kaiser zwischen den Zeiten*, 1965) and Fritz Hochwälder (*Das heilige Experiment*, 1943, 1947; *Der öffentliche Ankläger*, 1948, 1954; and *Donadieu*, 1955), who thus continued a tradition unbroken in Austria since the time of Franz Grillparzer thanks to the work of conservative writers Friedrich Schreyvogl, Max Mell and Rudolf Henz.

If there is a turning-point in the development of German drama corresponding to the *annus mirabilis* 1959 for fiction, it is the première of Rolf Hochhuth's *Der Stellvertreter* in 1963. Although it was far from being the first play on the question of guilt for atrocities committed during the Third Reich, its impact exceeded that of all previous treatments, whether realistic or parabolic. Hochhuth turned the theatre into a tribunal and passed judgement on Pope Pius XII, a person recognised by millions as the ultimate moral authority, for failing publicly to condemn the Holocaust and, by presenting in a Jesuit who voluntarily joined a deportation to Auschwitz one who was prepared to die for his convictions, indicated an alternative to the tactical restraint which had been the position of the Pope and the majority of his flock. The play's production and reception, however controversial, were symptomatic of a general revision in attitudes to the Third Reich, prompted also by the Frankfurt trial of Auschwitz guards, which became the subject of Peter Weiss's *Die Ermittlung* (1965), a play with a comparable impact. Hochhuth took his stand on the authenticity of the material on which his play is based and thus initiated the documentary phase in German drama which continued well into the 1970s and has not yet been abandoned by its originator. His principal plays differ however from the major examples of the genre by adapting the classical theatre of empathy to twentieth-century themes, as if the experiments in didactic/epic theatre undertaken during the Weimar Republic and the period of exile by Brecht and others had never taken place. There are features common to all his plays, whether tragedies (*Soldaten. Nekrolog auf Genf*, 1967 – on the justification of carpet-bombing of civilian targets and the *Realpolitik* of Churchill's alleged decision to ensure the 'accidental' death of the Polish general Sikorski in order to placate Stalin; *Guerillas*, 1970 – an unconvincing treatment of the relation between the First and the Third Worlds) or comedies (*Die Hebamme*, 1971 – on the remedial action taken by a vigorous midwife to alleviate a housing shortage; and *Lysistrate und die NATO*, 1974 – which updates Aristophanes by confronting men and women on a Greek island on the issue of the construction of a Nato base). They all share a hectoring discursiveness, black and white characterisation, melodramatic elements which strain credibility and thus ill accord with the aim of authenticity. These deficiencies are however outweighed by the conviction and intellectual force of the author, whose work is grounded in a philosophy of history which raises him above both investigative journalism and the nostra of ideology.

A 'purer' form of documentary drama was achieved by Heinar Kipphardt, who had begun his career as a dramatist in the GDR, before moving (back) to the West in 1959. *Der Hund des Generals* (1962) was a reworking for the stage of one of several stories set in the Second World War. *In der Sache J. Robert Oppenheimer* (1964) took up the theme of the responsibility of the scientist by presenting the hearing before the government committee which eventually deprived the 'father of the atom bomb' of his security clearance. Although he based the play on the official record, Kipphardt ensured additional dramatic interest by rigorously reducing the material at his disposal and introducing Brechtian alienation effects. The result is an austere court-room drama which allows the fundamental issues to emerge clearly without sacrificing authenticity (although Oppenheimer himself protested against aspects of his portrayal). Kipphardt returned to the Third Reich in *Die*

Geschichte von Joel Brand (1965) on the deal almost made between the title figure and Adolf Eichmann to secure the immunity of the Hungarian Jews in exchange for heavy vehicles desperately needed by the Wehrmacht. The play marks a stage in Kipphardt's fascination with the architect of the Holocaust (whose trial and execution in Israel had taken place only a few years before), which reached its climax in *Bruder Eichmann* (1982), his last work for the stage, in which an attempt is made to broaden and deepen the matter of the Holocaust by focusing on Eichmann's psychology and suggesting parallels to post-war atrocities tainted with genocide.

Martin Walser's early plays have domestic settings and mix absurdist and Brechtian features. In the early 1960s, however, he approached the heritage of the Third Reich in two plays which achieve their dramatic effect either by juxtaposing time levels and contrasting a 'holy fool' figure with the cynical opportunists who surround him (*Der schwarze Schwan*, 1964), or by skilfully adapting the 'Hamlet' model (the exposure of truth through a 'play within a play' engineered by an alienated member of a new generation) to a situation in which former Nazis make desperate efforts to suppress the facts of their involvement in a criminal system (*Eiche und Angora*, 1962). *Stienz* (1963) and *Helm* (1965), by Hans Günter Michelsen, both heavy with dialogue, approach the same theme in similar fashion.

If the course of German drama after 1945 may be described as an assimilation of influences, native and foreign, which had been marginalised by the distorted Classicism of the Third Reich, this process reached its climax and took a new turn with the first performance in 1964 of Peter Weiss's *Die Verfolgung und Ermordung Jean Paul Marats, dargestellt durch die Schauspielgruppe des Hospizes zu Charenton, unter Anleitung des Herrn de Sade*, known generally as the *Marat/Sade*. Weiss, who had briefly experimented with the theatre of the absurd, here broke new ground by combining Brechtian techniques of alienation and the epic theatre, complicated by a Chinese box structure adopted to convey three time levels, with a cultivation of the theatricality of excess which can be associated with the 'theatre of cruelty' of Antonin Artaud. The play confronts 'the divine marquis', representing extreme individualism, and the revolutionary 'friend of the people', representing political and social transformation, in debates set against the background of the minimal plot of Marat's murder by Charlotte Corday acted out under de Sade's direction by the inmates of a mental asylum. The play struggles to define the nature of emancipation, foreshadowing that unstable balance of political activism and self-absorption which marks the late 1960s and 1970s in Germany, although its style in the theatre was soon to be superseded by documentary drama.

It was natural for the writers of the inner emigration to cultivate poetry as an outlet for sentiments which could not find expression in the public art of drama and had to take coded or indirect form in fiction. Even in the lyric there were constraints, and the laments for the destruction of war and the perversion of values which accompanied it by the mainly Christian writers Elisabeth Langgässer (*Der Laubmann und die Rose*, 1947), Gertrud von Le Fort (*Gedichte*, 1949), Werner Bergengruen (*Dies Irae*, 1945; *Die heile Welt*, 1950), Rudolf Hagelstange (*Venezianisches Credo*, 1945) were for the most part written late and not published until after 1945. A greater measure of continuity with the pre-war years was provided by the nature poetry of Wilhelm Lehmann and the distilled modernism of Gottfried Benn, whose influence proved so great that the tentative initiatives of the 'Kahlschlag' poets were almost stifled. In fact the development of poetry in the Federal Republic is a process of gradual absorption of international modernism, of which Benn was the only true surviving representative in Germany. Günter Eich, who wrote the quintessential 'Kahlschlag' poem 'Inventur' and adopted the tone of Borchert in the title and closing exhortation of 'Wacht auf, denn eure Träume sind schlecht', was basically a nature poet close to Loerke and Lehmann. However, under the influence of the language scepticism characteristic of modernism he gradually abandoned the faith which underlies much German lyric poetry that the phenomena of the natural world might communicate a metaphysical message. This development had an unexpected outcome: Eich's last works (*Maulwürfe*, 1968, and *Ein Tibeter in meinem Büro*, 1970) consist of collections of whimsical fantasies in prose, intriguing combinations of word-play and satire which can be related to the playful experimentalism of concrete poetry.

Although Benn's influence is apparent in the work of some much younger poets at this time, it was brief and formal, a cultivation of his rhythms and preciosities rather than an adoption of the Nietzschean artistic credo on which they were based. Like another high priest of modernism, T.S. Eliot (who quoted from Benn's

'Probleme der Lyrik'), Benn occupied a position of lonely emi-
nence, even if admiration for the Indian summer of his last creative
phase (*Statische Gedichte*, 1948) compensated for the lack of echo
after his temporary accommodation with Nazism. He had nothing
to offer the original members of Gruppe 47, who concentrated on
fiction and essays, and when in the early 1950s poets gained a hearing at its meetings, they proved to be individual voices whose debt
to modernism took other forms. Paul Celan's hermeticism is a
response to the Holocaust, to which his parents fell victim, and
involves a drastic reduction of the formal options open to the poet
and at the same time an openness to the liberation of imagery
characteristic of modernism, especially French Surrealism. More
important, however, is Celan's Jewish heritage, which conditions
his negative mysticism, his cultivation of paradox and his attempt
to extract an intrinsic spiritual potential from the varied juxtaposi-
tions of a small number of elemental images, each with its own
peculiar resonance. His verse aims to both express and challenge
the tendency to silence which is the initial response to the sudden
supersession of poetry's celebratory function after Auschwitz and
Hiroshima. The poet is caught between the desire to communicate
and the impossibility of doing so in traditional poetic language.
Unlike Brecht and the political poets who adopted the laconic style
of his later work, Celan does not invite the reader to reconstruct a
rational train of thought with a clear socio-political dimension;
even when references to personal experiences and historical events
can be identified – and exegesis and commentary are still in their
early stages – the full implications of Celan's technique of embedding these in a complex network of ambivalent signals produced
by the multiple associations of abstract–concrete compounds have
not been exhausted.

Ingeborg Bachmann's poetry, although more accessible, is the
testimony of an equally vulnerable sensibility responding to
the same spiritual situation and questioning traditional poetic
resources with similar radicality, so that eventually poetry is abandoned in favour of prose. Initially, however, she had succeeded
in articulating a prevalent malaise, that post-war mood of uncertainty, a sense of exposure to forces beyond individual control,
which other writers had conveyed in the form of political allegory
or by more direct recourse to existentialism, in rich imagery and in
a flexible free verse which allowed scope to the expression of
exhortation and lament. Her poetry conjures a personal utopia by

means of imagery drawn from nature, religion, myth and folklore, yet it criticises those factors which prompt the desire to escape from reality; a fear that the tension between these two aims could not be resolved, that poetry could not engage with reality in a language that might transform it, may have led to her silence.

A sharper critique of an unacceptable and clearly recognisable reality emerges in the poetry of Hans Magnus Enzensberger, who more single-mindedly rejects the traditional role of the poet than any of his predecessors except Brecht, from whom he learnt much. Poetry for him is neither a vehicle for the expression of personal feeling nor a 'pure' work of art divorced from reality or the poet's personal situation; its subject is the contemporary scene which it explores in order to alert the reader to its deficiencies. Enzensberger has remained throughout his career soberly aware of the limits of the poet's power; indeed, at one stage he endorsed the proclamation of the 'death' of literature in the pages of *Kursbuch*, the periodical he edited during the 1960s. Before then he had hovered between the view, characteristic of Brecht, that the poet might change reality, and that of Adorno, the influential polymath and philosopher, who interpreted the progress of modernism (culminating in Beckett) as the only adequate and valid protest against a reality which the poet could not hope to engage with directly without making concessions to it.

Enzensberger combines direct exhortation to the reader ('Lies keine Oden, mein Sohn, lies die Fährpläne') and demonstration of real situations based on the view of the poem as an object for use, with the cultivation of a wide range of formal innovations drawn from international modernism, which he presented in the anthology *Museum der modernen Poesie* (1960). The view implied by the title, that modernism has run its course, that it marks the end of a heroic period of advance initiated by the enlightenment, and that the present age demands alternative solutions to its problems, or mankind (or at least western civilisation) is doomed, forms the basis of his later long poems *Der Untergang der Titanic* (1978) and *Mausoleum* (1975). Although criticism of a vacuous and febrile economic miracle is eloquently conveyed in the early collections (e.g. 'schaum'), they also contain pieces which celebrate a threatened natural world which is the poet's temporary refuge from a high-tech culture under the shadow of an apocalypse.

7

The Literature of the German Democratic Republic

In retrospect the GDR appears to have been an artificial construct, born of the defeat of Germany in 1945 (although, like the Federal Republic, it was founded in 1949) and fostered by the Cold War. The construction of the Berlin Wall in 1961 had been a sign that its political system was never accepted by a majority of its citizens. They declared their desire for unification with their western neighbour as soon as it became clear that the Soviet Union, itself undergoing a process of transformation, would not intervene in order to maintain a regime which, unlike some other states in eastern Europe, had taken no steps along the road to reform.

Literature under these conditions took a different course from that in the German-speaking democracies; indeed, there are grounds for claiming that the GDR represents a special case even amongst the countries of the former eastern bloc in the way in which the relation between writers and the state developed. As in all Communist countries writers were in a sense subject to an unwritten contract with the authorities, enforced through membership of the Schriftstellerverband (Writers' Union), which functioned to some extent as a forum for their concerns but more often than not as a controlling institution. Membership was necessary if writers were to gain a hearing in the GDR and other countries of the eastern bloc; in return for conformity, however, they were ensured freedom from commercial constraints and privileges denied to their fellow citizens. The crucial difference between GDR writers and those of other Communist countries lay in the availability of alternative publishing outlets in the West for those who sought a wider readership. (These also existed for non-German writers of the eastern bloc, but usually in the form of

151

émigré publishing houses committed primarily to the propagation of non-conformist literature.) For much of the period 1945–90 it was not possible to draw a clear distinction between conformist and dissident writing in the GDR, between those who whole-heartedly (or opportunistically) supported the system, enjoyed massive print-runs for their work and official approval in the form of prizes, and those who were content to spread their work within the GDR by alternative means (like the samisdat writers – authors of clandestine publications – from the Soviet Union and elsewhere) and otherwise depended on sales in the West. Instead, a broad spectrum existed between extremes of conformity and dissidence which was transformed into a confrontation between two clearly · defined groups only when Wolf Biermann, after performing his critical songs during a concert tour in the West in 1976, was deprived of his citizenship. Even when the lines were clearly drawn on that occasion, the authorities attempted to defuse a potentially explosive situation by the simple expedient of allowing the protesters to leave the GDR temporarily or permanently, resulting in an exodus of writing talent for which there was no equivalent in other east European countries.

In the end it became possible to divide the spectrum into three fairly homogeneous groups: the conformists, the dissidents (a convenient term, although it was not customary in either German state), and a further category which contained figures whose position was less easily defined but who deserve by any criterion a prominent place in any account of twentieth-century German literature. Indeed, there are writers of stature in all three groups (as well as others whose work has had little impact or staying-power), and any survey of GDR literature, while it gives due attention to the political background of its development, has to make a distinction between political stance (*vis-à-vis* the Communist system and the progress of the Cold War) and literary merit, so that works of ephemeral political notoriety are not given inflated significance, while others of real quality which cannot be classified as 'dissident' or political are given their due.

Such a distinction is especially important against the background of the new conditions created by unification. All German-speaking writers are now working in a free market economy, that is, they are no longer subject to direct or hidden censorship, but at the same time they are for good or ill no different from other citizens in their relationship to the state. They are in fact cushioned against the unpredictable pressures of commercial exploitation to a greater degree than the writers of other western democracies by the existence of a large number of (sometimes valuable) prizes, which can be defined as a form of subsidy by independent institutions. However, the new environment will undoubtedly affect the literature produced by writers resident in the former GDR. The conformist group will either change tack or cease to work, the 'dissident' group will end their protests or find other targets; the third group may also make adjustments, although these are less predictable. More important in the context of the latter pages of this chapter is the fact that this group contains five authors – Stefan Heym (born 1913), Christa Wolf (born 1929), Heiner Müller (born 1929), Volker Braun (born 1939) and Christoph Hein (born 1944) – whose work has gained pan-German, and in the case of the three older figures, international, recognition.

The roots of GDR literature lie in the Weimar Republic. The failure of the Spartacist uprising in 1919 ensured that Germany after defeat in the First World War would not immediately follow the path of the Soviet Union. However, the foundation of the KPD (the Communist Party of Germany), which immediately preceded it, represented a challenge to the Weimar political system which could not be ignored by intellectuals on the left. In the Bund proletarisch-revolutionärer Schriftsteller and its magazine *Die Linkskurve* (1929–33), always close to the party, indeed its cultural arm, a forum was established in 1928 for Communist writers, including J.R. Becher, Anna Seghers, Kisch, Renn, Marchwitza, Weinert, Weiskopf, Bredel and Grünberg. (Other literary figures on the left, however, such as Döblin and Brecht, kept their distance.) The Berlin branch of the Bund, led by Jan Petersen, maintained a precarious existence for a time after the Nazi takeover. The leading members, on the other hand, went straight into exile, spent eventually by most in Mexico and the Soviet Union, where after the Stalin purges they supported the Soviet anti-Nazi propaganda effort, before returning to Germany and settling in the Soviet Zone. The work they produced in the early years of the GDR conformed to the tenets of Socialist Realism, which some (Bredel, Marchwitza, Grünberg) had adopted from the beginning of their careers, before they were officially prescribed in the Soviet Union.

Anna Seghers is a more complex case, as her best work was written in Mexico during her exile and represents a less restricted view of the political options for the future. It can be claimed that *Das siebte Kreuz* was inspired by a Volksfront of all anti-Fascist forces, supported by European Communists during the 1930s in the face of the Nazi threat; here and in *Transit* (1944), which traces the fortunes of refugees congregating in Marseille in a desperate attempt to flee the Nazi occupation of France, the positive hero demanded by Socialist Realism is conspicuously absent, while in *Der Ausflug der toten Mädchen* (1946) Seghers aimed to provide a broader view of the involvement of her compatriots in the fateful developments in Germany by having her narrator, from the standpoint of the safe haven of Mexico, follow the lives of her class-mates, as they each make different political commitments during the years since they together took part in a school excursion in the vicinity of Mainz in 1911.

A similar panoramic survey appears on a much larger scale in *Die Toten bleiben jung* (1949, much of it written before Seghers returned to Germany in 1947); while *Der Ausflug* closed with the deaths of all the women with whom the narrator had shared her education, whether or not they had supported the Nazis, *Die Toten bleiben jung* attempts to establish continuity by bridging the hiatus of the Third Reich, while at the same time drawing a clear distinction between those responsible for the Nazi catastrophe and its opponents. Seghers here elaborates the technique of parallel strands of plot evident in some of her earlier works (e.g. *Die Gefährten*), identifying with each the actions and reactions of a small group of characters defined in class terms. Beginning with the killing of the young Communist worker Erwin, in flight from Berlin after the failure of the Spartacist uprising, *Die Toten bleiben jung* contrasts the murderers, who make differing accommodations to civilian life during the Weimar Republic, with Erwin's friends and work-mates, especially the Communist Martin. Erwin's girl-friend Marie gives birth to his son Hans after joining the much older widower and Social Democrat Geschke in order to care for his three children. While one of these becomes a fanatical Nazi, Hans finds in Martin a mentor who influences him in the spirit of Erwin. Although Hans has been engaged in the illegal Communist resistance during the early years of the Third Reich, he is conscripted into the Wehrmacht in 1939 and takes part in the invasion of the Soviet Union, resolving to desert only during the final battle for Berlin in February 1945. When he attempts to persuade his comrades to follow his example, he is executed on the orders of von Wenzlow, the man who had shot his father. While von Wenzlow prefers suicide to surrender, Emmi, Hans's pregnant girl-friend, finds refuge with Marie Geschke, who undermines the Nazi war effort by sabotage in the armaments factory where she works. The novel thus demonstrates the validity of its title, while basing its confrontations on the idea of a class conflict expanded to international dimensions. While there is a tendency to idealise the proletarian figures, the tactical errors resulting from divisions on the left and blindness to the Nazi danger are not glossed over, and although the officers are uniformly condemned, they do not form a homogeneous group. In its historical range and approach to characterisation the novel owes a debt to Tolstoy, whose objectivity Seghers had supported in a controversy with Georg Lukács during the exile years, yet by ensuring that all the figures tainted by Nazism fail to survive the defeat of Germany, she offers a simplistic view of the future. *Die Toten bleiben jung* is therefore, chronologically and ideologically, a transitional work.

With the novels *Die Entscheidung* (1959) and *Das Vertrauen* (1968) Seghers attempted to treat the early years of the GDR in a spirit of loyalty to the regime tempered by concern for the extreme positions it adopted under the influence of the post-war consolidation of Stalinism in the eastern bloc. Continuity with *Die Toten bleiben jung* is maintained by the introduction of some of its figures. The title *Die Entscheidung* signifies the decision between East and West, Communism and capitalism, against the background of a state-run steel-works, which in 1947 becomes the scene of a tug-of-war between the new authorities and the former owners, who by means of infiltration, rumour, the blocking of deliveries and inducement to emigration ('Republikflucht') attempt unsuccessfully to restore the old system. The story of the principal figures is continued in *Das Vertrauen*, in which the uprising of 17 June 1953, although interpreted according to the official line as a counter-revolutionary putsch, allows Seghers to point to factors which had led to the alienation of some of the workers. Here the title indicates the trust placed in the employees of the steel-plant by the party secretary when he decides not to call in Soviet tanks. The novel is thus inspired by a faith in mass support which the regime in fact had good reason to suspect was limited, while on the other hand it implicitly criticises its tendency towards intransigence in the face of dissatisfaction with such particular measures as the unilateral raising of work norms. The result is a stance typical of many writers in the early years of the GDR: acceptance of the parameters of Socialism, the dogma of class conflict and the consequent view of western policy as the work of the class enemy, at the same time a plea for a more flexible and open attitude to the workers in the context of the temporary thaw which followed Stalin's death. *Das Vertrauen* therefore goes beyond the conventions of Socialist Realism, to which its more superficial features can be so readily assigned.

Other novels which eventually achieved classic status in the GDR, yet adopt a more sceptical view of the possibility of harmony between party and individual, include Erwin Strittmatter's *Ole Bienkopp* (1963), set in a rural community during the changes to agriculture, and Erik Neutsch's *Spur der Steine* (1964), which, much influenced by Soviet models, concerns the tensions emerging during the construction of a chemical plant. All these novels, along with many others, can be classified as *Aufbauromane*, novels portraying the construction of Socialism.

Another group of novels, normally defined as *Ankunftsliteratur*, after the title of one of them – *Ankunft im Alltag*, by Brigitte Reimann (1961) – is mainly devoted to the commitment made by young members of the middle class to the establishment of a Socialist order and to the necessarily complex personal and professional relations between such figures and both the party and the working class. They testify to the need of the SED (Sozialistische Einheitspartei – Socialist Unity Party) to extend its power base beyond the traditional working class to include technical experts and other professionally qualified people. In some instances (Dieter Noll, *Die Abenteuer des Werner Holt*, 1960, Max Walter Schulz, *Wir sind nicht Staub im Wind*, 1962, Socialist adaptations of the *Bildungsroman*) they point to the place of culture in the formation of attitudes and implicitly advocate the reassessment of a cultural heritage which had been of such decisive influence in Germany on the attitude of the middle class to political activity.

In the *Aufbau-* und *Ankunftsromane* the memory of the Third Reich had been a factor influencing actions and opinions, but 'Bewältigung der Vergangenheit' (or coming to terms with what happened in the Third Reich) had been viewed as a simple matter of conversion to the new order, occasionally after a period of social disorientation and ideological limbo. However, the portrayal of life under Hitler has a special place in the literature of the GDR, not only because of the regime's claim to have made a total break with the immediate past, but also because many GDR authors had been actively involved in the struggle against Nazism, mainly in exile, but in some cases in Germany and the occupied countries. Of even greater impact than the relevant chapters of *Die Toten bleiben jung* was the account by Bruno Apitz in *Nackt unter Wölfen* (1958), based on eye-witness experience although with strong fictional trimmings, of the efforts by the inmates of Buchenwald to secure the safety of a three-year-old Jewish child smuggled into the camp by a Polish prisoner. The danger of discovery creates a conflict amongst prisoners forced to balance tactical and humanitarian considerations and tests their moral commitment to its limits.

The approach to the experience of the Third Reich by those who had not resisted its propaganda was necessarily more complex. True, the value of the best GDR treatments of the Nazi phenomenon lies in their emphasis on honesty and authenticity, on typical decisions of conscience in which ideological allegiance is not a primary factor; they therefore do not differ in general character from those of West German authors. Significant differences nevertheless emerge. While Alfred Andersch's desertion as recounted in *Die Kirschen der Freiheit* (and *Flucht in Etrurien*) is presented in existential terms, the change of heart experienced by Wehrmacht soldiers in the early stories of Franz Fühmann (*Kameraden*, 1955; *Kapitulation*, 1958; *König Odipus*, 1966) can be defined as a 'conversion' from one ideology to another, as the propaganda clichés of a crusade of western civilisation against Asiatic barbarity are abandoned; these works are accounts, concentrated by the circumstances of war, of the much slower and more circumstantial process followed by the author while a POW in the Soviet Union and traced also in *Der Hohlweg* by Günter de Bruyn, and the novels of Schulz and Noll. The examination of the impact of Nazism on a small community in the far east of pre-war Germany in Johannes Bobrowski's *Litauische Claviere* (1966) gains from its narrow focus on the ethnic tensions characteristic of an area which (with the exception of Siegfried Lenz) West Germans either ignored or pined for as an idealised lost homeland. Personal experience of the resistance was no safeguard against the romanticisation of anti-Fascist heroism and demonisation of unreconstructed Nazis in the stories of Stephan Hermlin ('Die Zeit der Einsamkeit', 'Die Kommandeuse'), although their formal qualities raise them above the level of West German works with similar deficiencies (e.g. the late novels of Remarque).

More interesting are the autobiographical accounts of the unquestioned indoctrination of youth from humbler backgrounds in the work of the middle generation (Erich Loest, Christa Wolf, Hermann Kant). In *Pistole mit sechzehn* Loest wrote in conscious reaction against the tendency in the GDR to fictionalise a worker resistance with only a tenuous relation to historical reality and to ignore the process by which the mass of Germans (including the working class) had become willing instruments of Nazi policy. Christa Wolf's *Kindheitsmuster* (1976) is a reconstruction of an identity which has become so alien to the narrator that she can approach it only by describing it in the third person. Kant's *Der Aufenthalt* (1977) offers a more conventional view of 'conversion' in a POW context; the exchange of identities, however, is complicated by the fact that the central figure, having accepted Nazism when his horizons were confined to the small town of his birth, is falsely accused of an atrocity against a civilian after capture as a POW in Poland. After he is forced to join a group of hardened Nazis, their company induces a distancing process which might not otherwise have taken place.

The everyday aspects of life in the Third Reich are illuminated by Helga Schütz in *Vorgeschichten* (1970), *Das Erdbeben bei Sangershausen* (1972) and *Jette in Dresden* (1977); their method of presenting slices of life and their faithfulness to a limited point of view bring them close to the west German chronicler Walter Kempowski. Jurek Becker's *Jakob der Lügner* (1968) belongs in subject and style to a long Jewish story-telling tradition; its narrator, who is never clearly identified, recalls from a post-war perspective an episode from a ghetto in Nazi-occupied Poland. Having been arrested for missing the curfew, Jakob accidentally hears in the police station a radio announcement that the Red Army is approaching. When he passes on the information to his fellow Jews, claiming that he has heard it on his own clandestine radio, he is forced to follow up this truth with hastily concocted lies in order to maintain morale. Because there is no attempt at concerted action against the Nazis in anticipation of liberation, Jakob's lies, it could be claimed, are merely sedative, and the novel ends with the deportation of the ghetto's inhabitants to a death-camp, which only the narrator survives. The absence of heroic confrontation challenges what had become the conventions of resistance literature and is based on a realistic view of the options open to the victims of Nazi persecution. At the same time it presents indirectly a plea for the utopian function of art in the form of 'story-telling', the white lie which by raising morale makes life more tolerable under conditions which cannot be materially changed without outside military help.   ·

Changes to the management of the economy after the initial years of reconstruction, in particular the introduction of the *Neues Ökonomisches System der Planung und Leitung der Wirtschaft* (NÖS-PL), which involved modernisation by means of high technology and the deployment of appropriate skills, were bound to have an effect on GDR literature. The working-class hero of high Stalinism soon appeared dated and authors turned to the 'Königsebene' or managerial level or to the educational infrastructure for their protagonists. The transition is marked by Kant's *Die Aula* (1965), in which the central character Robert Iswall, invited to give a speech at the closing-down ceremony of the *Arbeiter-und Bauernfakultät* (Faculty of Workers and Peasants) at a GDR university, looks back over his student days and the different courses taken by the lives and careers of his former class comrades in the intervening years. Within the framework of a wholly positive view of the system, which through the ABF had made it possible for the educationally deprived to challenge the cultural and professional hegemony of the old middle class, Kant offers sidelights on the tensions which this social engineering produced, although his gift for comic caricature and dazzling verbal dexterity tends to reduce them to a minimum, with the effect of papering over cracks which in the work of more intellectually probing authors would have been explored with less concern for a harmonious consensus. Thus the motivation for the 'Republikflucht' of Quasi Riek, Iswall's most gifted friend, is left deliberately unclear; when the former friends meet in Hamburg, where Quasi is found in charge of a pub called 'Zum toten Rennen', the atmosphere is frosty, and the reader is left with the impression that whatever dissatisfaction prompted the move is insignificant beside the loss of illusions suffered after it; at the same time Iswall's discovery that his friend's file has been removed from the ABF archive could imply either that he has been declared a non-person by the authorities or that he has been engaged in clandestine activities on their behalf. A similar ambivalence is evident in the novel's treatment of personal relationships. When Iswall finds that he and his friend Trullesand are rivals for the attentions of Vera Bilfert, the problem is solved by the party, which arranges a lengthy study tour in China for Trullesand and another girl, during which their attachment grows, leaving Iswall free to marry Vera. Kant portrays a conflict with potentially tragic consequences in such a way that feelings are defused and their manipulation for personal ends appears as the operation of a higher (political) wisdom.

Kant's second novel, *Das Impressum* (1972), follows a similar pattern. Its hero David Groth, having risen from a messenger to an editorial position in a leading newspaper, is offered the post of minister, and before agreeing to accept he looks back on his career, considering above all the older people he had encountered and their influence on him. Most form counterparts to the mentor-figures who had appeared in *Die Aula*, boosting his self-confidence and conveying through personal example the values which will continue to guide him. With such a clearly affirmative structure the novel's interest lies chiefly in the episodes Groth recalls, which demonstrate Kant's talent to create cameos (evident also in his short stories) symptomatic of broader historical tensions, turning-points and historical allegiances.

The unbroken progress to the top experienced by Iswall and Groth is absent from the other novels of this phase (by de Bruyn, Jakobs and Neutsch), in which the emphasis lies on the contrast between the idealism and untainted commitment of youth and the disillusionment of middle-age. Already in *Beschreibung eines Sommers* (1961) Karl-Heinz Jakobs had modified the traditional Socialist Realist formula (in which a worker without political consciousness or a disorientated bourgeois aesthete develops towards Socialist commitment) by narrating from the point of view of an unpolitical anti-hero. In *Eine Pyramide für mich* (1971), also by Jakobs, a professor returns to the site (a dam) of his first professional triumph and becomes aware of the contrast between the idealism and comradely feelings of his youth and the cynicism and personal betrayals which have accompanied his later professional advancement. In Jakob's next novel *Die Interviewer* (1973) a similar figure is brought to realise that planning from above must take into account the needs and problems of those subject to it and that the planners themselves, by allowing a purely rational approach to problems to influence their domestic lives, have undermined their closest relationships. The following novel, *Wilhelmsburg* (1979), which did not appear in the GDR, approaches the same theme in a more radical manner by linking doubts concerning the ultimate purpose of professional activity (here the manufacture of weapons) with the Warsaw Pact invasion of Czechoslovakia in 1968, against which the central figure brings himself to protest, a decision which however fails to save his marriage or his relationship to his daughter, who commits suicide.

The same conflicts between professional advancement (and by implication, the political conformity which must accompany it) and private obligations mark de Bruyn's *Buridans Esel* (1968), although here an irony reminiscent of the nineteenth-century realist Fontane might be said to reduce the impact of a critique of bourgeois accommodation to routine. However, by confining himself to a small number of characters in a restricted setting de Bruyn is able to allow problems contingent on professional life in the GDR to emerge with symptomatic force, whether in the triangular relationship of *Buridans Esel*, the ideologically motivated intrigues surrounding a literary award in *Die Preisverleihung* (1972) or the rivalry between literary historians in *Märkische Forschungen* (1978).

Erich Loest, a highly productive author who had fallen foul of the regime in 1957 because of his association with a political reform group, produced in *Es geht seinen Gang oder Mühen in unserer Ebene* (1978) a further contribution to the theme of professional disillusionment and marital disharmony, while in *Auf der Suche nach Gatt* (1973) even the more conformist writer Erik Neutsch dealt with it in a much more radical manner than in his *Spur der Steine*, although in the later novel a changed attitude enables the central figure to overcome his personal and professional crisis and reintegrate himself into the working community; it thus represents a 'catching up' with the development of society rather than a questioning of it which might lead to an advance beyond its premises. In its form, Neutsch's novel, like Gerti Tetzner's *Karen W.* (1974), shows the influence of the most important novel of this more critical phase, a turning-point in the development of a more subjective approach to the exploration of problematic relationships and their breakdown, Christa Wolf's *Nachdenken über Christa T.* (1968).

Wolf had already brought herself to the attention of a wide readership with *Der geteilte Himmel* (1963), in which Rita, although given the opportunity to join her lover in the West after the construction of the Wall, voluntarily abandons the relationship and returns to her work in the East. The theme as presented in the novel reads like a nineteenth-century conflict between duty and inclination in which the former is triumphant. In the circumstances of the time, however, it was a bold step to treat the effect on personal relationships of the division of Germany. Despite the possibility left open at the end of the novel that Rita has attempted suicide (like the corresponding figure in Johnson's *Zwei Ansichten*, which offers a more balanced but also more schematic view of the theme), Wolf could claim that there was ultimately no clash between personal self-realisation and social duty by at least implying that any other decision would have meant abandoning ideals to which she was committed, whereas her boy-friend takes a more pragmatic view. The problems arising in the social transformation of the GDR are presented as challenges; those who meet them, choosing 'das härtere strengere Leben' (the more arduous, regimented life), are granted heroic status, those who evade them by committing 'Republikflucht' are seen as resigned and disorientated, without comparable ideals. Rita's position is in many ways similar to that of the title figure in Brigitte Reimann's *Franziska Linkerhand*; both women leave sheltered middle-class homes for employment in difficult conditions, Rita in a railway waggon factory, Franziska in an architect's office supervising the construction of a vast and soulless housing estate.

In *Nachdenken über Christa T.* the title figure studies, teaches, then withdraws to a rural hermitage, where, after fragmentary attempts at writing, she dies of leukaemia. Here there is no question of harmony between individual aspiration and social duty, rather the implied plea for an understanding of those who are temperamentally incapable of adapting to a social system in which culture and the finer feelings must take second place to a criterion of performance which harnesses more aggressive human impulses. Although a west German critic concluded that Christa T.'s problems are specific to the GDR, Wolf's definitions of alienating factors in society could apply equally to the West, and the reader cannot help sharing instead the doctor's post-mortem verdict: 'Todeswunsch als Krankheit, Neurose als mangelnde Anpassungsfähigkeit an gegebene Umstünde' (death-wish as illness, neurosis as failure to adapt to given circumstances). Christa T. thus anticipates figures in later works by Wolf and other authors with an interest in artists of the past whose failure to accommodate themselves to their respective social environments led to suicide or insanity. These include Kleist and Caroline von Günderode in Wolf's *Kein Ort. Nirgends* (1979) (a title signalling uncompromising utopian aspirations, utopia being the Greek term for nirgends/

nowhere); the eponymous heroine of her *Kassandra* (1983), in which the critique is broadened to absorb issues raised by the women's and peace movements; the portrayals of vulnerable geniuses in Gerhard Wolf's *Der arme Hölderlin* (1976); Hermlin's *Scardanelli* (1970) (Hölderlin's pseudonym after the onset of madness); the 'Prussian' plays of Heiner Müller, in which representatives of the enlightenment are forced into sycophancy by Prussian absolutism; critical-biographical works on E.T.A. Hoffmann and Trakl by Fühmann, on Jean Paul Friedrich Richter by de Bruyn, on Günderode and Bettina von Arnim by Christa Wolf and on Kleist by Günter Kunert.

Christa T. also anticipates the problematic hero(in)es who populate the fiction of the 1970s after Erich Honecker, who had succeeded Walter Ulbricht as SED General Secretary and Head of State, made in 1971 a speech which appeared to signal liberalisation in the following words: 'Wenn man von der festen Position des Sozialismus ausgeht, kann es meines Erachtens auf dem Gebiet von Kunst und Literatur keine Tabus geben. Das betrifft die Fragen der inhaltlichen Gestaltung als auch des Stils' ('If one bases oneself on the firm position of Socialism, then in my opinion there can be no taboos in the area of art and literature, in questions concerning the shaping of content or style'), to which he added the significant qualification that 'keine Konzessionen an Anschauungen, die unserer Ideologie fremd sind' ('no concessions to views which are alien to us') were thus implied. The statement has since been quoted repeatedly and subjected to as much exegesis as the most cryptic piece of Holy Writ. In fact certain taboos remained in force until November 1989: the fundamental tenets of Marxism-Leninism, the armed forces, the security services (Stasi), the pollution which was a side-effect of the single-minded promotion of heavy industry, the military influence on education, and the division of Germany insofar as the human suffering it caused was given greater emphasis than the security it ensured to the system. However, certain liberal causes which received equal or more support in the West were taken up in published work. The GDR developed its own type of *Frauenliteratur* without challenge from offialdom, and science fiction, detective stories, historical and children's fiction poured from the presses.

The factor which more than any other strained relations between the state and the writing community was the absence of a public forum for genuine debate, available elsewhere in democratically elected local and national institutions and a free press. The ensuing vacuum was filled to some degree by creative writers, who however were forced to avoid open confrontation by resorting to various forms of coding. The special quality of later GDR literature arises from the literary ingenuity necessary to devise codes which would satisfy or hoodwink the censor yet be transparent to the normal reader. Traditional Socialist Realism was *in extremis* by 1970, but the need to supply a coded statement gave it the *coup de grâce*. Meanwhile, the relaxation following the 'no taboos' speech led to the publication of two works which in their different ways broke with the conventions accepted by even the most critical and formally innovative of the writers discussed so far. Ulrich Plenzdorf's *Die neuen Leiden des jungen W.* (1972) was above all significant in taking account of the popular culture (and its effect on the life-style of the young) which had been such a marked feature of all advanced industrial societies in the late 1960s. Just as in the West it undermined the bourgeois-Protestant ethic and the cultural norms associated with it, so in the East it challenged the image of the heroic Stakhanovite (one who models himself on the Soviet miner Stakhanov, whose achievements were exploited for propaganda purposes) and anti-Fascist which had been such a potent role model throughout the history of Communism. In fact Plenzdorf's novel hardly appears explosively dissident in retrospect; its (anti-)hero, reporting from the beyond, to which an accident with a tool he invented has consigned him, challenges the views expressed about his personality, his work and his affair with Charlie (Charlotte) by those who had been close to him, but neither these interventions nor the implications of the contrafacture of Goethe's *Die Leiden des jungen Werther* amount to a political statement.

Volker Braun's *Unvollendete Geschichte* (1975), on the other hand, in referring in passing to Plenzdorf's work, points up its own radical departure from a tendency to tone down dissatisfaction with accepted norms. By its subject-matter – a young couple suffer harassment when the man attempts 'Republikflucht' – it also invited comparison with Christa Wolf's *Der geteilte Himmel*. Instead of the voluntary return of the female protagonist to a firm place in GDR society (at the cost of separation from her lover), Braun, as his title suggests, leaves the ending of his story open; both she and her boy-friend are suspected, indeed ostracised by their superiors in their employment and the party, and any alternative to the uncertainty of isolation in a society from which they cannot escape has to be supplied by the reader.

Stefan Heym's *Collin* (1979), which, unlike Braun's work, could not appear in the GDR, is equally subversive; by placing the title figure, a member of the intelligentsia, side by side with a senior Stasi official in neighbouring hospital beds, Heym is able to develop a sharp critique of party privilege and blindness, taking a stage further the examination of middle-age crises of identity found in the novels of Jakobs and others. The opposition between intellectual and party official, however, is not simple, as Collin has throughout his career made accommodations to the system which he now reappraises. Similarly, Jurek Becker's later intellectual protagonists are forced to confront their relations to their work and their family. In his *Irreführung der Behörden* (1973) an author deceives his way to success by satisfying the expectations of readers in search of simple escapism and is brought to realise that the dishonesty involved both ruins his private life and runs counter to Socialist principles. The central figures in his novels *Der Boxer* (1976), *Schlaflose Tage* (1978) and *Aller Welt Freund* (1982) find themselves increasingly isolated in the GDR, the first as a Jew unable to come to terms with his experiences in the Third Reich who escapes to the West, the second as a schoolteacher who falls foul of the authorities when he abandons ideological indoctrination of his pupils (and whose girl-friend escapes to the West), the third as a journalist who attempts suicide after failing to please everyone (to be 'aller Welt Freund') and ends as a paranoiac who cannot reintegrate himself into work and personal relationships. In these novels, as in de Bruyn's *Neue Herrlichkeit* (1984), the authors contrive an indirect critique of a system viewed as at best unsympathetic, at worst vindictive.

Others directed their attention to the problems of young people, either in the spirit of Plenzdorf (Rolf Schneider, *Die Reise nach Jaroslav*, 1974) or in a more openly critical manner (Reiner Kunze, *Die wunderbaren Jahre*, 1976; and Thomas Brasch, *Vor den Vätern sterben die Söhne* and *Kargo*, both 1977).

The tensions, acute in GDR society, between the desire for individual self-realisation and the pressures to conform, were not always approached as directly as in these examples. Writers coded their criticisms, either by adapting the forms of fantasy and science fiction, or by turning to history, especially, as already noted, by exploring the precarious psychosocial position of artist-intellectuals in the past. The indirection of this method is in part a consequence of the Biermann affair, which brought to an end the brief period of 'thaw' after Honecker's 'no taboos' speech; however, it can also be seen as prompted by the growing dissatisfaction with conventional realism (Socialist or other), which places unacceptable limits on the expression of utopian aspirations, for which the free imagination had been, especially during the Romantic period, an appropriate vehicle. The store of images, motifs and archetypes available in the Bible, Greek mythology and German folklore became a source for writers' investigation of the contemporary human condition. A distinction has to be made here between the coded discourse necessary to evade censorship and the more traditional concern to present by means of fantasy and myth constants in human nature or contemporary features not confined to the eastern bloc, although the fusion of more than one discourse is characteristic of the most memorable and distinguished examples of this trend (Christa Wolf, *Kassandra*; Fühmann, *Die Schatten/Das Ohr des Dionysos*; Stefan Heym, *Ahasver*; Morgner, *Trobadora Beatriz* and *Amanda*; Stefan Schütz, *Medusa*).

Occasionally the allegory is so cryptic as to defy interpretation (as in Fritz Rudolf Fries's *Verlegung eines mittleren Reichs* (1984)), or it approaches the technique of the traditional satire of human foibles (as in Günter Kunert's *Im Namen der Hüte* (1967), in which the clairvoyant powers of a picaresque hero enable him to survive the chaos of post-war Berlin and gain some enlightenment on his confused ancestry). Such devices are more transparent in the stories collected in Hans-Joachim Schädlich's *Versuchte Nähe* (1977) and Erich Köhler's *Der Krott* (1976); in the second of these the substance defined by the title is a scab-like formation on the skin symbolising the productive fantasy by which a dull routine (here the work of a cultural official in a power station) may be enlivened.

In *Der König David Bericht* (1972) Heym provides his most successful exploration of his preferred theme, 'Macht' versus 'Geist'. Although it recalls similar treatments in the historical novels of Feuchtwanger and Alfred Neumann, it is primarily a critique of the manipulation of the historical record in the interests of ideology and existing power-structures within the Communist system. Ethan, historian at the court of Solomon, suffers when he exposes the discrepancy between truth and image in his biography of David. More elaborately allegorical (and less specific to a political system) is *Ahasver* (1981), in which three narrative strands are

skilfully juxtaposed: the Wandering Jew's own account of his relation to God, Adam and his fellow fallen angel and antipode Lucifer
who, in contrast to Ahasver's revolutionary dissatisfaction with the
status quo, represents elements apparently impervious to change.
Christ fails to live up to Ahasver's hope that he will extend his
mission from love of man to struggle against the conditions which
restrict his progress. In an apocalyptic ending God, Christ and
Ahasver are reconciled under the threat of nuclear catastrophe.
Having presented his left-wing credentials in this strand, Heym
criticises the ossification of revolutionary dogma and the related
careerism of its supporters in the second and third strands, set in
sixteenth-century Germany after the impetus of the Lutheran
Reformation has given way to stagnation, and the contemporary
GDR, establishing a clear parallel between both.

In other examples of critical fantasy the guiding spirit proves to
be a feminism which has its analogues in the literature of the
Federal Republic and Austria. Whereas, however, western feminist
literature concentrates on the development of a specifically femi-
nine discourse, the reworking of myth and the cultivation of surreal fantasy in GDR feminist writing allow a broader treatment of
feminist issues, mainly by linking these formal innovations to the
exposure of sexual discrimination within the GDR or patriarchal
values at the root of international tensions and other problems
which transcend those specific to the Communist system. In the
later novels of Irmtraud Morgner, *Leben und Abenteuer der Trobadora
Beatriz nach Zeugnissen ihrer Spielfrau Laura* (1975) and *Amanda. Ein
Hexenroman* (1983), two parts of an uncompleted trilogy, equality of
the sexes as proclaimed in the GDR constitution is contrasted with
a reality in which women are burdened with their former role and
the additional stress of employment, often in low-paid jobs under
trying conditions. In *Amanda* fantasy is allowed greater scope in a
radical reinterpretation of the myth of the *Walpurgisnacht*, the
annual gathering of witches on the central peak of the Harz range
(which forms an episode in Goethe's *Faust*); the witch and the
siren, traditionally images deriving from male fears of female
emancipation, are given positive definition in an archetypal confrontation with an old patriarchal value system represented by the
chief devil Kolbuk and the chief angel Zacharias, under whose
joint hegemony the harmony within each sex of rational and sensual impulses and a balanced relationship between the sexes have
become utopian dreams. Morgner remains loyal to the hope that

the emancipation thus implied is compatible with the abstract tenets of Socialism, while a critique of 'really existing Socialism' emerges incidentally in certain episodes.

In Stefan Schütz's monumental *Medusa* (1986), however, the reality of the Communist system as represented by the GDR is more openly and radically criticised. The central female figure, Marie Flaam (with the features of Molly Bloom), experiences in the first part, 'Kathedrale des Ichs', in the Palace of the Republic in East Berlin, a series of constricting controls designed to reduce the individual to docile acceptance of a false harmony and extinction of identity in the name of equality. In the second part, 'Anabasis' (warriors' march), this process is demonstrated in a children's concentration camp; its relation to Buchenwald, built by the Nazis close to Weimar (the residence of Goethe and symbol of German Classicism), is more than hinted at in a sequence which points to the degeneration of the values associated with the enlightenment in both Nazism and Stalinism, as reason is made the instrument of terror and totalitarianism. Marie Flaam's odyssey ends on a precariously positive note in the third part, 'Free play of love' (*sic*); she finds a matriarchal mentor in Gorgo Sappho, a reincarnation of Medusa, with whom she eventually merges, and a male partner in the Jew Naphtan, with whom she enjoys a brief fulfilment in a utopia lacking any social constraints on feeling, while the battle of the sexes continues in the background. There is a striking resemblance between *Amanda* and *Medusa* in the constellation of characters which emerges; in both, the female protagonist has a mentor who stands for her unrealised self. The symbiosis of Laura and Amanda and of Marie Flaam and Gorgo Sappho is a sign that the utopian self is attainable – a conclusion which contrasts positively with that of Bachmann's *Malina*, in which the female is deprived of her identity, the price paid for the survival of her male alter ego (the title figure).

The work which most closely combines a revision of myth and feminism with the aim of an understanding and possible cure of contemporary international tensions and has in consequence had greater resonance, is Christa Wolf's *Kassandra* (1983, published in the GDR as an epilogue to the Frankfurt poetry lectures *Kassandra. Voraussetzungen einer Erzählung*, which in the West appeared separately). The lectures describe how during a trip to Greece (in particular Athens, Crete and Mycenae) the plan for a new version of the Cassandra myth was conceived, in which the Trojan priestess would represent first a cult in transition, as the mother goddess Gaia is superseded by the patriarchal Apollo, and then a renunciation of cults both old and new in favour of a utopia in which the true self would be realised. In the story Kassandra looks back over her life, her initial awareness of her prophetic powers, her part in the war (a pawn in Troy's search for an ally) and her death-sentence at the behest of Achilles. Before she is taken away to be sacrificed she recalls a reserve of dissident women in the caves outside the fortress of Troy, led by Arisbe (who becomes Kassandra's mentor), where an alternative model of human relationships, based on a harmonious interaction of 'Leben' and 'Geist', had been briefly put to the test. Here Aeneas joins his father Anchises before departing to found a new Troy. Kassandra rejects his plea to accompany him, suspecting that heroic status will be a precondition of his expedition's success and render love between them impossible. The identification of patriarchal values with military power must be read in connection with the renewed arms race during the late 1970s and the early 1980s and the peace movement it prompted in both German states and elsewhere. The feminism thus defined can also be traced back to 'Selbstversuch', Wolf's contribution to the anthology *Blitz aus heiterm Himmel*, which consists in the GDR edition of stories and an essay by male and female writers on the subject of sex change.

The principal GDR writers of the 1980s also developed a form of critical realism which supersedes *Aufbau-* und *Ankunftsliteratur* and the fiction of middle-age crisis on the technical-managerial level. Volker Braun's *Hinze-Kunze-Roman* (1985) focuses on the new GDR hierarchy of functionaries and their minions, here a state official of working-class origin (Kunze) and his chauffeur (Hinze), son of a white-collar employee. Kunze uses the numerous opportunities provided by official trips for sexual adventure and even conducts an affair with Hinze's wife Lisa. She however breaks free of domestic confinement and after qualifying for a leading political position starts a new life separated from both men. Hinze remains in a subordinate position, despite the intellectual equality manifested in the arguments with his 'master' and the theoretical equality implied by both the formula 'Hinze und Kunze' and the Socialist claims of their society.

A woman occupies a more central position in Christoph Hein's *Der fremde Freund* (1982, published in the following year in the Federal Republic as *Drachenblut*), which concerns the discrepancy between the outward stability and professional success of Claudia, a forty-year-old doctor, and the inner emptiness experienced after the senseless death in a pub brawl of the architect Henry, with whom she had had a year-long affair, in which a fear of total trust and intimacy had characterised both parties. The blood of the dragon had made her invulnerable, obscuring the lime leaf which marks a residual sensitivity. While Claudia thus comes to terms with her isolation, she recalls her former self in nostalgic memories of her school-friend, who eventually fell foul of the authorities. The hint here offered of a link between emotional stagnation and political repression is made more explicit in Hein's second and third novels *Horns Ende* (1985) and *Der Tangospieler* (1989). The former adopts the technique of multi-perspective narrative in order to throw light on the mystery surrounding the suicide in 1957 of the director of the museum in the small town of Guldenberg, to which he had been transferred in 1953 from Leipzig after expulsion from the SED. Five local inhabitants present their memories of the affair from the standpoint of the 1980s, revealing a web of criminality, corruption and denunciation which extends from the Third Reich through the years of Stalinism. Like Jurek Becker and de Bruyn, Hein avoids stridency; instead he allows a state of emotional atrophy and social apathy to emerge from the statements and interactions of his characters and allows the reader to draw the appropriate political conclusions.

Hein's novels can be defined as historical fiction on the Stalinist heritage, which, like that of the Third Reich, demands confrontation. Stefan Heym also approaches political questions through history; here however a distinction exists between the novels based on the Bible and myth already noted, those on political and intellectual revolutionaries of the past (*Lassalle*, 1969 – on the founder of the first German workers' party; *Die Papiere des Andreas Lenz*, 1963 – set during the revolution of 1848–9; and *Die Schmähschrift*, 1970 – on Daniel Defoe) and those which take place during Heym's own lifetime. To the last category belong not only the novels written first in English before he settled in the GDR, but also *5 Tage im Juni* (published in the West in 1974, but written much earlier) and *Schwarzenberg* (1984), both of which have a direct bearing on post-war German history. The first examines the uprising of 17 June 1953 from the standpoint of a union official, a working woman and a stripper, thus modifying the official views of East and West; the second provides a fictional reconstruction of how an independent state in southern Saxony survived for seven weeks in 1945 between evacuation by the Nazis and the arrival of occupying troops – a testimony to the ability of local Germans, unhindered by the tensions which were to lead to the Cold War, to make their own fresh start.

The view from below which is a feature of these two novels is also prominent in the recent fiction of Erich Loest (*Völker-schlachtdenkmal* 1984; *Zwiebelmuster*, 1985), Klaus Schlesinger (*Leben im Winter*, 1980), de Bruyn (*Neue Herrlichkeit*, 1984) and Monika Maron (*Flugasche*, 1981).

Among the returning exiles who settled in the Soviet zone/GDR were two dramatists, Bertolt Brecht and Friedrich Wolf, whose careers had run parallel since they wrote their first plays immediately after the First World War. The former became a figure of such popularity and influence that his work was canonised in the GDR and performed throughout the capitalist, Communist and developing worlds; the latter, who had been almost as productive, writing one of the most effective of the exile plays, *Professor Mamlock*, and holding the same political views, has been almost totally forgotten. The reason lies in their different approaches to dramatic form and audience response, which emerged clearly in a discussion after the first GDR production of *Mutter Courage und ihre Kinder*. Wolf favoured the traditional act structure and characters with whom one might readily identify (or conversely from whom one might feel repelled); Brecht, on the other hand, developed his own form of epic theatre in which dramatic illusion was subverted in order to encourage a rational, critical response to the contradictions of a social situation, indeed of life itself. The dramatists of the GDR followed Brecht's example as manifested in the work of the Berliner Ensemble, the company he founded on his return to Germany. This became a magnet not only for audiences but for playwrights keen to observe in practice techniques which would supersede the worn-out classicism cultivated in the Third Reich as well as the more well-meaning (but equally antiquated) appeal to humanitarian sentiment evident in exile drama and some of the post-war plays which developed its themes (e.g. Günther Weisenborn's *Die Illegalen*, 1946, on a German resistance group).

The three principal dramatists of the GDR, Peter Hacks (who moved from the West in 1955), Volker Braun and Heiner Müller (both of whom were employed for a time at the Berliner Ensemble) began as disciples of Brecht, supplying, it can be claimed, the works which Brecht himself might have written had he not been mainly occupied with supervising productions of plays written during exile. Only *Die Tage der Commune* (1949, première in 1956), untypical of his work in any phase, was conceived, written and performed during the GDR years, although *Turandot* (begun in the 1930s) and *Der aufhaltsame Aufstieg des Arturo Ui* (written in 1941) were first performed in 1969 (1973 in the GDR) and 1958 (1959 in the GDR) respectively.

Hacks began with historical plays in which enterprises traditionally associated with heroic initiative and enlightened despotism are viewed from a Marxist perspective: *Das Volksbuch vom Herzog Ernst* (1953, première 1967), which exposes the link between medieval heroism and feudal power structures; *Eröffnung des indischen Zeitalters* (1954, later version *Columbus, oder: Die Weltidee zu Schiffe*, première 1975), which presents the discoverer of America as a precursor of reason; *Die Schlacht bei Lobositz* (1955) and *Der Müller von Sanssouci* (1957) on the relations of Frederick the Great to his subjects and mercenary employees; and *Margarete von Aix* (1969), in which the vengeful plans of a former queen of England are opposed to the humanism embodied by her father René of Provence. Significantly, Hacks wrote only two plays with GDR settings, both of which were controversial. In *Moritz Tassow* (1965) the title figure, an impetuous eccentric, wants to introduce collectivisation at a time – 1945–6 – when the party is dividing estates into smaller units and distributing them to landless peasants; in the end the party has the last word and Tassow chooses the outsider position of writer. In *Die Sorgen und die Macht* (various versions between 1959 and 1962) a briquette factory producing shoddy goods in order to fulfil imposed norms comes into conflict with the glass factory dependent on them; harmony is ensured not only by an agreement between the factories, but also by the acceptance of Socialism by a boy from one factory who falls in love with a girl from the other. Hacks's work since is marked by the transition from dialectical drama to what he has called 'sozialistische Klassik', in which myth plays a prominent role. Besides providing versions of Aristophanes, he has updated Greek legends in *Amphitryon* (1968), *Omphale* (1970), and *Die schöne Helena* (1964), in which, as in his version of the Creation, *Adam und Eva* (première 1973), there is a tendency to reconcile an optimistic Marxism with traditional postulates of the enlightenment, apparent also in *Prexaspes* (1976), a

coded but anodyne treatment of contemporary Communist government. Hacks achieved his greatest success in both German
states with *Ein Gespräch im Hause Stein über den abwesenden Herrn
von Goethe* (première 1976), in which the status of Germany's greatest literary icon is subverted in the monologue of his most articulate lover.

Volker Braun began as a dramatist with a more drastic treatment
of the problem Hacks had approached in *Moritz Tassow*. In Braun's
Die Kipper (1972, first version entitled *Kipper Paul Bauch* 1962–5) an
unskilled worker fires his team to greater performance, causes an
accident and emerges from prison to learn that the men he had led
no longer need him. The play shows the failure to overcome the
contradiction implicit in the desire to achieve self-realisation in
work which is merely a stage in the progress towards a situation
in which such work will no longer be necessary, thanks to the
collective liberation represented by rationally planned co-
operation. The enforcement of a similar claim to individual fulfilment in work has tragic consequences in *Tinka* (1975) and *Schmitten*
(1981), in which female protagonists are unable to adjust their
aspirations to the working practices and personal prejudices of
their colleagues. Braun went on to deal with crises in the infant
Soviet system and other revolutions in *Lenins Tod* (première 1988),
Guevara oder der Sonnenstaat (1978) and *Großer Frieden* (1979), before
offering in *Die Übergangsgesellschaft* (1987) a coded treatment of the
GDR in the 1970s.

Apart from the last of these, Braun's later plays (for example
Simplex Deutsch, 1980, and *Siegfried Frauenprotokolle Deutscher
Furor*, 1986) resemble in style, breadth of historical range and depth
of political concern the more recent work of Heiner Müller, who
has succeeded in claiming the attention of directors and audiences
in both German states. On the face of it Müller's work is marked by
the same thematic emphases as Hacks and Braun (and other GDR
dramatists); his 'Produktionsstücke' (shop-floor plays) *Der Bau*
(two versions, 1963 and 1964) (based on Neutsch's *Spur der Steine*)
and *Der Lohndrücker* (1956), and his play on land reform *Die
Umsiedlerin* (published as *Die Bauern* in 1975), have GDR settings,
yet his debt to Brecht is more apparent in his radical conflation of
historical realism and revised myth. In *Philoktet* (1966) he modifies
Sophocles, who introduces Hercules as *deus ex machina* to ensure
the title figure will return home to assist the Greeks, by having
Neoptolemos murder Philoktet at the prompting of Odysseus, thus

turning the story into a parable on the conflict between *Realpolitik* and the free individual. The problem of means and ends which had preoccupied Brecht, the question whether an ideal is tainted by the shoddy means adopted to approach it, is given a radical twist not only here, but also in plays which have as their background the Soviet Union in revolution (*Zement*, 1974) or war (*Wolokolamsker Chaussee*, 1988) or the Third Reich (*Die Schlacht*, 1975) or an archetypal situation of the kind which Brecht had made the subject of *Die Maßnahme* (*Mauser*, 1970). With *Germania Tod in Berlin* (1977) and *Leben Gundlings Friedrich von Preußen Lessings Schlaf Traum Schrei* (1977) Müller depicted German history as a process in which a slavish and fratricidal mentality comes to fruition in events which echo one another from the defeat of the Romans in the Teutoburger Wald to the uprising of 1953 in the GDR. The surreal nightmarish images evident in these plays and *Hamletmaschine* (1978), which were to influence younger dramatists such as Thomas Brasch (*Rotter*, 1977) and Stefan Schütz, are developed in *Der Auftrag* (1980), *Verkommenes Ufer Medeamaterial Landschaft mit Argonauten* (1983), *Bildbeschreibung* (1985) and *Anatomie Titus Fall of Rome* (1985).

The lyric poetry of the GDR can be divided initially into works by those who continue the tradition of the party *Kampflied*, epitomised by the publicly read and sung poems of Erich Weinert, and the Socialist classicism developed by Johannes R. Becher in exile celebrations of German landscapes and major cultural figures from the past presented in sonnets and similarly strict and conventional forms. Becher, who had begun as the most strident of the Expressionists and had been brought to trial in the Weimar years for his anti-war novel *Levisite*, became as a leading figure of the Bund proletarisch-revolutionarer Schriftseller and its exile successors the most prominent German advocate of the Communist cause in literature, a role which predestined him for the office of Minister of Culture in the GDR. Yet the aesthetic conservatism of his later verse should be seen in the context not of Stalinism, but of the general trend in exile literature towards toning down or replacing the innovations of modernism in favour of more accessible forms in the service of a broad anti-Fascist front and the definition of a challenge and an alternative to the Nazi misappropriation of German culture.

Brecht too gave priority to clarity and simplicity, cultivating a 'gestische Schreibweisel' in rhymeless verse and irregular rhythms which allows an expression which is both personal and characteristically indirect. The growing laconicism of his later poetry culminates in the poems written after his return to Germany, especially the cycle *Buckower Elegien* (1953), in which ostensibly pastoral themes inspired by the surroundings of Brecht's weekend retreat on the edge of Berlin mask a concern for the future of Germany and his own role in it. It was on these foundations, rather than Becher's classicism or the modernism of Stephan Hermlin, whose contact with French resistance circles had prompted him to combine anti-Fascist commitment with the florid imagery characteristic of French symbolism and successive movements, that younger GDR poets were to build. Like the dramatists Hacks, Braun and Müller, the poets Günter Kunert, Heinz Kahlau, Kurt Bartsch and Wolf Biermann adapt Brecht's language of 'Gestus', in which a characteristic mode of action or behaviour finds expression, to new public themes and personal preoccupations. However, the course taken by the more important of these, Kunert and Biermann, indicates the impossibility in the long term of reconciling the critical rationalism of Brecht with either commitment to a public role in the context of 'really existing Socialism' or the demands of a subjectivity uneasily responding to a socio-political nexus in which former imperatives no longer have meaning. Both these poets were to leave for the West after years of official criticism and surveillance, but while the former withdrew into an understated pessimism prompted mainly by disillusionment with the 'progress' of the whole of advanced western civilisation, the latter remained for a time determined to maintain a public role despite the official ban on publication and performance and eventual expatriation, in order to proclaim a populist Socialism which could not be accommodated to the fossilised structures of the eastern bloc.

Three poets are best considered in isolation from these developments, as they each contribute to and extend in their own way the long German tradition of the humanised landscape in lyric poetry. Erich Arendt had been detached from contemporary debates during exile in Spain and Latin America, although a clear anti-Fascist commitment inspired poems written in response to the Spanish Civil War. In his later work hymnic forms are used to convey austere reflections on the spirit of Greek landscape and ancient monuments or to assess the convulsions in man's view of the cosmos brought about by scientific advance in a style increasingly concentrated and hermetic; indeed, the concentration on a few basic images (stone, sand, lava and dust) encourages comparison with Paul Celan. Peter Huchel, whose career likewise began in the 1920s and then proceeded via a loose attachment to inner emigration to the editorship of the GDR's most prominent literary magazine *Sinn und Form*, from which he was dismissed in 1962, had his roots in the melancholy landscape of Mark Brandenburg, and while he remained open to international modernism as editor and poet, his interweaving of mythical references and motifs drawn from literature and nature in densely textured ruminations recalls Loerke and Lehmann. Johannes Bobrowski achieved before his early death a reputation in the West which owes as much to his skilful handling of multiple perspectives in his two novels and numerous short stories as to his poetry, in which his homeland, the frontier of East Prussia and Lithuania, is viewed with an empathy which brings to the fore not only the characteristic features of the landscape, but also an awareness of the various ethnic groups who have populated it in uneasy condominium over a long period of history.

Another strand of GDR poetry can be traced back to the Johannes R. Becher Institute of Literature in Leipzig, where another poet of an older generation, Georg Maurer, originally from a German-speaking enclave in Romania, succeeded in adapting in odes and sonnets images marked by a restrained modernism and the expansive tone of Hölderlin and Rilke to themes which made occasional concessions to Socialist Realism. By conveying a positive view of human achievements in art, love and work he avoided confrontation with official prescriptions. Maurer has been almost ignored in the West; his influence, however, may prove to have been seminal on what has been called the 'sächsishe Dichterschule', although its members (Volker Braun, Rainer and Sarah Kirsch, Karl Mickel) went on to develop in different directions.

Braun occupies a crucial position, not only because of his prominence in all three major genres, but in his determination to push to the limit the strains induced by combining Socialist commitment, openness to international modernism and the expression of personal dissatisfaction with really existing Socialism. From the beginning his poetry is marked by an attempt to balance between conflicting impulses and loyalties, for which a Brechtian dialectic is the main vehicle, and a steadily expanding thematic and tonal range eventually provides a panoramic view of the GDR and the monuments of earlier civilisations. Gradually the strong subjective element, apparent at first as youthful hope and frustration, finds muted and tentative expression in fragmentary forms which aim to explore the factors which have contributed to angry bewilderment at the fate of utopian ideals.

Sarah Kirsch, who has lived in the West since 1977, is at first sight a lyrical talent in a more conventional mould, whose work lacks a political dimension. Her characteristic tone arises from the flowing quality of her largely unpunctuated verse, in which travel, nature and love and the ethereal metamorphoses of the moods associated with them are central. Yet the emphasis on the intimate, the microscopic and the local is grounded in a melancholy awareness of overshadowing global issues. Other poets on the margin of this 'Saxon' group include Reiner Kunze, in whose work laconicism became largely a transparent code for a firm stance against the Communist system, Heinz Czechowski and Wulf Kirsten, both of whom have supplied further variations on the landscape poem, with special attention to the ravages of war – Czechowski witnessed the destruction of Dresden as a child – and of the contemporary environment, thus contributing to an ecological consciousness of growing pan-German significance.

The convergence of the two German literatures over recent years is as apparent in poetry as in the other genres, but in some respects the GDR lyric has retained a special character in its awareness of literary forebears and contemporary fellow-writers, epitomised by the numerous portrait poems by all the poets mentioned, in which the reader experiences a series of wide-ranging dialogues.

Since unification it is natural to ask whether the term 'literature of the GDR' can have any further meaning except as a historical category. Even before the *Wende* or historical turning point marked by November 1989 it became more and more difficult to define, in the face of growing exodus to the West of most of the writers critical of 'really existing Socialism'. It seems reasonable to include as part of GDR literature works by such writers composed after their departure which take the GDR as their subject, as well as those works produced in any part of Germany since the *Wende* which do likewise. One would have to count amongst them the dramas *Schlußchor* by Botho Strauß and *Iphigenie in Freiheit* by Volker Braun, the stories *Die Birnen von Ribbeck* by F.C. Delius, *Auf Sand gebaut* by Stefan Heym and the novel *Stille Zeile sechs* by Monika

Maron. Christa Wolf's *Was bleibt*, on a brief invasion of privacy by the Stasi, occupies a special position as a scapegoat text in a literary debate to which reference is made in the next chapter. Other writers, who underwent much more intensive surveillance (Erich Loest, Reiner Kunze, Wolf Biermann) have documented its extent since the files became available to public scrutiny. Martin Walser's *Die Verteidigung der Kindheit*, which traces the life of a lawyer from Dresden who studies and qualifies in West Berlin, then makes a career in the Federal Republic, but retains an irrational attachment to his mother who remains in the East, demonstrates the human cost of the division of Germany for those who were not content to accept it. So far the most interesting and symptomatic responses to the *Wende* have been in the form of essays, reportages and auto-biographies by a number of figures in this chapter and poems by Heiner Müller and Volker Braun.

8

The Literature of the Federal Republic of Germany and the Second Austrian Republic from 1968 to 1990

The student movement was not confined to Germany, but in other countries (mainly the USA and France) it was conditioned by other factors (in the USA by the war in Vietnam and by the civil rights campaign, in France by dissatisfaction with the personal rule of President de Gaulle). In Germany it can be interpreted as an extreme manifestation of a general shift to the left which led to the formation first of a Great Coalition of the CDU (hitherto the main ruling party) and the SPD, then of a coalition of SPD and FDP, which continued under Chancellors Willy Brandt and Helmut Schmidt until 1982. The late 1960s saw a vast expansion in higher education throughout the West, and much student protest was directed against the fossilised structures, antiquated courses and authoritarian government of the universities, as well as against the inadequate facilities available to a rapidly rising student population. However, expansion meant the end of the university as an élite institution inducing conformity to a rigid ethos and resulted in the questioning of norms in all aspects of political, social and personal life. A further complicating factor was the generation gap, which in Germany was exacerbated by the involvement of the older generation in the Third Reich and its consequent suppression of this experience in the early post-war period. Furthermore, the demand for the revision of the curriculum led to the rediscovery in some subjects, especially *Germanistik*, of neglected areas such as working-class writing and the left-wing literature of the Weimar

Republic. Insofar as the student movement aimed to overturn capitalism and the bourgeois-individualist work ethic which supports it, it failed totally, and the withdrawal from political activity of many students and intellectuals during the early 1970s into a semi-private area where an alternative culture and life-style could be pursued on the margins of society has been interpreted as the consequence of frustration and disillusionment with the course the movement had taken. Certainly, this mood led to the foundation of terrorist groups who despaired of transforming society by any means other than violence, and the activities of this tiny extreme minority prompted counter-measures which for a time encouraged the view that the state was arrogating to itself powers which would undermine civil liberties, including the free expression of opinion. However, many causes supported by the student movement remained the subject of debate at all levels of society and led to changes in the law, while the democratic system at the centre and at local level remained intact, indeed was given new life through the formation of new pressure groups ('Bürgerinitiativen') which either grew out of the student movement or independently of it. If therefore the student movement fragmented into a number of conflicting factions occupied with fruitless theoretical debate and increasingly eccentric provocations of majority opinion, that is only one aspect of a process which can be traced to the present, in which a consensus, however precarious, is maintained on the need to combine and harmonise the productivity demanded by the successful operation of a market economy with aspirations to individual freedom. In the end the two are seen as ideally interdependent, as long as the development of high technology allows greater leisure even to the employed, and the obstacles to self-realisation are no longer political or social but economic or existential. The difficulties which accompany this process arise mainly in the area of personal relations and apply not only to marginalised minorities with which artist-intellectuals identify, but to all social groups, as they attempt to reconcile the mental demands made by employment in a sophisticated high-tech ambience, the temptations of consumerism and the competing blandishments of the media with an awareness of global problems and the traditional expectations of what constitutes a proper role in the family and the community. (Of course this social diagnosis applies only to the western democracies at the close of the 1980s when employment is relatively high.)

If the history of literature in the Federal Republic is viewed against this background, it is possible to provide definitions of the politicisation of literature and the ensuing trend of *neue Subjektivität* (new subjectivity) and see them in clearer perspective. The advocates of *neue Subjektivität* did not see their work as apolitical, while most of the writers who took up political issues of the moment were well aware of the difference between their work and direct political action.

The novels which describe the student movement were retrospective and naively adopted the model of the *Bildungsroman* (Uwe Timm, *Heißer Sommer*, 1974; Peter Schneider, *Lenz*, 1973), while the most impressive examples of politically inspired literature were prompted by later phases of protest and the ensuing reaction: the *Radikalenerlaß*, a law of 1972 which barred from state employment those deemed to hold extreme political views (Peter Schneider, . . . *und schon bist du ein Verfassungsfeind*, 1975) and the anti-terrorist campaign which culminated in 'der deutsche Herbst' of 1977 (Heinrich Böll, *Die verlorene Ehre der Katharina Blum*, 1974, and *Fürsorgliche Belagerung*,1979). Furthermore, the experience of the public dimension of the student movement plays only a marginal role in works characteristic of *neue Subjektivität* or *neue Innerlichkeit* (new subjectivity) – Nicolas Born, *Die erdabgewandte Seite der Geschichte* (1976), Elisabeth Plessen, *Mitteilung an den Adel* (1976), Bernward Vesper, *Die Reise* (1977), Karin Struck, *Klassenliebe* (1973) – some of which can also be linked to depictions of the urban underground and the alternative scene in the novels of Hubert Fichte and Peter-Paul Zahl.

The subjectivity which here finds expression differs from its more conventional form in the autobiographical works of representatives of an older generation: Elias Canetti's *Die gerettete Zunge* (1977), *Die Fackel im Ohr* (1980) and *Das Augenspiel* (1985), Wolfgang Koeppen's *Jugend* (1976), Ernst Jünger's diaries *Siebzig verweht* (1981) and Max Frisch's semi-autobiographical stories *Montauk* (1975), *Blaubart* (1976) and *Der Mensch erscheint im Holozän* (1979), yet it has its precursors in older writers (Nossack, Frisch, Hildesheimer) discussed above. Indeed, *neue Subjektivität* has received different diagnoses and been traced to different roots. It can be interpreted as a reaction against the 'death' of literature and the concomitant elevation in status of documentary investigation proclaimed in the journal *Kursbuch* 15, and as a consequence of withdrawal into the private sphere by those whose attempt to reconstruct society had failed. (*Kursbuch*, in which literature took second place to reportage and sociological investigation, became staple reading for the generation of 1968.) Any assessment of its relation to the student movement must depend on one's view of whether the public dimension of the movement was ever of great significance, at least in literature. It is doubtful whether any advanced industrial society could or can be transformed in the spirit which initially imbued the movement, however convinced the students were that Marxist theory and practice would provide valid solutions to economic and social deficiencies. In fact, the thought which supported and was generated by the student movement was concerned as much with the liberation of the psyche and interpersonal relations as with the reform of a rigid social structure and economic organisation; indeed, the criticism levelled against the latter was based primarily on concepts developed by the early Marx and then linked to radical psychoanalysis by Herbert Marcuse, and exploitation and alienation were terms ready to hand to define whatever hindered the ultimate ideal of self-realisation. Yet extremism and disintegration characterised the private as well as the public dimensions of the student movement. The lack of a common view of the self and the manifest differences between selves, actual and potential, meant the process of self-realisation could take the form of a complex quest, a process of action and reaction which might end in isolation, confusion and breakdown. The more radical examples of *neue Subjektivität* demonstrate the dangers inherent in this process, the aporia of emancipation (Born, *Die erdabgewandte Seite der Geschichte*; Brinkmann, *Keiner weiß mehr*, 1968; Struck, *Klassenliebe* and other novels; Theobaldy, *Spanische Wände*, 1981; and Vesper, *Die Reise*), while others end in the precarious attachment of the protagonist to an alternative community (Schneider, *Lenz*; Martin Walser, *Die Gallistl'sche Krankheit*, 1972) or in his or her illness or insanity, which may be implicitly or explicitly diagnosed as socially or domestically conditioned, (Fritz Zorn, *Mars*, 1977; Kipphardt, *März*, 1976; Dieter Kühn, *Die Kammer des schwarzen Lichts*, 1984; Adolf Muschg's *Albissers Grund*, 1974 and *Das Licht und der Schlüssel*, 1984).

During the 1980s two major authors, Peter Handke and Botho Strauß, develop these concerns on the basis of an awareness of these dilemmas and false solutions, and what had too often been a straightforward confession of personal malaise is gradually transformed into a more distanced account of the processes which lead to a psychological cul-de-sac, accompanied by ever more articulate diagnosis and suggestions for therapy. Handke's later work is best considered in an Austrian context. Strauß's ruminatory explorations of self-absorption, identity crisis and obsessive emotional dependence in *Marlenes Schwester* (1975), *Die Widmung* (1977), *Rumor* (1980) are in their style quintessential examples of 'new subjectivity', yet implicitly criticise its excesses in the egocentricity of their central figures, while in the aphoristic *Paare Passanten* (1981) and *Niemand anderes* (1987) he switches between a registration of the surface phenomena of contemporary urban life and reflective passages in an attempt to reveal the causes of the spiritual malaise of which his fictional and dramatic characters provide symptoms. The development from the political commitments of the late 1960s to the search for a new form of personal stability in the 1980s corresponds to a *Tendenzwende* or shift of view within society as a whole and leads to a reassertion of intellectual traditions which had lain dormant and ignored in the emancipatory enthusiasms of the student movement and its aftermath and a consequent preoccupation with literary precursors. This last new direction transcends the inner German frontier and therefore includes, besides the GDR works mentioned in the last chapter, Hildesheimer's *Marbot* (1981), Harig's *Rousseau* (1978), Peter Schneider's *Lenz*, Gert Hofmann's *Gespräch über Balzac's Pferd* (1981), Adolf Muschg's *Kellers Abend* (1975), Hermann Lenz's *Erinnerung an Eduard* (Mörike) (1981), Peter Härtling's *Hölderlin* (1976), *Niembsch oder Der Stillstand* (on Lenau) (1964), *Die dreifache Maria* (on Mörike) (1982) and *Waiblingers Augen* (1987), Dieter Kühn's *Ich Wolkenstein* (1977), *Der Parzival des Wolfram von Eschenbach* (1977) and two biographies of Neidhart von Reuenthal (1981 and 1988), and Grass's *Das Treffen in Telgte* (1979).

There were forms of realism marginal to the student movement and the agitatory and subjective forms of literature which were its primary and secondary products. A 'new realism' which aimed at a spontaneous and intense experience of reality at the expense of rational, social and psychological penetration of the broader forces which influence daily lives developed under the influence of Dieter Wellershoff. Basing themselves on Camus, the *nouveau roman* and the *Sekundenstil* of the Naturalists, the members of this Cologne group (Günter Seuren, Nicolas Born, Günter Herburger, Gisela Elsner and Rolf Dieter Brinkmann) later drew away from their mentor and from one another. Wellershoff applied film techniques to novels which centre on figures who under the pressures of life in the city resort to crime (*Die Schattengrenze*, 1969; *Einladung an alle*, 1972; *Die Schönheit des Schimpansen*, 1977; and *Der Sieger nimmt alles*, 1983). Herburger combined microscopic realism with large-scale futuristic dystopias which extrapolate observed tendencies in contemporary German society: *Jesus in Osaka* (1970) and the Thuja trilogy (1977–92). Gisela Elsner, having attained overnight fame with a grotesque portrayal of family life in *Die Riesenzwerge* (1964), continued with *Der Nachwuchs* (1970) and *Der Punktsieg* (1977) in the same vein, which shades off into more conventional forms of social realism in *Das Berührungsverbot* (1971), *Abseits* (1982) and *Das Windei* (1987). Brinkmann's short career culminated in *Rom. Blicke* (1979), in which words and photographs are juxtaposed in an attempt to portray a metropolis from the point of view of a radically alienated consciousness.

It is ironical that in the GDR the efforts of the ruling party to encourage the portrayal of the work-place by workers and writers bore little fruit, despite the proclamation of the 'Bitterfelder Weg' at conferences held in an industrial town near Leipzig in 1959 and 1964, yet a vigorous *Arbeiterliteratur* developed in the Federal Republic when local initiatives in the Ruhr led to the formation of the Dortmund Gruppe 61, eventually dissolved in 1972. Its most prominent member was Max von der Grün, who based his early novels *Männer in zweifacher Nacht* (1962) and *Irrlicht und Feuer* (1963) on his experience of work as a miner. Here and in *Stellenweise Glatteis* (1973), on a lorry fitter, and *Zwei Briefe an Pospischiel* (1968), on a power-station worker, Grün focuses on the growing alienation of a figure who fails in an attempt to create solidarity on the shop-floor in order to challenge the silent collusion of management and unions when particular abuses (inadequate safety standards and the installation of a bugging device) come to light. This type of formally conventional social realism was also practised by Franz Josef Degenhardt, Bernt Engelmann, Uwe Timm, Gerd Fuchs, Christian Geissler, F.C. Delius and Otto F. Walter, most of whom were associated with the publishing venture Autorenedition.

Meanwhile a more radical fraction within Gruppe 61 broke off to form Werkkreis Literatur der Arbeitswelt in 1969, establishing branches ('Werkstätten') throughout the Federal Republic with the aim of fostering a political consciousness which would produce changes in organisational structures and working practices. To this end the convention of the solitary protagonist battling against alienating apathy and sinister machinations (occasionally linked to neo-Nazism) in a plot spiced with sentiment and sensationalism was abandoned in favour of documentary and reportage, modelled on the committed journalism of Egon Erwin Kisch in the Weimar Republic. Günter Wallraff, the most dedicated member of the group, aimed at maximum authenticity by gaining hands-on experience of working environments as a disguised employee. While closer to investigative journalism than to literature, Wallraff's series of collections (*Wir brauchen Dich. Als Arbeiter im deutschen Industrieleben*, 1966; *13 unerwünschte Reportagen*, 1969; *Neue Reportagen. Untersuchungen und Lehrbeispiele*, 1972) provide a broad cross-section of working routines in the Federal Republic and demonstrate the human price paid for the efficiency and productivity of the economic miracle. His resort to supporting documentation and statistics and sober style do not preclude a subjective element, as he concentrates on the mechanical tasks which leave the piece-worker no room for personal initiative or interest in the end product. Some of the reportages appear dated now that the main problem confronting the workers is redundancy caused by automation, while many of the situations he describes appear merely occasions for comedy if one ignores his intellectual utopianism and morally dubious methods of infiltration. The tendency to hector and repeat is less evident in those investigations which expose management strategies (*Wie hätten wir's gerne*, 1975) and Germany's principal tabloid (*Der Aufmacher. Der Mann, der bei 'Bild' Hans Esser war*, 1977; *Zeugen der Anklage. Die 'Bild'-Beschreibung wird fortgesetzt*, 1979), in which he takes up themes which were central to the campaigns of the student movement and its sympathisers (F.C. Delius, *Wir Unternehmer*, 1966, *Unsere Siemenswelt*, 1972; Böll, *Berichte zur Gesinnungslage der Nation*, 1975).

The treatment of the Third Reich in the fiction of this period can be related to the formal approaches which writers develop in response to contemporary events and the changing intellectual climate. An effective fusion of experimental and documentary techniques marks Alexander Kluge's *Schlachtbeschreibung* (1964), which seeks to provide by means of a montage of anecdotal material and documentation an insight into the battle of Stalingrad which adds a further dimension to the historical record, and Manfred Franke's *Mordverläufe 9/10.XI.38* (1973), which performs the same task in following the course of the pogrom of that date

('Reichskristallnacht') in a provincial town. The child's point of view directs the reader's response in more conventionally narrated accounts of crucial events (for example, the outbreak of the Second World War in the first volume (*Die erste Polka*, 1975) of Horst Bienek's 'Gleiwitzer Trilogie') and moral dilemmas (as in Siegfried Lenz's *Deutschstunde*, 1968, in which the tribulations of an artist, modelled on Emil Nolde, who is forbidden to paint are interwoven with a boy's growing alienation from his policeman father, who dutifully attempts to enforce the ban). From these it is only a short step to the many *Väterromane*, in which writers retrospectively explore their relations to their fathers, all of whom belong to the generation which had reached adulthood shortly before or during the Third Reich. There had been strong allegorical elements in those early treatments of the Third Reich which placed it in a metaphysical framework (Kasack, Andres, Langgässer, Thomas Mann), and in the following phase writers concentrated on the moral and political dimensions of the Nazi phenomenon. Now, however, in accordance with the trend towards 'new subjectivity', as writers delve into childhood memories of their domestic and educational background and growth in awareness, a psychological approach is dominant in Bernward Vesper's *Die Reise* (1977), Günter Seuren's *Abschied von einem Mörder* (1980), Christoph Meckel's *Suchbild* (1980), Peter Henisch's *Die kleine Figur meines Vaters* (1975), Peter Härtling's *Nachgetragene Liebe* (1980) and Ludwig Harig's *Ordnung ist das ganze Leben* (1986). The attitudes which emerge are varied – the first and second can be described as bitter recollections of active Nazis, while the third and fourth concern fellow travellers enabled by their professions (writing and photography) to maintain a distance from the commitments and horrors of the time, and Härtling and Harig offer rounded portraits inspired by affection – but all throw light on the authoritarian structures which public and family life shared during their childhood. Women writers provide similar insights (see below) and the theme is also present in contemporary GDR literature (C. Wolf, *Kindheitsmuster*).

Meanwhile the *Zeitroman*, which had brought German literature international recognition in the 1960s, retained its range, quality and appeal. Works which make minimum concessions to modernism and offer a panoramic view of German society often in the form of the family saga include Hans Werner Richter's *Rose rot, Rose weiß* (1971), *Die Stunde der falschen Triumphe* (1981) and *Ein Julitag* (1982), Ralph Giordano's *Die Bertinis* (1982), Dieter

Lattmann's *Die Brüder* (1985) and the novels of Manfred Bieler, Heinz Piontek and Hermann Lenz. Such accessible works differ profoundly from Peter Weiss's *Die Ästhetik des Widerstands* (1975, 1978, 1981), which appears as an erratic block in the literary landscape, although with it its author regained a respect which he had largely lost with his later documentary dramas. An ambitious combination of political and aesthetic theory, would-be autobiography (in the sense that it recounts a life the author wishes in retrospect had been his own) and proletarian *Bildungsroman*, the three monumental volumes tackle a thesis central to cultural debates on the left throughout the century, that ruling elites have based their hegemony not only on political and military power, but also on the control of knowledge and culture. The relation between artistic creativity and power, the function of art in the context of class conflict are the themes implied in the lengthy discussions of cultural artefacts, whether the Pergamon altar, Picasso's *Guernica*, Géricault's *The Raft of the Medusa* or the novels of Kafka. Weiss offers Marxist insights into works to which they are normally considered irrelevant; in an analysis of *Das Schloß*, for example, the castle is equated with the crumbling structures of capitalism and K. defined as a proletarian hero. However misplaced such an interpretation may appear, it allows Weiss to integrate into a Marxist canon the classics of modernism, which had been dismissed as formalist testimonies to the decadence of bourgeois society by Stalinist critics; thus not only Kafka, but also Joyce, Schönberg, Stravinsky, Klee and Picasso all make their contribution to a 'kämpfende Ästhetik'. Weiss traces the trials and tribulations of the left between 1937 and 1945, as his proletarian protagonist passes from Germany to Czechoslovakia, Spain, France and Sweden, gaining contact with numerous historical figures including Brecht, members of resistance groups and the exiled Social Democratic and Communist parties, but remaining a shadowy figure, a vehicle for the exploration of abstract themes.

Walser's work maintained an ironic stance *vis-à-vis* contemporary extremist follies, tempered by a sympathy for central characters whose awareness of the passage of time prompts them to indulge in them. The problems of Walser's always male protagonists, as they negotiate a series of intricate, tortuous and ultimately unsatisfying sexual, social and professional relationships, merely exacerbate a condition in which existential fears and psychological vulnerability create a need for an inner life which may act as a bastion against a hostile world, yet the necessary adjustments to reality are handled with such ironical verve, arising from the contrast between the inner man and the mask he is forced to show to the world, that a melancholy undercurrent only emerges sporadically. Usually threatening disasters are circumvented and a precarious survival, often with the help of a long-suffering but understanding wife, is ensured. Since his brief divergence from this basic orientation during the politicised 1960s Walser has provided a series of variations on this predicament in *Jenseits der Liebe* (1976), *Ein fliehendes Pferd*, (1978), *Seelenarbeit* (1979), *Das Schwanenhaus* (1980), *Brandung* (1985) (the best German example of the campus novel), *Brief an Lord Liszt* (1982) and *Jagd* (1988).

Johnson's *Jahrestage* (1970, 1971, 1973, 1983) hinges on the crucial year 1968, marked by the climax of the Vietnam war (at least in its impact on American and world opinion) and the invasion of Czechoslovakia by the Warsaw Pact, both epitomising East–West tensions. It also represents a turning-point in the *Zeitroman*, looking back to earlier treatments by Johnson and others of the east–west dichotomy and the generation gap, made especially virulent in Germany by the problem of coming to terms with the memory of the Third Reich. Johnson focuses on these themes by means of multiple perspectives and a strong documentary element, anticipating a similar combination of theme and form in later novels, such as Christa Wolf's *Kindheitsmuster*. Johnson's cool neutrality conveyed in a mannered, rough-hewn prose could hardly be further from the rampant self-absorption and flowing style of *neue Subjektivität*. Siegfried Lenz, a writer of similar temperament and provincial north German roots, remains even more conservative in style after *Deutschstunde*, but by concentrating in *Das Vorbild* (1973), *Heimatmuseum* (1978), *Der Verlust* (1981) and *Exerzierplatz* (1985) on a few figures in a restricted setting he reflects changing attitudes to social and political questions as they affect much wider sections of the community.

Böll remained true to himself to the end, although his novels became increasingly diffuse in form. In *Gruppenbild mit Dame* (1971) he created a heroine who embodies the values he held most dear, embedding her life in a rich social microcosm and reconstructing her personality by means of interviews undertaken by a distanced narrator, whose impersonality is ensured by the abbreviation 'Verf.' *Die verlorene Ehre der Katharina Blum* (1974), although centred on a similar female protagonist, is a much more concentrated work and perhaps the most lasting fiction to emerge from the political phase of literature in the Federal Republic. However, as a defence of the inviolability of the private sphere it has little bearing on the ideological struggles on the radical margins of its political life. At its centre is not the traditional conflict between 'Geist' and 'Macht', the intellectual and the state – a perennial theme of German literature – but that between genuine and instinctive fellow-feeling and a stupefying mass medium which alienates ordinary people from their real interests and their true selves. Yet although Böll's interest in theoretical debates on revolutionary change was minimal, he was seen here to join forces with the student movement, for which the Springer press was a main target. *Fürsorgliche Belagerung* extends the defence of privacy by examining the predicament of all the members of an extended family divided by age and economic interest. Here Böll avoids a simple confrontation of political extremism and state power and instead concentrates on the wide spectrum of opinion represented in a varied cast of characters caught between these polarities, denying a simple identification of a person with his or her social role. Böll shows that extraordinary measures of the kind taken against terrorism during 'der deutsche Herbst' can release an insidious poison into the body politic which undermines social and domestic cohesion. Finally, in the semi-dramatic *Frauen vor Flußlandschaft* (1985) he offers a threnody on the malign effects on personal relations of the political culture of the economic miracle.

In Grass's work apocalyptic fears become more and more evident, as he adopts a Cassandra-like role in his public pronouncements. His response to the socio-political crisis in west German society between 1968 and 1977 finds expression in *örtlich betäubt* (1969) and *Aus dem Tagebuch einer Schnecke* (1972), which can be seen as parallel works, for while the first contrasts the middle-aged school teacher Starusch with his hot-headed pupil Scherbaum, who aims to challenge the bourgeois complacency of the habitués of West Berlin's most elegant café by incinerating a dog in protest against the Vietnam war, the second retraces the author's participation in the general election campaign of 1969, in which the SPD became for the first time the senior partner in a government coalition, initiating that gradual social transformation symbolised by the path of the snail and advocated by the author in opposition to the demand for volcanic upheaval made by the radical students. The historical scope of Grass's fiction, already broad, is steadily expanded. His deep concern with Germany's cultural past and its bearing on the present is reflected in the speech on Albrecht Dürer in *Aus dem Tagebuch einer Schnecke*, in the significance accorded to the folk tale 'Vom Fischer und syne Frau' and the Grimms' fairy tales in *Der Butt* (1977) and *Die Rättin* (1986), and above all in the comparisons implied in *Das Treffen in Telgte* between the relations of 'Geist' und 'Macht' during the Thirty Years War and in the present, when the position of Gruppe 47 in the initial post-war years could no longer be maintained and its dissolution became inevitable. In *Kopfgeburten* (1980) he exposed the well-meaning liberalism of a young school-teacher couple with reservations about the wisdom of procreation to the teeming life and ineradicable poverty of India, while a cosmic view of ecological catastrophe and nuclear holocaust is offered in *Die Rättin*. However, it is in *Der Butt* that Grass presents his most comprehensive account of human development; in a richly textured web of myth and history he traces the conflict between the sexes in an account of nine female cooks from the Stone Age to the present whose biographies correspond to the nine months of his wife's pregnancy. Considered as a contribution to the feminist debate the device has proved more controversial than was perhaps intended, for while the majority of the historical women are portrayed as hapless victims of male hegemony, radical feminism is ridiculed in the 'Vatertag' episode and the subtext makes an explicit connection between male domination and aggression and an inventiveness which has marked the progress of civilisation, thus insinuating that women cannot occupy man's place without severing that connection and bringing progress to a halt.

The term *Frauenliteratur* covers a series of partially overlapping definitions: literature by men about women, literature by women, literature aimed at women and all literature about women, and a feminist stance is possible in all four categories. Although female writers have been active in Germany since the early Middle Ages and although feminist themes appear in German literature since the eighteenth century, contemporary German feminism can be described as an offshoot of the student movement and has had repercussions in German society far beyond the literary landscape. The most striking features of German literary feminism are the variety of positions adopted *vis-à-vis* female self-realisation and the personal and professional relations in which women engage and the formal strategies adopted to convey these themes. Women writers of an older generation (Marieluise Kaschnitz, Luise Rinser, Ingeborg Drewitz) recognised the conflict of independence and subjectivity with traditional female roles but accepted its inevitability in their lives and their writing. Women writers of the exile and the early years of the GDR, of whom Anna Seghers is representative, saw the problem of female emancipation in the context of the struggle against Nazism (or Fascism in other parts of the world), to which more often than not it had to be subordinated, or, according to the Marxist model, against the background of class conflict, the end of which would create the right conditions for the self-realisation of both sexes. The writer who made the most substantial contribution to the themes and styles of more recent writing, before the women's movement of the 1960s had set a new agenda, was Ingeborg Bachmann, in her radio play *Der gute Gott von Manhattan*, her stories 'Ein Schritt nach Gomorrha' and 'Undine geht' and her unfinished novel cycle *Todesarten*. *Malina* (1971), its overture, traces the failure of an unnamed narrator to find and express a female identity by means of memory-work which attempts to come to terms with the trauma of childhood, personified by a father-figure who in her dreams threatens, rapes and kills her and stands for the social forces which prevent self-realisation; instead, she is eventually absorbed by her male alter ego Malina. She projects all her hopes for a fulfilled emotional life on to the 'real' male figure Ivan, an average family man with whom she has an affair, and for a time is freed from her obsessions and comes close to the utopia of limitless love and freedom adumbrated in the *Märchen* of the princess of Kargan. Ivan, however, forces her into the traditional female role defined by housework, mothering and sexual availability and ignores the rational part of her personality represented by Malina. She seeks to integrate male and female, intellect and emotion, but Malina demands that she kill Ivan and his children, that is banish them from her life. This allegorisation of female psychology points to the loss of feminity which ensues when a woman makes claims that go beyond a role defined by men. In the following almost complete *Der Fall Franza* (1978) Bachmann links the same problem more explicitly with the perpetuation of Fascist attitudes. The protagonist Franziska is reduced by her husband, a Viennese psychiatrist, to an object of scientific interest, a clinical case deprived of positive qualities. She flees to her childhood home, then accompanies her brother to the north African desert, only to find there a world even more deeply marked by male hostility, from which only death can provide an escape. When a former concentration camp doctor whom she consults in Cairo refuses her request to kill her she dies in sordid circumstances in Gizeh as an act of protest against a society in which the vulnerable, the eccentric and the weak, who include women, Jews and Australian aboriginals, are oppressed. The surviving sketches for the next part of the cycle, *Requiem für Fanny Goldmann* (1978), concern a famous actress, whose lover exploits her in order to make a career and betrays their intimacy by describing their relationship in a marketable book.

The search for a female identity remains the central theme of German feminist literature. Women writers are not content to focus on professionalisation and consequent economic independence, which along with the pill are the main factors in the liberation of women in the West from traditional role models. Professionalisation can lead to deformations as damaging as enforced domesticity in a patriarchal household, as some of the novels of Gabriele Wohmann, Margrit Schriber, Gerlind Reinshagen and Elfriede Jelinek indicate. The more distinctive and radical treatments of feminist issues, however, while giving due weight to social conditioning, trace quests which take place on the margins of a society which perpetuates patriarchal values in the name of competition and material productivity. In some instances the alienation produced by these values can be total, leaving only the retreat to death (Bachmann), Lesbianism (Verena Stefan, Christa Reinig) and a mythical hypostatisation of motherhood (Karin Struck, *Die Mutter*). The strong confessional element in German women's writing, the urge to authenticity which informs it, the emphasis on familial influences and personal relationships, give it an important place in the 'new subjectivity' of the 1970s. It is significant that in works of this type, parents (usually of the Nazi generation) assume dimensions which overshadow other persons, including husbands and lovers, in the lives of the (often autobiographical) protagonist (Elisabeth Plessen, *Mitteilung an den Adel*, 1976; Barbara Bronnen, *Die Tochter*, 1980; Brigitte Schwaiger, *Lange Abwesenheit*, 1980; Jutta Schutting, *Der Vater*, 1980; Ruth Rehmann, *Der Mann auf der Kanzel*, 1979; Karin Struck, *Zwei Frauen*, 1983 (father); Elfriede Jelinek, *Die Klavierspielerin*, 1983; Waltraud Anna Mitgutsch, *Die Züchtigung*, 1985; Karin Struck, *Die Mutter*, 1975; Helga M. Novak, *Die Eisheiligen*, 1979; Gabriele Wohmann, *Ausflug mit der Mutter* 1976 (mother)).

Although all these writers make the crucial distinction between sex and gender – in one instance (the GDR anthology *Blitz aus heiterm Himmel*, 1975, containing contributions by Christa Wolf and Sarah Kirsch) base on it a series of variations on the theme of sex change – female sexuality, both hetero- and homosexual, is not ignored; indeed, in the work of Elfriede Jelinek (especially *Lust*, 1989) it is given a scope which allows woman a role as subject and object of lust. More often female erotic power is seen as just part of a potential creativity which might find expression in all aspects of private and public life, provided women are not cut off from the springs of their true feminity. In order to discover those springs some writers resort to myths from various sources in the belief that they provide archetypes of a primeval human nature since distorted by the instrumental reason that has ensured both material advances and a growth in man's destructive capacity. Such distortion is evident in those myths which depict the supersession of matriarchal by patriarchal values. The most ambitious works in which myth is harnessed to feminist themes are Christa Wolf's *Kassandra* and Irmtraud Morgner's *Amanda* (see Chapter 6), but Barbara Frischmuth's trilogy *Die Mystifikationen der Sophie Silber* (1976), *Amy oder die Metamorphose* (1978) and *Kai und die Liebe zu den Modellen* (1979) and the work Gertrud Leutenegger are equally relevant, as well as Stefan Schütz's *Medusa* (1986). In Frischmuth's novels elementary fairy spirits originating in the Alps ensure access to mother, earth and death goddesses, whose positive role is also evident in Leutenegger's dramatic poem *Lebewohl*. *Gute Reise* (1980), which gives the myth of Gilgamesch a new interpretation.

The strong presence of myth and legend in German literature has its roots in Classicism, in which myth is as prominent as in the art of the Italian Renaissance, and in Romanticism, which initiated a preoccupation with German folklore and legend which gradually developed nationalist overtones. The contemporary interest results from a post-Nietzschean and post-Freudian belief that myth is related to the chthonic depths of the psyche and that the· traditional Christian framework for understanding human aspirations and the dangers which threaten them is no longer adequate. As we have seen, Greek myth was conceived by GDR writers in Marxist terms as an instrument for the exposure of those forces which inspire and hamper man's conquest of nature and the man-made obstacles to his self-realisation within a society. With the 1970s and 1980s however, a more diffuse mythical conscious-ness gains ground in both German states, which can be related to the cult of the subjective and the irrational. Here the aim is to bring to light a mystery which is obscured by reflection on the course of man's social progress through history and may be revealed by self-communion and intimate contact with the phenomena of nature.

In the later work of Peter Handke what began as awareness of and rebellion against social conditioning by the imposition of linguistic formulae has developed to become a permanent exploration of the self through its multifarious responses to the world (or of the world through the self) unhampered by abstract commitments and the practical accommodations of domestic and professional life. All Handke's protagonists are in flight from normality and often signal their break with it by a motiveless crime; they include the goalkeeper in *Die Angst des Tormanns beim Elfmeter* (1970), the press attaché in *Die Stunde der wahren Empfindung* (1975), the young man with literary ambitions in *Falsche Bewegung* (1975), the alienated wife in *Die linkshändige Frau* (1976), the geologist in *Langsame Heimkehr* (1979), the teacher and amateur archaeologist in *Der Chinese des Schmerzes* (1983), the narrator in *Die Wiederholung* (1986) and the motley group of drop-outs in *Die Abwesenheit* (1987). Handke's characters, projections of his own ego, are hardly social beings who relate to one another. While he has been seen as the most prominent advocate of 'new subjectivity', the reader gains little sense of a concrete self but of the author as medium, a camera eye registering a series of snap-shots conveying a silent, frozen reality. His hypersensitivity leads to a growing detachment which is occasionally accompanied by revulsion from what in the opinion of most would be considered the stuff of life. Its stylistic consequence is an artificial, ceremoni-ous tone, a converse with nature which is marked by both micro-scopic precision and ritualisation, for which Handke finds analogies in admired writers of the past, references to whom fill his ruminative notebooks *Das Gewicht der Welt* (1977), *Das Ende des Flanierens* (1980), *Die Geschichte des Bleistifts* (1982) and *Phantasien der Wiederholung* (1983). The crossing of thresholds and frontiers becomes a key image, especially in *Der Chinese des Schmerzes* and *Die Wiederholung*, yet the expansion of awareness which this implies does not transcend the real world and Handke is forced to make a virtue out of the repetition ('Wiederholung', another key term) of attempts to assign significance to the ordinary;

consequently the further development of this variety of 'new subjectivity' must be uncertain.

The dissolution of plot which follows from the exclusion of human inter-action takes extreme form in the novels of the German Brigitte Kronauer (*Frau Mühlenbeck im Gehäus*, 1980; *Rita Münster*, 1983; *Berittener Bogenschütze*, 1986; and *Die Frau in den Kissen*, 1990), who contrives a diffuse pattern of delicate perceptions and intricate reflections which culminate in dazzling but transient epiphanies in which a figure explores the possibilities of grasping reality and its own identity. These features also define the iridescent prose of the Swiss Gertrud Leutenegger in *Vorabend* (1975), *Ninive* (1977), *Gouverneur* (1981) and *Meduse* (1988) and the work of two other Austrians, Gerhard Roth and Peter Rosei. Roth began with *Die autobiographie des albert einstein* (1972) and *Der Wille zur Krankheit* (1973), explorations of mental illness which allow an eccentric view of reality to emerge; the experience of the protagonists is registered in short, disparate units which are also a feature of the later fiction, in which mental disorientation is marginal. The remark of one of these figures: 'Ich litt an meinen Wahrnehmungen wie an einer Krankheit' (i.e. 'I suffered from my perceptions as if from an illness'), can be related to the sense the reader gains of threatening malevolence beneath the idyllic surface of the rural settings of his novels. The flight from the everyday to rural and exotic locations, a theme as consistent in the work of Roth and Rosei as in that of Handke, proves futile, because dissatisfaction with normality has as much to do with a personal view of the world suffused by existential fears from which there is no escape, as with the deficiencies of normality and its alternatives. These, however, undermine any expectation of finding in rural community and landscape a haven of values associated with the homeland and cultivated in the *Heimatroman*. This had enjoyed, especially as represented by Stifter, Rosegger and Waggerl in Austria, a long tradition but had become an object of suspicion for the part it played in the cultural transformation accompanying Austria's transition from democracy via Austrofascism to absorption into the Third Reich.

These strictures against the *Heimatroman* are implicit also in the work of lesser-known writers, some of whom have seen in rural and small-town environments ideal conditions for the survival of a Fascist mentality (Gerhard Fritsch, *Fasching*, 1967; Hans Lebert, *Die Wolfshaut* 1960, *Der Feuerkreis*, 1971), as in the much more substantial oeuvre of Thomas Bernhard, whose bleak view of provincial life arises not so much from the wish to challenge cosy complacency as from a consistently held *Weltanschauung* encapsulated in the statement 'Es ist nichts zu loben, nichts zu verdammen, nichts anzuklagen, aber es ist vieles lächerlich; es ist alles lächerlich, wenn man an den Tod denkt' (i.e. 'There is nothing to praise, nothing to condemn, nothing to accuse, but a great deal is ridiculous; everything is ridiculous when you think of death'). (Cf. Gerhard Roth's statement 'Schreiben ist zwangsläufig eine Auseinandersetzung mit der eigenen Sterblichkeit und damit den Nachkommen.' 'Writing is perforce an argument and coming to terms with one's own mortality and one's descendants.') Whether one places Bernhard in a long line of melancholy misanthropes whose jaundiced view of the human condition does not preclude philosophical depth and stylistic finesse (e.g. Pascal, Schopenhauer), whether one sees his manic dedication as an attempt to exorcise a personal trauma arising from the childhood circumstances described at length in the five volumes of his autobiography, whether one interprets the solipsism of his central figures, often isolated from the common herd by their social standing and their intellectual and artistic gifts, as an opportunity to exploit the humorous potential of exaggeration in obsessive monologues, Bernhard's work is both repellent and addictive. This paradoxical effect arises from the contrast between the negativity of the content, largely consisting of cataracts of acidulous invective, and the narrative energy which informs its delineation. As with Kafka, the reader is left wondering whether there is any distance between author, narrator (where present) and figures whose obsessions exert such a magnetic force that no alternative view from minor characters can emerge; in the end that distance is abolished, as in *Auslöschung* (1986), the summa of Bernhard's achievement, in which his sure control of narrative structure reaches ultimate refinement.

Another recent trend in Austrian literature continues to reflect on language as a determining factor in human behaviour by demonstrating the interrelationship of prescription and cliché and social norms. Here the writers associated with the Forum Stadtpark in Graz and its magazine *manuskripte* (Alfred Kolleritsch, Wolfgang Bauer, Michael Scharang, Klaus Hoffer, Elfriede Jelinek, Gert F. Jonke, as well as Frischmuth, Handke, Roth, and Rosei) develop the initiatives of the Wiener Gruppe in different directions. A new social realism is evident in the work of

Franz Innerhofer, Josef Winkler, Gernot Wolfgruber, Peter Turrini, Handke in the biography of his mother *Wunschloses Unglück* (1972) and Scharang in *Charly Traktor* (1973) and *Der Sohn eines Landarbeiters* (1976).)

During the 1960s and later, the German theatre turned against its museum-like role of institution for the preservation and communication of the classics as repositories of timeless cultural values. Documentary drama was not the only form to fill the void. A model with stronger and older roots was found in the *Volksstück*, especially as represented by the work of Fleißer, Zuckmayer and Horváth in the 1920s and 1930s, which in turn continues and updates a tradition originating in the popular theatre of early nineteenth-century Vienna. Of the *Volksstück* authors (Kroetz, Sperr, Fassbinder, in Austria Sommer and Turrini) Kroetz has proved the most prolific and most often performed. His portrayal of the most inarticulate members of marginal sections of society in Bavaria and Austria seems at first sight to mark a revival of the style and social concerns of Naturalism. Yet in focusing more and more on more typical working-class and petty bourgeois figures as they confront the pressures of the consumer society and are forced to adapt to the new working practices which it demands he joins the mainstream of the new *Volksstück*, sharing the linguistic concerns of Horváth and (for a time) the pedagogic aims of Brecht. Later still, he makes the *Volksstück* a vehicle for conveying his own feelings in a non-naturalistic manner. *Neue Subjektivität*, although less amenable to dramatic presentation than to the other major genres, is increasingly evident in the move away from documentary drama. However, this trend does not signify a return to the 'poetic' theatre of the 1950s typified by the early Frisch; rather authors resort to a combination of realism and extreme theatricality to convey a distinct personal vision.

The historical plays of Dieter Forte (on Luther and Münzer, Henri Dunant, and Kaspar Hauser) are closest to documentary drama in their exposure of the economic forces underlying the idealism of their protagonists and the resistance it encounters. Tankred Dorst's *Toller* (1968) (set during the short-lived Munich Räterepublik in 1919) and Martin Walser's *Das Sauspiel* (1975) (set in Nuremberg after the defeat of the peasant uprising in 1526) examine the role of the artist-intellectual (represented in the first by Toller, Mühsam and Landauer, in the second by Dürer, Hans Sachs and Faust) in times of political confusion with analogies to the rise and fall of the student movement. Both authors' other plays, how-ever, while occasionally retaining a broad historical sweep, focus on the complexity of human relationships, especially within the family, as in Walser's grotesque exposures of the fellow-travelling mentality in the Third Reich and after, and of bourgeois self-deceptions in a domestic setting, and on situations in which char-acters are forced to come to terms with historical turning-points or react to imposed social forces, as in Dorst's Merz cycle, an exten-sive chronicle in various media of a middle-class family between the 1920s and the present. Both authors also share with others a preoccupation with the relation of the artist to his time (Dorst, *Endzeit*, 1973, on Knut Hamsun's accommodation with Nazism; and *Goncourt oder die Abschaffung des Todes*, 1977, on the Paris Commune; *Der verbotene Garten*, 1982, on D'Annunzio; Salvatore, *Büchners Tod*, 1968; Weiss, *Hölderlin*; Walser, *In Goethes Hand*, 1982), which in the case of Salvatore and Weiss is clearly linked to the slackening of revolutionary impetus in the student movement.

Dorst's more recent work is best viewed in the context of a post-modern mythical awareness, grounded in both pessimism as to the fulfilment of grander human aspirations and a playful scepticism as to the nature of illusion and reality, which gains ground throughout the 1980s in literature, philosophy and all the perform-ing arts. The essentially theatrical interest in existence as a role, apparent from the beginning of his career, attains monumental dimensions in the ten-hours-long reworking of Arthurian myth *Merlin* (1980), which follows misplaced idealism to its tragic conse-quences and offers in Arthur a figure comparable to the artists of his earlier plays caught up in a process beyond their control. The author to whom the elastic label of post-modernist is more readily applied is Botho Strauß, whether one defines him as a unique talent or a mere exploiter of contemporary neuroses. In his plays, of which the most important are *Trilogie des Wiedersehens* (1976), *Gross und klein* (1978), *Kalldewey Farce* (1981), *Der Park* (1983) (a recreation of *A Midsummer Night's Dream*) and *Die Fremdenführerin* (1986), mental disorientation in all its forms becomes a symptom or metaphor for the general state of the individual at present in a society which oppresses in the name of reason. Despite their grotesque features, obscure symbolism and surreal ambience in which a series of mysterious metamorphoses are depicted, they do not represent a revival of the theatre of the absurd, but focus on failed human relationships and the frustrations of attempts to find a role and identity which combine personal fulfilment and social effectiveness. The undirected awareness and confused consciousness of Strauß's figures are expressed in an amalgam of disparate elements: monologue, dialogue, intense lyricism, pantomime, recondite reference, dialect and crude urban slang, and cinematic techniques are applied to introduce a metaphysical dimension. Behind Strauß's fantasies is the view that modern civilisation has robbed individuals of their capacity for profound experience, secure identity and action marked by personal integrity; it thus challenges the progress of enlightenment towards utopia which had been an undercurrent of most intellectual trends in the two German states.

The work of the other major dramatist of the 1970s and 1980s, Thomas Bernhard, is more radical in its exposure of the human lot, his bleak vision of human nature allowing merely monotonous variations on limited themes. The world is presented as a house of correction in which there are only powerful megalomaniacs and their terrorised victims, deformed creatures performing meaningless rituals in a restricted space. Yet Bernhard differs from Beckett, of whom much the same might be said, by adding a dimension of comic exaggeration in the torrential speech of his principal figures, who can be seen on the one hand as vehicles for the communication of Bernhard's view that death overshadows all human activity, condemning it to futility, and on the other hand as monomaniacs in a long line of characters whose obsessions contrast with a moderate norm, and who provoke laughter by challenging or departing from it. It is difficult to establish whether that norm is implied (as in Molière and the tradition of social comedy which stems from him) or supplied by the audience, and to categorise the plays accordingly. *Vor dem Ruhestand* (1979) and *Über allen Gipfeln ist Ruh* (1981), in which the central figures are monsters of vanity and tyrannical egotism, can be defined as satires; *Der Weltbesserer* (1979) and *Immanuel Kant* (1978), in which they appear as in love with their own eccentricity, uttering voluble monologues devoid of sense, are close to the theatre of the absurd, while *Minetti* (1977), in which the title figure emerges as a heroic figure, can be called a grotesque tragedy.

The more recent work of Kroetz demonstrates ever more clearly a failure to sustain the critical potential of the *Volksstück*. In focusing on unemployment and the unequal struggle between the old peasant culture and the economic dominance of urban capitalism he continues to show an awareness of social problems in the Bavarian society he knows best. However, the increasingly tragic tone of his plays indicates neither a Brechtian conviction that a solution can be found by embracing ideology or advocating pragmatic political measures, nor the implication present in Horvath's *Volksstücke*, that a clear-sighted view of what an individual can achieve and reasonably expect in the pursuit of his or her aspirations is the only alternative to shallow escapism and the constrictions of a dishonest appeal to conventional morality. Yet such an assessment cannot detract from the emotional impact of his work, which arises from a profound sympathy with his figures, or from his mastery of dialect and colloquial speech as a vehicle for the revelation of complex human predicaments.

The poetry of this period represents a reaction against two earlier trends: the hermeticism which culminated in Celan, and the political-didactic verse which blossomed during the student movement, although the first type continued to be represented by Ernst Meister, the second by Erich Fried. Walter Höllerer, as much a literary manager as a poet, initiated a controversy on the viability of the long poem, which found practitioners in Günter Herburger and Rolf Dieter Brinkmann. There followed a wave of poetry on everyday themes, marked by the dissolution of traditional forms, the inclusion of contemporary diction and slang, in which the influence of pop-culture (especially in the work of Brinkmann) is strong. As with the prose fiction of this phase, it is difficult to draw a temporal or stylistic line between the political and the private, as the freer forms of personal and social interaction and their attendant frustrations which are a major theme of this poetry can be linked to the direct political action of demonstrations and campaigns. This fusion is evident in words from the introduction to an anthology published in 1977:

Worum es geht ist, daß die Sprache, in der sich die Lyrik derzeit organisiert, eine der persönlichen Erfahrungen ist, ein Widerstand gegen die Massenmedien, Wirtschaftsverbände, Parteien und Ministerien mit ihren verstümmelnden, wirklichkeitsverzerrenden oder synthetischen Produkten. Der Bezug auf das Selbsterlebte ist der Versuch, Verläßliches, Überprüfbares zu sagen angesichts der öffentlichen Parolen.

[What counts is that the language in which lyric poetry at present is organised is drawn from one's personal experiences, forms resistance to mass media, economic interest groups, parties and ministries with their mutilating, distorting and synthetic products. The relation to what one has oneself experienced is the attempt to say something reliable and testable in the face of slogans from the public domain.]

The emphasis on directness, spontaneity and authenticity leads to a rejection of symbolism and metaphor, which are replaced by contrasting registers juxtaposed to produce collage effects. The most representative poems register contemporary urban reality in a relaxed conversational style (Jürgen Becker, Brinkmann, Born, Theobaldy), in which symptomatic detail is preferred to abstraction. However, such poetry soon degenerates into series of snapshots or disparate banalities, countered in some instances by a return to the disciplines of traditional forms, while older poets, such as Enzensberger and Peter Rühmkorf, publish sporadically in their own distinctive styles.

Much attention has been given recently by critics and academics in Germany to the differences between modernism and post-modernism and the position of contemporary German literature in the gradual displacement of the one by the other. No one looking back on the course of German literature over the century can deny that its contribution to international modernism has been considerable. The Expressionists, Thomas Mann, Musil, Broch, Canetti, Kafka, Döblin, Brecht and Benn all responded in their different ways to the crisis of values which arose from the development of bourgeois industrial society in a period marked by war and political turmoil and from the 'Umwertung aller Werte' in Nietzsche's diagnosis of post-Christian disorientation. Most retained a residual faith in an intellectual project inspired by the enlightenment hope that a combination of progress and stability within a framework of humanism was valid and practicable. Strenuous abstraction, socio-historical awareness and psychological depth ensured that their work also contained certain traditional features (progress to a goal by means of linear narration within a system of definable binary oppositions in a fictional world with firm contours, with the aim of discovering, establishing and validating an identifiable *Weltbild* or *Weltanschauung*). Much of the literature published since 1970, however, is marked by different tendencies: a multiplicity of styles and disconnected images, many of which are drawn from myth, folk memory and the more imaginative literature of the past, giving rise to an intertextuality in which parody and pastiche play a prominent role. The influence of the photographic and electronic media, of commercial design and advertising, leads to the levelling of the formerly sharp divisions between high culture and popular entertainment, the creation of new realities, each equal in status to any formerly acknowledged reality. Whether one uses the terms post-modernism or magic realism to define this trend, one cannot help noting how the traditionally valued qualities of depth, coherence, meaning, originality and authenticity are dissolved and superseded by semiotic volatility, 'depthless' fabulation, a bricolage of fragmentary sensations, disposable simulacra, a free play of multi-media forms and effects, in which contradictory orders of reality metamorphose into one another or the fabulous irrupts into the 'normal' world. Such synchretism, with the sensual appeal of its potentially endless play of transitory impulses, its promiscuous superficiality, gives priority to the medium over the message, to performance over content, to unstable variations over binary opposition and semantic stability, and its function and effect have been described as 'die ästhetische Entsorgung der Modernisierungsschäden' (compensation through art for the damage done by modernisation). Its character can be linked to those aspects of contemporary literary theory which emphasise 'jouissance'.

There is, however, in the German literature which possesses one or more of these features a note which is less evident elsewhere, an acopalyptic tone which can be related either to the profound unease arising from the threat of nuclear catastrophe and ecological disaster, or to the continued awareness, with its roots in the experience of the Third Reich, of the sinister and destructive potential of human nature. Indeed, the literature of the 1980s in Germany has been defined as 'Angstliteratur', devoid of human warmth, communication and action, overshadowed by death and hopelessness, the consequence of a loss of faith in the enlightenment belief in progress by means of reason. 'The dream of reason gives birth to monsters' is the title of a famous Goya etching and could stand as a motto over much contemporary German literature. The purpose behind the resort to myth is not only to gain access to a rich storehouse of signs to be manipulated according to whim, but to explore a deeper mood, born of the recognition that: 'Die Aufklärung hat die Welt zerstört, den Menschen nicht verbessert, die Revolution zu neuen Mordmaschinen pervertiert – vom Thermidor zum Gulag!' (The enlightenment has destroyed the world, it has not improved mankind, the perversion of revolution has produced murder machines – from Thermidor to the Gulag.) The enlightenment, far from liberating man from a self-imposed immaturity, has subjected him to a new form of slavery, to an atrophied, stunted psyche incapable of contact with his fellows or with the numinous, represented by myth, a dimension inducing fear and awe and therefore counter-acting the 'flattening' influences of modern life. Such views directly challenge the strong tradition of political and philosophical engagement in German literature and the varying combinations of abstraction and moralism which served it, whether in the ideological commitments of left and right, or in the belief that the springs of human behaviour can be reached by analysing language as well as action. They also leave open the possibility of access to an alternative tradition of radical aestheticism which has been stronger elsewhere,. especially in France, but which has occasionally had advocates and representatives in Germany, such as the early Romantics, Gottfried Benn, Ernst Jünger, and at present the critic Karl Heinz Bohrer, who has claimed that 'geschichtliche, politische und gesellschaftliche Erfahrungen dem deutschen literarischen Bewußtsein Zonen der Phantasie verboten haben' (historical, political and social experiences have closed off areas of the imagination from German literary consciousness), leading to the dominance of post-war German literature by writers (Böll, Grass) whose work functions as 'säkularisierte Erbauung' (secularised edification).

It is in the context of a sense that this tradition can no longer be renewed that the so-called 'deutsch-deutscher Literaturstreit', an acrimonious debate on the responsibility of GDR intellectuals who had neither openly challenged the regime nor espoused the western norm of democratic pluralism, must be seen. Occasioned by the publication shortly after the *Wende* of Christa Wolf's *Was bleibt*, a semi-fictional account of her surveillance by the Stasi written mainly in 1979, the controversy possessed from its beginning wider ramifications. Wolf came to be seen as representing, along with Stefan Heym, Heiner Müller, Volker Braun and Christoph Hein, a 'third way', which might have led to a reformed, de-Stalinised GDR, had it not been rejected in favour of unification by its people. Equally significant was the implication throughout the debate that the 'third way' was not only illusory and a mark of political naivety which failed to take account of the ground swell of popular opinion, but also a feature of post-war literature in both German states, from the publication of *Der Ruf* onwards, and could be associated with a 'Gesinnungsästhetik' (a blanket term best rendered by 'the aesthetics of ethos'). Having run its course in the West such a position had only remained immune in the GDR from the developments which had superseded it elsewhere because GDR literature had had a social function which would now be performed by investigative journalism and political debate in the press and other media, thus rendering unnecessary the preservation of the former territory of the GDR as a 'Kulturschutzgebiet' or haven for the protection of an endangered species. It is undoubtedly true that there is at present no dominant trend more clearly definable than post-modernism; instead there is a 'neue Unübersichtlichkeit', a situation of confusion in which literature is forced to fight a rearguard action against the competition of the electronic media which in some respects have raised themselves to the level of art but which are at one in reducing the significance of the committed subject who alone is the source of 'Gesinnung'. Such a diagnosis is confirmed by an assessment of those works which have found favour both with the critics and the reading public during the last decade in the West, above all Patrick Süskind's *Das Parfum* (1984) and Christoph Ransmayr's *Die letzte Welt* (1988), but also the work of Handke, Bernhard, Botho Strauß and Dürrenmatt, and such lesser-known figures as Klaus Hoffer, Gert F.Jonke, Peter Rosei, Gerhard Roth, Urs Widmer, Hermann Burger, Gerold Späth and Adolf Muschg. It is perhaps no coincidence that with the exception of Strauß (who in any case may be said to be developing an ethos, albeit radically different from that which had for a while formed an east–west consensus), all of these are Austrian or Swiss. In the end the most memorable of recent texts are those which combine a free-flowing fantasy with an urge to warn against those threats to a humane future which would stifle utopian strivings: Stefan Heym's *Ahasver*, Grass's *Die Rättin*, Morgner's *Amanda*, Hans Wollschläger's *Herzgewächse* (Part I, 1982), Carl Amery's *Die Wallfahrer* (1986) and *Das Geheimnis der Krypta* (1990), Michael Ende's *Die unendliche Geschichte* (1979), Günter Herburger's Thuja trilogy, Stefan Schütz's *Medusa* and *Katt* (1988), Gerd Heidenreich's *Belial oder die Stille* (1990) and Botho Strauß's *Der junge Mann*

(1984). A new development easily ignored by critics who share many authors' preoccupation with German identity encouraged by its bitter past and (until 1990) divided state, is the growing interest in the Third World and other exotic locations, evident in Hubert Fichte's non-fictional investigations of Afro-American cultural syncretism in the Caribbean and Central and South America in *Xango* (1976) and *Petersilie* (1980); Adolf Muschg's observations of culture clash in Japan in *Im Sommer des Hasen* (1965) and China in *Baiyun oder die Freundschaftsgesellschaft* (1980); Grass's accounts of India in *Kopfgeburten* and *Zunge zeigen* (1988); Nicolas Born's view of the internecine conflicts in Lebanon in *Die Fälschung* (1979); Dieter Kühn's prescient scenario of a Middle East oil crisis in *Und der Sultan von Oman* (1979); and Uwe Timm's exposure of colonialism in *Morenga* (1978) and his sober assessment of the tensions arising between European technical expertise and native labour on a construction site in the South American jungle in *Der Schlangenbaum* (1986). Equally striking is the steadily growing involvement of writers from all German-speaking areas in other media, especially film (Süskind, Jurek Becker, Handke, Kluge, Turrini, Dorst, Achternbusch), comparable to the place of radio in the 1950s and 1960s in the careers of Eich, Böll, Wellershoff, Hildesheimer, Bachmann, Dürrenmatt, Frisch, Aichinger, Andersch, Kaschnitz, S. Lenz and M. Walser, or of graphic art in the activities of Dürrenmatt, Hildesheimer, Meckel, Peter Weiss, Grass, Kunert.

Whether, as has been claimed, the demise of the GDR marks the end of the unquestioned role in West German intellectual life of the left–liberal consensus, is however by no means certain. Intellectuals not only from the GDR but throughout Germany know well that the freedom of the market means subjection to the market, that the removal of borders and the accessibility of the supermarket have not resulted (yet) in a homogeneous nation, and therefore Cassandra warnings from them, amongst whom Günter Grass has been the most vociferous, will continue. Furthermore, it will be realised, when the dust has settled after the 'deutsch-deutscher Literaturstreit', that the particular value of those works which can be defined as 'Gesinnungsliteratur', whether written east or west of what used to be called the iron curtain, lies not in their more or less coded stance towards the Communist system, but in their position on such global issues as the threat to the ecological balance of the planet, the destructive potential of western technology in nuclear and non-nuclear forms, a Eurocentrism which ignores the Third World, instrumental reason and patriarchal deformations, all of which transcend the old ideological divisions and which will continue to preoccupy thinking people as long as we can reasonably foresee.

Bibliography

REFERENCE

Heinz Ludwig Arnold (ed.), *Kritisches Lexikon der deutschen Gegenwarts-literatur* (Munich 1978–). Critical surveys of the work of contemporary writers, including minor figures, in loose leaf form with periodic updates.

Henry and Mary Garland, *Oxford Companion to German Literature* (1976). Covers the whole span of German literature and includes entries on movements, styles, figures and events in history.

Raymond Furness and Malcolm Humble, *A Companion to Twentieth Century German Literature* (London 1991). Over four hundred entries on writers active since 1900.

Hermann Kunisch and Herbert Wiesner (eds), *Lexikon der deutschsprachigen Gegenwartsliteratur* (Munich 1981). Substantial entries on writers active since 1930.

Dietz-Rüdiger Moser (ed.), *Neues Handbuch der deutschen Gegenwartsliteratur seit 1945* (Munich 1990). Substantial entries, including contemporary writers not treated elsewhere.

LITERARY HISTORY

Viktor Žmegač (ed.), *Geschichte der deutschen Literatur vom 18. Jahrhundert bis zur Gegenwart*, Band III, 1918–1980 (Königstein 1984). The most thorough, comprehensive and balanced survey. Austria and GDR receive separate treatment.

Wolfgang Beutin *et al.*, *Deutsche Literaturgeschichte. Von den Anfängen bis zur Gegenwart*, 3rd edn (Stuttgart 1989). Concise and cogent.

Erhard Bahr (ed.), *Geschichte der deutschen Literatur*, Band 3, *Vom Realismus bis zur Gegenwartsliteratur* (Tübingen 1988). A movement-by-movement survey.

Jan Berg *et al.*, *Sozialgeschichte der deutschen Literatur von 1918 bis zur Gegenwart* (Frankfurt 1981). Gives much attention to minor but socially and politically relevant works, including reportage.

Ronald Gray, *The German Tradition in Literature 1871–1945* (Cambridge 1965). Provocative considerations of major authors.

Raymond Furness, *The Twentieth Century* (A Literary History of Germany. Volume 8) (London 1978). Covers period to 1945, with emphasis on earlier movements in both Germany and Austria.

207

Michael Hamburger, *A Proliferation of Prophets. Essays in Modern German Literature*. Volume 1 (Manchester 1983). Concentrates on the major figures in fiction and poetry before 1945.

Michael Hamburger, *After the Second Flood. Essays in Modern German Literature*. Volume 2 (Manchester 1986). Concentrates on fiction and poetry since 1945.

FROM THE GRÜNDERZEIT TO EXPRESSIONISM

Herbert Lehnert, *Geschichte der deutschen Literatur vom Jugendstil zum Expressionismus* (*Geschichte der deutschen Literatur von den Anfängen bis zur Gegenwart*, Band 5) (Stuttgart 1978). A substantial survey in a traditional style, covering personalities, themes, genres and movements.

Frank Trommler (ed.), *Jahrhundertwende: Vom Naturalismus zum Expressionismus 1880–1918* (Horst Albert Glaser (ed.), *Deutsche Literatur, Eine Sozialgeschichte*, Band 8) (Reinbek 1982). Articles on themes, movements, genres and major authors.

Roy Pascal, *From Naturalism to Expressionism. German Literature and Society 1880–1918* (London 1973). A major study of literature's maladjustment to the spirit of Wilhelminian society.

Walter Sokel, *The Writer in Extremis* (Stanford 1959) (German edn entitled: *Der literarische Expressionismus*). A standard work.

THE WEIMAR REPUBLIC

Wolfgang Rothe (ed.), *Die deutsche Literatur in der Weimarer Republik* (Stuttgart 1974). Articles on movements and trends.

Alan Bance (ed.), *Weimar Germany. Writers and Politics* (Edinburgh 1982). Essays on the major writers in relation to political developments.

Ronald Taylor, *Literature and Society in Germany 1918–1945* (Brighton 1980). Less social background than the title suggests, but a substantial survey.

Alexander von Bormann and Horst Albert Glaser (eds), *Weimarer Republik – Drittes Reich: Avantgardismus, Parteilichkeit, Exil 1933–1945* (Horst Albert Glaser (ed), *Deutsche Literatur. Eine Sozialgeschichte*, Band 9) (Reinbek 1983). Articles on themes, movements, genres and major authors.

THE THIRD REICH AND EXILE

J.M. Ritchie, *German Literature under National Socialism* (London 1983). Includes chapters on the literature of exile and inner emigration.

Horst Denkler and Karl Prümm (eds), *Die deutsche Literatur im Dritten Reich. Themen – Traditionen – Wirkungen* (Stuttgart 1976). Articles on themes, traditions and effects.

Manfred Durzak (ed.), *Die deutsche Exilliteratur 1933–1945* (Stuttgart 1973). Articles on conditions in countries of exile and on principal exile writers.

AFTER 1945

Manfed Durzak (ed.), *Die deutsche Literatur der Gegenwart. Aspekte und Tendenzen* (Stuttgart 1971). Articles on aspects and tendencies.

Manfred Durzak (ed.), *Deutsche Gegenwartsliteratur. Ausgangspositionen und aktuelle Entwicklungen* (Stuttgart 1981). Updated version of the above, with articles on literature in all German states and its relations to other media.

Peter Demetz, *Postwar German Literature* (New York 1970) (German edn entitled: *Die süße Anarchie*, Frankfurt 1970). Focuses on principal figures in major genres.

Peter Demetz, *After the Fires. Recent Writing in the Germanies, Austria and Switzerland* (San Diego 1986) (German edn entitled: *Fette Jahre, magere Jahre. Deutschsprachige Literatur von 1965 bis 1985*, Munich 1988). Focuses on principal figures against the background of social and political trends.

Thomas Koebner (ed.), *Tendenzen der deutschen Gegenwartsliteratur* (Stuttgart 1984). Substantial surveys of major genres, including radio and television plays. The GDR receives separate treatments.

Fritz J. Raddatz, *Die Nachgeborenen. Leseerfahrungen mit zeitgenössischer Literatur* (Frankfurt 1983). Idiosyncratic but illuminating considerations of major figures against background of changing mood of the times.

Fritz Raddatz, *Eine dritte deutsche Literatur. Stichworte zu Texten der Gegenwart* (Reinbek 1987). Postulates a 'third' German literature transcending east–west divisions.

THE FEDERAL REPUBLIC OF GERMANY

Paul Michael Lützeler and Egon Schwarz (eds), *Deutsche Literatur in der Bundesrepublik seit 1965. Untersuchungen und Berichte* (Königstein 1980). Articles on themes, trends and relations to other media.

Ralf Schnell, *Die Literatur der Bundesrepublik. Autoren, Geschichte. Literaturbetrieb* (Stuttgart 1986). Concentrates on literature as political and apolitical protest in name of alternative views of individual and society. Valuable for chapter on 'Literaturbetrieb'.

Bernd Balzer *et al.*, *Die deutschsprachige Literatur in der Bundesrepublik Deutschland. Vorgeschichte und Entwicklungstendenzen* (Munich 1988). Covers the period in four chronological divisions.

Ludwig Fischer (ed.), *Hansers Sozialgeschichte der deutschen Literatur vom 16. Jahrhundert bis zur Gegenwart*, Band 10: *Literatur in der BRD bis 1967* (Munich 1986). Articles on social parameters, concepts and strategies, genres, groups, relations to other media, developments in Austria and Switzerland.

Richard Hinton Thomas and Keith Bullivant, *Literature in Upheaval. West German Writers and the Challenge of the 1960s* (Manchester 1974). Considers the response of writers to the political radicalisation of the period.

Keith Bullivant (ed.), *After the 'Death' of Literature. West German Writing of the 1970s* (Oxford 1989). Articles on themes, trends and individual authors by (mainly) British Germanists.

Klaus Briegleb and Sigrid Weigel (eds), *Hansers Sozialgeschichte der deutschen Literatur vom 16. Jahrhundert bis zur Gegenwart*, Band 12: *Gegenwartsliteratur seit 1968* (Munich 1992). As in volume 10 of the same series.

THE GERMAN DEMOCRATIC REPUBLIC

Wolfgang Emmerich, *Kleine Literaturgeschichte der DDR*. Erweiterte Ausgabe (Frankfurt 1989). Considers literature in all genres in chronological phases marking ideological changes.

Hans-Jürgen Schmitt (ed.), *Hansers Sozialgeschichte der deutschen Literatur vom 16. Jahrhundert bis zur Gegenwart*, Band 11: *Die Literatur der DDR* (Munich 1983). As in volume 10 of the same series.

J.H. Reid, *Writing without Taboos. The New East German Literature* (New York 1990). A substantial survey, with the emphasis on prose fiction.

Martin Kane (ed.), *Socialism and the Literary Imagination. Essays on East German Writers* (Oxford 1991). Considers key aspects of work of principal figures.

AUSTRIA

C.E. Williams, *The Broken Eagle. The Politics of Austrian Literature from Empire to Anschluß* (London 1974). Considers the major figures in relation to political and ideological upheavals of the period.

Alan Best and Hans Wolfschütz (eds), *Modern Austrian Writing. Literature and Society after 1945* (London 1980). Articles on all major figures of the period.

Donald G. Daviau (ed.), *Major Figures of Modern Austrian Literature* (Riverside 1988). Articles on all major figures and others.

Donald G. Daviau (ed.), *Major Figures of Contemporary Austrian Literature* (New York 1986). Articles on all major figures and others.

SWITZERLAND

Malcolm Pender and Michael Butler (eds), *Rejection and Emancipation. Writing in German-Speaking Switzerland 1945–1991* (New York 1991).

Klaus Pezold *et al.*, *Geschichte der deutsch-sprachigen Schweizer Literatur im 20. Jahrhundert* (Berlin 1991).

Index

211

Index